C000265376

The Ties That Bind

Migration is among the central domestic and global political issues of today. Yet the causes and consequences – and the relationship between migration and global markets – are poorly understood. Migration is both costly and risky, so why do people decide to migrate? What are the political, social, economic, and environmental factors that cause people to leave their homes and seek a better life elsewhere? Leblang and Helms argue that political factors – the ability to participate in the political life of a destination – are as important as economic and social factors. Most migrants don't cut ties with their homeland but continue to be engaged, both economically and politically. Migrants continue to serve as a conduit for information, helping drive investment to their homelands. The authors combine theory with a wealth of micro and macro evidence to demonstrate that migration isn't static, after all, but continuously fluid.

David Leblang is Ambassador Henry Taylor Professor of Politics and Professor of Public Policy at the University of Virginia.

Benjamin Helms is Postdoctoral Fellow at the Institute for Politics and Strategy at Carnegie Mellon University.

The Ties That Bind

Immigration and the Global Political Economy

DAVID LEBLANG

University of Virginia

BENJAMIN HELMS

Carnegie Mellon University

CAMBRIDGE
UNIVERSITY PRESS

CAMBRIDGE
UNIVERSITY PRESS

Shaftesbury Road, Cambridge CB2 8EA, United Kingdom

One Liberty Plaza, 20th Floor, New York, NY 10006, USA

477 Williamstown Road, Port Melbourne, VIC 3207, Australia

314–321, 3rd Floor, Plot 3, Splendor Forum, Jasola District Centre, New Delhi – 110025, India

103 Penang Road, #05–06/07, Visioncrest Commercial, Singapore 238467

Cambridge University Press is part of Cambridge University Press & Assessment, a department of the University of Cambridge.

We share the University's mission to contribute to society through the pursuit of education, learning and research at the highest international levels of excellence.

www.cambridge.org
Information on this title: www.cambridge.org/9781009233224

DOI: 10.1017/9781009233248

© David Leblang and Benjamin Helms 2023

This publication is in copyright. Subject to statutory exception and to the provisions of relevant collective licensing agreements, no reproduction of any part may take place without the written permission of Cambridge University Press & Assessment.

First published 2023

A catalogue record for this publication is available from the British Library.

Library of Congress Cataloging-in-Publication Data
NAMES: Leblang, David, author. | Helms, Benjamin, 1994– author.
TITLE: The ties that bind : immigration and the global political economy / David Leblang, Benjamin Helms.
DESCRIPTION: Cambridge ; New York, NY : Cambridge University Press, 2023. | Includes bibliographical references and index.
IDENTIFIERS: LCCN 2022022796 (print) | LCCN 2022022797 (ebook) | ISBN 9781009233224 (hardback) | ISBN 9781009233279 (paperback) | ISBN 9781009233248 (epub)
SUBJECTS: LCSH: Emigration and immigration–Economic aspects. | Globalization. | BISAC: POLITICAL SCIENCE / General
CLASSIFICATION: LCC JV6217 .L43 2023 (print) | LCC JV6217 (ebook) | DDC 304.8–dc23/ eng/20220729
LC record available at https://lccn.loc.gov/2022022796
LC ebook record available at https://lccn.loc.gov/2022022797

ISBN 978-1-009-23322-4 Hardback
ISBN 978-1-009-23327-9 Paperback

Cambridge University Press & Assessment has no responsibility for the persistence or accuracy of URLs for external or third-party internet websites referred to in this publication and does not guarantee that any content on such websites is, or will remain, accurate or appropriate.

To my mother, Susan, and the memory of my father,
Larry D.L.
To my mother, Janet, and my father,
Clay B.H.

Contents

Figures and Tables

Figures

Tables

Appendix Figures

Appendix Tables

Acknowledgments

This collaboration was born in the fall of 2016, when David was awarded a contract from the Department of Homeland Security (DHS) to support a project modeling the determinants of migration to the United States. The project, motivated by the 2015–16 presidential campaign, sought to answer the following question: Would supporting development programs, engaging home countries in trade and investment practices, and/or expanding opportunities for remittances be more effective strategies to decrease migration than spending money on border walls? Funding from Grant Award Number 2015-ST-061-BSH001, awarded to the Borders, Trade, and Immigration (BTI) Institute – A DHS Center of Excellence led by the University of Houston – allowed us to hire students, collect data, and do preliminary writing on a number of topics covered in this book.[1] Revisions to our contract were such that we were not obligated to produce any research papers for DHS; they are in no way responsible for the analyses or conclusions included in this book.

The DHS contract provided funding to support Ben's work. The College and Graduate School of Arts and Sciences at the University of Virginia (UVA) and the Bankard Fund for Political Economy also provided support necessary for the completion of the project. The Global

[1] Some of this work was supported by the US Department of Homeland Security under Grant Award Number 2015-ST-061-BSH001, awarded to the Borders, Trade, and Immigration (BTI) Institute: A DHS Center of Excellence led by the University of Houston, and includes support for the project "Modeling International Migrant Flows." The views and conclusions contained in this document are those of the authors and should not be interpreted as necessarily representing the official policies, either expressed or implied, of the US Department of Homeland Security.

Policy Center at UVA's Batten School supported some of David's time, as did the Ambassador Henry Taylor Professorship. Financial support from DHS was essential as it allowed us to hire some outstanding undergraduate and MA students – Rebecca Brough, Kelsey Hunt, Alexa Iadarola, Ankita Satpathy, and Eric Xu – who contributed to data collection and cleaning, translation of primary source documents, and some of the research underlying Chapter 6.

This work rests on foundations developed in earlier work. We are grateful to Jennifer Fitzgerald and Jessica Teets for allowing us to draw on their collaboration with David. Some of this work was presented at different venues, and we appreciate comments from conference participants at the International Political Economy Society and the Annual Meeting of the American Political Science Association, and seminar participants at the University of Colorado, University of Michigan, University of Texas, University of South Carolina, Columbia University, New York University, UCLA, London School of Economics, Oxford University, University of Pennsylvania, Université Laval, University of Maryland, and University of Virginia.

From David: I have been fortunate to have amazing colleagues who have influenced my thinking about immigration and political economy. I am privileged to count Jennifer Fitzgerald, Sarah Bermeo, Sonal Pandya, Maggie Peters, and Alexandra Zeitz as co-authors and collaborators; they have pushed me to explore several of the puzzles explored in this book. Human mobility does not just occur when people cross international borders. Co-teaching courses on migration, borders, and humanitarian response with Jennifer Rubenstein and Kirsten Gelsdorf fundamentally broadened my perspective, challenging me to think differently about the nature of human mobility. Both David Singer and Sonal Pandya encouraged me to work on a book-length treatment of migration and political economy, a project that only came to fruition once I began collaborating with Ben.

I thank my wife Emily and our children Max and Samantha for their love, support, and sometimes unusual inspiration. When asked, "what does your father study?" the kids would often respond, smiling, "immigration, blah, blah blah." They all put up with too much typing, often at our kitchen table, as this book was coming together. Finally, my deepest thanks to my parents for their unfailing support and love over the course of my academic career; they have never been anything less than supremely proud that their son is a college professor. I dedicate this book to my mother and to the memory of my father.

From Ben: I have benefitted from a supportive network of mentors, colleagues, friends, and family, without which I could not have written this book. David has been an incredible mentor to me personally and professionally, and I feel fortunate to co-author this book with him. He sparked my interest in this topic as a young graduate student, and I cannot thank him enough. Sonal Pandya constantly inspires me to think harder about the dynamics of human mobility, and her mentorship has been indispensable. Philip Potter and John Owen gave me excellent advice and encouragement as I began this project. Colleagues and friends at the University of Virginia, including Richard Burke, Daniel Henry, Aycan Katitas, Kal Munis, Nicola Nones, and Anthony Sparacino, have been amazing sources of support and inspiration.

I especially want to thank my fiancée, Janet Lawler, for her love, support, and willingness to put up with late nights of fiddling with figures and tables while watching television. I also appreciated her friendly (but persistent) reminders to take a step back from a chapter for a while and gain a new perspective. I truly could not have written this book without her. Finally, I want to thank my parents, Janet and Clay, for their constant love and support throughout my life. I always know that they are incredibly proud of me, and for that I am so thankful. I dedicate this book to my mother and father.

Introduction

Immigration and Globalization

History abounds with stories and images of migration: Moses and the Israelites journey from Egypt to the Promised Land; the Celts leave Central Europe and settle in Gaul; the pilgrims sail from England to the New World; Italians, Irish, and Eastern Europeans travel through Ellis Island in the late nineteenth century; and East German residents move west when the Berlin Wall falls. While these images differ historically, socially, politically, economically, and geographically, they all illustrate the central role that migration – the act of leaving one's native land to settle elsewhere – plays in shaping the modern world.

Migration, along with commodity trade and capital mobility, is an integral component of globalization. When people move, they bring with them ideas, knowledge, and skills acquired in their homeland – attributes that influence political, economic, and social life in their host community. But the act of migrating does not mean that those who move leave behind their homelands: far from it. Migration – and migrants – form tight social networks linking home and host countries, facilitating transfers of both human and financial capital.

While essential to the stability of the global political economy, migration has often been treated as an economic and cultural threat, especially in advanced industrial democracies (Dancygier 2010; Fitzgerald 2018). Opponents of migration regularly mischaracterize existing evidence by arguing that migrants drive down wages, overconsume public goods, generate social conflict, and resist assimilation (Clemens and Hunt 2019; Clemens and Pritchett 2019). These arguments are seized upon by political parties which seek to make immigration control – and often anti-globalization efforts – a central part of their policy platform. Whether anti-immigration

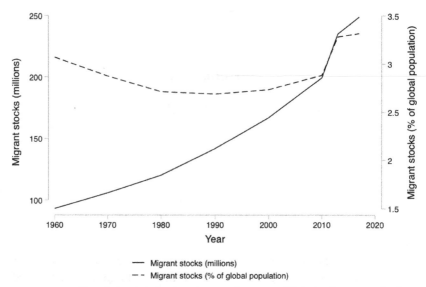

FIGURE 1.1 Trends in global migration, 1960–2017. Global migrant stocks in millions and as a percentage of global population.
Source: Özden et al. (2011) and UN (2019).

sentiment is a consequence of exposure to migrants, job loss associated with globalization or technological change, or a result of deeper cultural and/or political shifts is a question addressed by others (e.g., Peters 2017; Goodman and Pepinsky 2021). Our focus is on the ways in which migrant networks help construct and continually reconstitute the global political economy.

The consequences of anti-immigrant sentiment, however, are of relevance, as public attitudes and policies influence the attractiveness of different host countries. One of the arguments we advance in this book is that anti-immigrant policies have implications for global economic exchange. Well-regulated migration, we argue, is essential for global flows of capital. Disrupting flows of people through the construction of walls, implementation of anti-migration policies, or the fomenting of anti-immigrant sentiment, disrupts the flow of capital and commodity trade.

Despite increasing antipathy toward migration by politicians and political parties across the United States and the European Union, levels and rates of immigration remain consistent by historical standards. The International Organization for Migration (IOM) estimates (see Figure 1.1) that there were 272 million migrants globally in 2019, with approximately two-thirds being labor migrants or migrants in search of employment; this represents roughly 3.5% of the world's population (McAuliffe and Khadria

2020). Flows of labor migrants into wealthy countries have remained high over the last two decades, with more than five million new permanent residents in those countries arriving in 2019 (OECD 2020). It is difficult to predict the post-pandemic migration landscape, but evidence from globally representative survey data indicates that over 150 million people expressed a desire to move from their homelands in 2020 (Gallup 2021).

While international trade and capital mobility erode the separation between national markets, migration breaks down traditional barriers between nation-states, bringing together different cultures, customs, languages, and religions. Migration, unlike commodity and capital mobility, results in the movement of *people* – laborers, investors, students, and citizens. Migrants control both human and financial capital and bring with them social capital, knowledge, and network connections. The ability to migrate brings with it challenges and opportunities for nation-states as countries of origin – homelands – often work to maintain connections with those who have left, while countries of destination – host countries – compete to attract the "best and brightest."

Although humans have moved across long distances for millennia, migration takes on renewed political importance in the current era. Rising social and political conflict over human mobility – not just in advanced economies but also in the Global South – means that understanding the causes and consequences of international migration is more important than ever. Our point of departure is that migration, while an intrinsic part of globalization itself, facilitates deeper connections across countries and economies, acting as a conduit for information and knowledge and mobilizing investments in human and financial capital.

As we discuss below, migration had, until World Wars I and II, been part and parcel of globalization. Temporary and permanent migrants populated the New World, inhabiting new countries – often by force – with new languages, laws, and customs carried from their homelands. They developed trade and financial networks: opening banks and supplying credit, and acting as consumers and producers within global supply chains. Yet only recently has migration been considered an important component of global economic exchange. This lack of consideration may be due to the absence of a global organization to manage migration akin to the International Monetary Fund (IMF) or the World Trade Organization (WTO). Or it may be because the only global organization charged with population flows – the United Nations High Commission on Refugees (UNHCR) – focuses on individuals who are forcibly displaced due to conflict or natural disaster.

This book contributes to our understanding of migration as a global phenomenon. Our coverage is expansive, focusing on the dynamics, patterns, causes, and consequences of global migration. We begin by examining why people decide to migrate, exploring the political, social, and economic factors that influence an individual's decision to leave their homes and seek a better life abroad. Given a desire to leave one's homeland, we then explore the factors that influence the choice over different destinations, arguing that political factors – the ability to participate in the political life of a host country – are as important as economic and social factors. After migrants leave, they do not cut ties with their homeland. Rather, they continue to engage both economically and politically. We explore how migrants drive investment to their homelands, and how homelands work to harness the human and financial capital of their expatriate populations.

In the remainder of this chapter, we first situate globalization and migration in historical perspective. We then provide an overview of existing theoretical and empirical literature on the causes and consequences of migration. Within this historical and theoretical context, we describe the scope conditions for our argument before concluding with a roadmap of the arguments and evidence presented in the rest of the volume.

MIGRATION AND GLOBALIZATION IN HISTORICAL CONTEXT

The 19th century is often viewed as a period of unparalleled globalization, with almost unfettered movement of labor, capital, and commodities.[1] Technological advances and reductions in transportation costs, combined with the discovery of new markets and materials, resulted in a massive expansion of global trade and investment. Migration – among Europeans, at least – was relatively unconstrained, with some fifty million Europeans (and an equal number of Asians) moving abroad during this period (Frieden 2012). This era of globalization was fittingly summarized by John Maynard Keynes in *The Economic Consequences of Peace*:

"The inhabitant of London could order by telephone, sipping his morning tea in bed, the various products of the whole earth, in such quantity as he might see fit, and reasonably expect their early delivery on his doorstep; he could at the same moment and by the same means adventure his wealth in the natural resources and

---

[1] See Hatton and Williamson (2005) for a historical review of globalization and role of migration in that process.

new enterprises of any quarter of the world, and share, without exertion or even trouble, in their prospective fruits and advantages; or he could decide to couple the security of his fortunes with the good faith of the townspeople of any substantial municipality in any continent that fancy or information might recommend" (Keynes 1919, p. 11).

This period saw rapid global economic growth and convergence, as poorer countries grew faster than their richer counterparts. This was due, in large measure, to the expansion of international trade, the economic stability associated with the gold standard, and the ability of labor to move in pursuit of higher wages (Eichengreen and Flandreau 1997; Hatton and Williamson 1998).

If World War I put the lid on this era of globalization, the interwar period tightened it. Unemployment, coupled with debts accumulated along the way, led combatant countries to use economic policies to attempt to protect their labor markets. Governments imposed capital controls, competitive devaluations, tariffs, and migration restrictions to place the burden of economic adjustment on other countries. The Great Depression that followed reinforced these protectionist tendencies, eroding political support for open markets (Eichengreen and Leblang 2008).

The Bretton Woods Accords, negotiated primarily between the US and the United Kingdom and signed by forty-four countries in 1944, was an effort to resurrect key components of pre-World War I globalization. The creation of the IMF to manage exchange rates and the General Agreement on Tariffs and Trade (GATT) embodied the hope that global cooperation – at least among Western powers – could bring about trade and investment sufficient to drive growth and employment. The key compromise embedded in these agreements was an explicit acknowledgment – a compromise – that participant countries would balance international economic engagement with the political need to protect domestic laborers and labor markets (e.g., Ikenberry 2001). What is notable is that within this institutional framework, countries made no provisions related to international labor migration (Peters 2017; Goodman and Pepinsky 2021), likely because politicians needed to accommodate the demands of organized labor without external agreements tying their hands.[2]

Just because migration was not part of international agreements does not mean that there was no human mobility. The vast majority of border

---

[2] It is important to recognize that during this time, international agreements for the protection of refugees and asylum seekers were signed under the auspices of the newly formed United Nations (UN) and the United Nations High Commission for Refugees (UNHCR).

crossings – both after World War II and today – are not migratory; they are tourists, students, and business travelers who have no intention of remaining in the host country. And the lack of international agreements did not stop countries in the Global North from adopting their own unilateral policies regarding temporary and permanent labor migration.

Temporary labor agreements were an important and essential part of the postwar migratory environment. The United States and countries across Europe signed guest worker agreements with a wide range of countries (Messina 2007; Peters 2019). These agreements were designed to supply low-cost, temporary labor to countries rebuilding after World War II, providing a boost to agriculture and manufacturing and allowing for more rapid reentry into global supply chains. These agreements supplied advanced economies with low-cost labor while simultaneously providing sending countries with a mechanism to export surplus labor that may prove politically problematic (Miller and Peters 2020).

The relative lack of international agreements on global migration likely contributes to the relative paucity of comparable statistics on labor mobility. What data we do have comes largely from national censuses, collected by the United Nations Population Division (UNPD), aggregated and standardized by scholars interested in making cross-national and -temporal comparisons (Özden et al. 2011). Utilizing these data, in Figure 1.1, we show the growth of global migration since 1960, both in raw numbers and as a share of the world population.[3] In Figure 1.2, we show trends in migration across different country corridors. By far the largest growth is in the number of migrants from the Global South residing in the Global North, though in absolute number, South–South migrants remain the largest migration corridor.[4] This is due, in part, to large labor migration from Southeast Asia to countries in the Persian Gulf, as well as the fact that

---

[3] It is important to emphasize the difference between *stocks* and *flows* of migrants. Statistics reported in national censuses refer to the *stock* of individuals born in country *o* who are currently residing in the country *d* where the census was collected. Information on migration *flows* is generally collected by border agencies or immigration authorities and refer to either the number of individuals entering a country *d* at time *t* or the number of individuals who have obtained citizenship in country *d* at time *t*. The information in Figures 1.1 and 1.2 refer to *stocks* of foreign-born populations.

[4] Throughout this book, we define the Global North as the following set of countries: Australia, Austria, Belgium, Canada, Denmark, Finland, France, Germany, Greece, Hungry, Iceland, Italy, Japan, Luxembourg, Malta, the Netherlands, New Zealand, Norway, Poland, Portugal, Slovenia, Slovakia, Spain, Sweden, Switzerland, United Kingdom, United States. This definition largely aligns with Organization for Economic Cooperation and Development (OECD) membership.

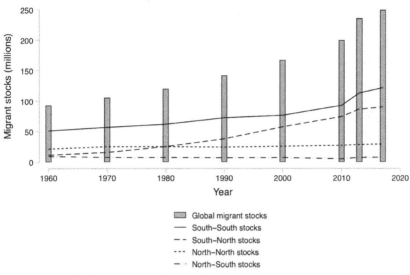

FIGURE 1.2 Global migration by corridor, 1960–2017.
Source: Ozden et al. (2011) and UN (2019).

when environmental crises or conflict occur, individuals are most likely to move to a neighboring country (Braithwaite, Salehyan, and Savun 2019).

What explains these patterns of migration? Why do some leave while others remain? And once individuals, families, and/or communities migrate, how and why do they remain connected to their homelands? These are the central questions we address in this volume; questions that are at the core of current policy debates across destination countries.

WHAT DO WE KNOW?

We are, obviously, not the first to ask this array of questions. Part of the draw of studying global migration is the opportunity to draw connections across scholarship that explores these questions from political science, economics, sociology, geography, and demography. One of the earliest theoretical perspectives on human mobility was Adam Smith's observation regarding *internal* migration in his 1776 *An Inquiry into the Nature and Causes of the Wealth of Nations*. "[T]he wages of labour vary more from place to place than the price of provisions" because, he wrote, "it appears evidently from experience that a man is of all sorts of luggage the most difficult to be transported" (Smith 1776|1977, pp. 83–84). Smith recognized not only that there is variation across localities regarding wages but also that migration – moving from market to market, even internally – is very costly.

Following Smith's conjecture, economic models of migration tend to argue that, all else equal, individuals will migrate from origin country o to destination country d if the expected wage in country d exceeds the expected wage in *country* o, minus the cost(s) associated with migrating (e.g., Borjas 1989). These models of individual wage maximization find favor among those seeking to understand migration between advanced economies, situations where policy and mobility constraints are minimal. Models focusing on decisions made by migrants in the Global South also assume that migration is rational behavior, but posit that the relevant unit of analysis is the household, not the individual. These New Economics of Labor Migration (NELM) models argue that migration decisions are made not by individuals, but rather are the product of family strategies to maximize income and diversify economic risk (e.g., Stark and Levhari 1982). While neoclassical models focus on wage maximization, NELM models focus on migrant remittances – funds transferred back home to friends, families, and households. Consequently, they predict different patterns of, and motivations for, migration.

Scholars interested in global migration hewed to Smith's observation about the costliness of moving. British geographer Ernst Georg Ravenstein (1885) and American sociologist George Zipf (1946) are two early examples. Studying British census data, Ravenstein concluded that migrants tend to move only short distances, and those moving a long distance will migrate to larger cities. Zipf built on Ravenstein, hypothesizing that the volume of migration is proportional to the size of the product of the populations of the origin and destination and inversely proportional to the distance between them. In this way, Zipf translated Newton's physical law of gravity to provide a framework for the study of migration. In this context, distance is the inverse of gravitational pull; the larger the distance between the origin and the destination, the more costly (and more difficult) it will be to move. This "gravity" approach is an influential framework used to study a broad range of internal and global economic activities including capital flows, international trade, and global migration – of which we make extensive use in this book (Beine, Bertoli, and Moraga 2016).

Current approaches to understanding the location choice – the destination – of migrants attempt to measure these "gravitational" forces from a variety of perspectives. Migration, unlike trade in commodities or capital, is a function of individual agency and, as such, there are linguistic, cultural, and ethnic differences between countries that present informal barriers to entry and integration. These barriers are in addition to formal policies that encourage or discourage migration between countries. Sociological approaches argue that we can understand current migration flows through an examination of migrant networks: social systems of connections among family members, co-ethnics, or fellow compatriots that share information between host and home countries (Massey et al. 1993). Information conveyed to potential migrants includes details about labor market opportunities and rules governing citizenship rights in host countries.

Beyond the decision to migrate and choice of destination, a variety of models have been used to better understand the nature and consequences of economic exchange. David Ricardo's canonical model of international trade emphasized the role of comparative advantage in helping predict which goods countries should specialize in producing and trading. With specialization comes a global increase in international trade. Specialization, however, generates winners and losers in the domestic economy, as owners of the relatively scarce factor suffer a decline in the value of returns to their factors, while owners of the abundant factor see an increase in the value of their factor.[5] While the Heckscher-Ohlin and Stolper-Samuelson frameworks help us identify which groups will lobby for protection – whether it be trade or labor – these models highlight the difficulty in assessing priorities when it comes to factor liberalization. One of the reasons, as Mundell (1957) pointed out, is that closing the market to trade may stimulate capital flows. It may, however, *decrease* the flow of capital if capital mobility complements trade flows.[6]

Empirical evidence, however, indicates a more pointed conclusion than envisioned by Mundell (1957), so far as migration is concerned. Trade and investment require that parties to the exchange believe that their counterparties will comply with any contractual agreement. In other words, for an investor in country o to invest in country d, she needs to believe that her counterparty in country d will follow through; she may be

---

[5] See Rogowski (1987) and Frieden (1994) for a discussion of these arguments in relation to international trade and exchange rate policies.

[6] There is increasing evidence that labor market concerns on their own do not affect opinions on immigration in the United States or Europe, as almost all immigrants living in the United States and Europe are complements for local labor. Highly developed economies such as the US and the European Union (EU) are composed increasingly of jobs that need language or other country-specific skills that immigrants are unlikely to possess. See Peters (2015a, 2017) for a review and discussion of these literatures.

secure in this belief if country d has transparent and credible mechanisms for contract enforcement. But what if country d does not have these mechanisms? Drawing on the history of the Maghribi Traders, Greif (1989, 1993) argued that co-ethnics substitute for formal contract enforcement, as they provide information about the reputation of potential counterparties and a sanctioning mechanism should a counterparty abrogate the agreement.

Greif's argument can be used to develop a framework that uncovers the complementarity between migration and global trade and investment. Gould (1994), Rauch and Trindade (2002), and Parsons and Winters (2014) show how trade follows patterns of international migration, while Leblang (2010) and Kugler, Levintal, and Rapoport (2018) do the same for capital flows. The mechanisms here are myriad: Migrants may have specific knowledge of regulations in their homelands, they may serve as a signal regarding the preferences of home-country consumers, or they may be able to leverage connections allowing for market entry.

Most research on the consequences of migration over the last two decades has primarily focused on destinations – host countries. There is a vast literature on the wage effects of migration – whether migrants increase, decrease, or have no effect on the wages of native workers[7] – and on the effects of migration on public opinion and support for populist movements in destination countries.[8] Drawing on theories of decision-making in liberal democracies, Freeman (1995) develops a schema to categorize whether destinations have open or closed immigration systems. Peters (2017) deploys insights from theories of firm behavior to explore where and when we might observe changes in the restrictiveness of migration policy across destinations.[9]

Much less has been written about the effects of migration on countries of *origin* – home countries. While early literature focused on the potential that migration, and the desire of wealthy countries to attract skilled migrants, would result in "brain drain," recent work has given pride of

---

[7] See Clemens and Hunt (2019) and Peri and Yasenov (2019) for a synthesis and review of this literature.

[8] See, for example Fitzgerald (2018), Margalit (2019), and Joppke (2020) for recent contributions.

[9] Hollifield (1992) argues that democracies, by construction, are designed to push towards restrictive immigration regimes, while at the same time capitalist economies compel policy-makers to adopt more open immigration systems. Looking outside the nation-state, Sassen (1996) and Joppke (1998) argue that the rise and soft power of international human rights regimes has pushed liberal democracies to provide entry rights for migrants.

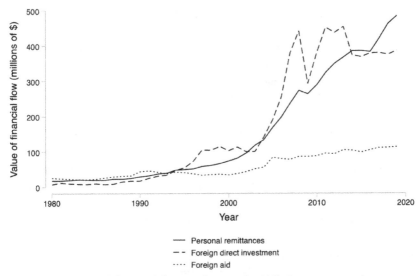

FIGURE 1.3 Global financial flows to low- and middle-income countries, 1980–2018.
Source: World Bank World Development Indicators.

place to migrant remittances.[10] And for good reason: In Figure 1.3, we show the evolution of global remittances flows alongside global flows of foreign aid and foreign direct investment (FDI) to low- and middle-income countries. As of 2017, remittances exceed global FDI flows and, importantly, they are more stable than other global financial flows.

Scholars interested in economic development emphasize the poverty- and inequality-reducing role of remittances. Because remittances flow directly to households, they have the potential to more directly and immediately affect consumption, allowing recipients to invest in health, education, and other public goods that may not be directly provided by the government (Adams and Cuecuecha 2010). Remittances – and their capacity to provide recipient households with financial resources – have important knock-on effects on our understanding of the political economy of development. While not our focus, recent research in political economy explores the political consequences of remittances, asking whether remittances contribute to democratization or the turnover of autocratic regimes (Escribà-Folch, Wright, and Meseguer 2022).

Global migration, then, both directly and indirectly, has important consequences for political and economic development. And, despite the

---

[10] See Kone and Özden (2017) for a review of the arguments and evidence surrounding brain drain, brain gain, and brain circulation.

claims of anti-globalization advocates, governments retain their sovereignty. This does not mean that borders are inviolate; rather, it suggests that countries have a range of options when it comes to managing population flows. On the sending country side, countries have developed a range of institutions designed explicitly to harness remittance flows. Destination countries, likewise, have an arsenal of policy levers that they deploy to manage the inflows of foreign populations.

It is important to qualify the scope conditions under which these conclusions apply. Our primary focus in this book is on labor migration: migration that policymakers tend to describe as "legal," "authorized," or "regulated" and which academics tend to term "economic." This language is used to distinguish migration that is "voluntary" from migration that is "coerced" or "involuntary." This "forced" migration is usually viewed as resulting from conflict (interstate or civil war), repression, and, recently, from natural disasters and climate change (Betts 2009).

The supposed distinction between "voluntary" and "forced" migration has outlived its usefulness, if indeed it ever was useful (Van Hear, Brubaker, and Bessa 2009). Labor migrants may not move just to maximize income, but because there are no economic opportunities in their home communities due to factors like climate change, natural disasters, or low-quality or repressive governance. These individuals and families "flee" economic insecurity, the prospect of malnutrition, violence, and, in some cases, a general lack of economic opportunity. They seek economic refuge and security in other countries. Similarly, those who seek asylum or refuge from political violence or oppression become economically and socially active in their host country in ways that make it difficult to distinguish them from the standard caricature of "labor migrants."

This analytical distinction is rendered more difficult by challenges associated with measurement. Most OECD countries record migrant *inflows* based on the migrant's country of origin, while others measure migration based on the migrant's country of birth. A smaller number of countries record migration based on the migrant's country of citizenship, which may or may not be their country of birth. Measures of migrant stocks – the accumulated number of migrants – measure migrants by their country of birth (for the most part) but do so, generally, every five or ten years, depending on when national censuses are performed. Census data typically do not distinguish between "voluntary" or "forced" migration; it simply asks where the respondent was born, and possibly how they entered the host country.

What this means is that when we discuss migrant flows, we are measuring those who have entered a host country through regular mechanisms for the purpose of work or family unification; we do not explore the determinants of refugee or asylum flows (see Hatton 2020). However, when we discuss migrant stocks, we refer to individuals present in a host country who were born elsewhere, without regard to whether they arrived through regular (versus irregular) means or whether they were granted refugee or asylum status.

CONTRIBUTIONS AND PLAN OF THE BOOK

This brief review situates our argument within the context of a growing and evolving literature from political science, economics, sociology, and demography on the causes and consequences of global migration. Besides articulating and empirically demonstrating that politics shapes human mobility, this book demonstrates that international migration is the glue that binds the global political economy together, benefiting both migrant-sending and -receiving countries in the process. Migrants are crucial facilitators of international capital flows, especially in contexts where formal political and economic institutions are weak or absent. We provide both theory and evidence that international migration brings benefits to home and host societies, and we focus on a range of policy tools that help sending and receiving countries reap these benefits while managing migrant flows. These benefits, however, generate a tension: Increasing globalization unleashes the very forces that seek to undermine its effectiveness, threatening the economic opportunity that migration represents.

Our contribution highlights how political conditions and institutions intimately shape each part of the migration process, from deciding to leave, to choosing where to go, to re-engaging with one's homeland. Because politics shapes whether and how people access resources that are critical for their own well-being, it plays a paramount role in determining individuals' mobility decisions. For example, poor public goods provision and weak political institutions drive emigration because they reduce well-being, and migrants choose destinations based on the political environment that will shape life in their new home. In essence, we argue that a comprehensive account of global human mobility must grapple with its political causes and consequences.

This book combines original theoretical developments with a diverse array of empirical analyses to make its case. Our theoretical frameworks are rooted primarily in rational choice theories of human decision-making, focusing on how political institutions and conditions shape the utility function of people considering and engaging in migration. Methodologically, we employ cutting-edge statistical models to systematically test our arguments in each substantive chapter. We harness both micro-level data on individual decision-making, as well as macro-level time-series data, to identify broader patterns of human mobility. Throughout our analyses, we pay close attention to accounting for alternative explanations and potential confounding factors.

The book is informally organized into three distinct parts. Following the introduction, the first two chapters investigate the decision to migrate, which we conceptualize as a two-stage process. Chapter 2 investigates how a person decides whether to emigrate. We review existing economic and sociological explanations and then build our own *political* explanation, focusing on the quality of local public goods, confidence in political institutions, and perceptions of physical safety in migrant-origin countries. We also explore how political conditions interact with and mitigate economic and sociological drivers of migration. In Chapter 3, we turn our eye to the second stage: a migrant's choice of destination. Here, we home in on the political environment in migrant destination countries, including the bundle of citizenship rights that countries afford migrants, the level of electoral support that anti-immigration parties enjoy, and corruption.

We shift the focus in the next two chapters away from explaining migration and toward how and why migrants foster global economic exchange. Chapter 4 investigates the role of migration in facilitating international flows of investment capital. We hypothesize that because migrants hold valuable knowledge about the economic environment and potential investment opportunities in their homelands, they help investors overcome transnational information asymmetries and increase investment toward their homelands. We use a wealth of cross-national data on migration and international investment capital flows to substantiate our argument empirically. Chapter 5 focuses on *personal* capital flows – the role of migrant remittances. Our original contribution in this chapter shows that migrant-sending countries can build political institutions that engage members of the diaspora to incentivize remittances and return migration. We also build a novel explanation, rooted in principal-agent theory, to explain why some countries have quickly adopted these institutions while others have not.

In the final two chapters, we turn our attention toward gleaning policy-relevant insights for migrant-receiving countries. Chapter 6 discusses how destinations can leverage labor market policies – notably, providing temporary labor market access to migrants – to encourage greater remittance flows that help dampen "root causes" of subsequent migration from low- and middle-income countries. In Chapter 7, our concluding chapter, we place each of our contributions into the broader context of rising anti-immigrant sentiment around the world. While we establish that migration generates significant benefits for the global political economy, we note that these benefits are increasingly threatened by political actors that seek to restrict immigration and villainize migrant populations. Successfully leveraging the economic opportunity that international migration represents is a political project that can be hampered by increasingly successful nativist political movements.

2

Origins

Why Do People Migrate?

International migration is one of the riskiest – and potentially costliest – individual behaviors examined by scholars of political economy. We often explore why people change their political and economic preferences, vote for one party or another, or participate in political protests. In many ways, emigration stands alone because of its costliness and potential permanence. In the simplest sense, an individual or household must use often-scarce financial resources, contemplate leaving behind friends and family, and make decisions among potential destinations for emigration to become a reality. Emigration is costly in other ways as well: It involves forgoing economic opportunity and accumulated social capital at home and risks the loss of proximate social ties in the emigrant's community. And emigration requires that individuals confront known unknowns: Economic opportunities abroad are uncertain, new social contexts can be difficult to navigate, and migrants often face political exclusion and discrimination in destination countries.

Despite these myriad costs, international migration is far from a rarity. In 2019, more than 270 million people resided outside their country of birth (McAuliffe and Khadria 2020). Figure 1.2 illustrates that the number of international migrants has steadily increased over time, with flows from the Global South to the Global North growing significantly (Özden et al. 2011; World Bank Group 2016). Why do people decide to leave their homeland? How can we understand the desire to migrate, and concomitantly, the decision to remain at home?

We answer these central questions by foregrounding human mobility and *im*mobility. Even though millions of people leave their home countries every year, an overwhelming majority of people never migrate internationally. In other words, most individuals either do not want to leave their home country or face constraints that prevent mobility. While the absolute number of migrants has increased over time, when expressed as a proportion of the global population, the size of the migrant population is relatively constant over time at around 3 percent (McAuliffe and Khadria 2020). Global public opinion data illustrated in Figure 2.1 suggests that regardless of region, only a small minority of people express a desire to migrate internationally, and an even smaller group are actively preparing to move. While it may seem odd to highlight *im*mobility in a book about the political economy of international migration, answering "Why do people leave?" requires recognizing that "Why do people stay?" is an equally important question (Schewel 2020).

To understand the decision to leave, we first analyze emigration as a micro-level behavior – a decision made by an individual or household. This micro-level analysis of emigration decision grounds our macro-level exploration of the causes and consequences of migration in the later chapters. Our approach is multifaceted. While scholars have invested considerable energy developing and evaluating economic and sociological explanations of emigration, these explanations are insufficient in that they largely ignore the *political* roots of the decision to leave or stay. Because politics and political institutions shape the environment in which potential emigrants live and because they have significant consequences for an individual's well-being, these factors independently shape preferences over staying and leaving.

While there are a multitude of political conditions that plausibly influence the decision to move or stay, we focus on three overarching features of an individual's political environment: satisfaction with the quality and delivery of public goods, confidence in national political institutions, and perception of physical safety. Classic theories of democracy suggest citizens reward governments that provide quality governance at the ballot box – and punish governments that fail to deliver public goods and physical safety (Lipset 1959; de Mesquita et al. 2003). We extend this logic to questions of human mobility: When citizens are satisfied with the political environment in which they live, they are more likely to remain in place.

This chapter proceeds as follows. We build a micro-level theoretical model of the decision to emigrate that not only includes common economic and sociological explanations for emigration but also draws out the political roots of mobility and immobility. We explore the importance of these variables in an empirical analysis of emigration intentions and concrete

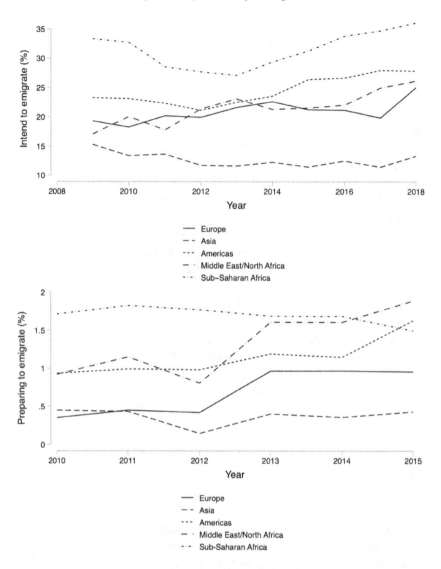

FIGURE 2.1 Potential emigration by region. Top panel: percentage of respondents who intend to emigrate by region, 2009–18. Bottom panel: percentage of respondents who are actively preparing to emigrate by region, 2010–15.
Source: Gallup World Poll.

emigration plans. Our findings indicate that political conditions are as important as economic and social drivers of emigration. Satisfaction with the quality of governance reduces emigration intentions, increasing the rootedness of populations who would otherwise aspire to emigrate.

Political conditions prove most important to highly educated individuals, who are most sensitive to weak governance and opaque political institutions. Meanwhile, quality governance mitigates the effect of other powerful migration drivers, such as deteriorating economic conditions and transnational social networks. Taken together, our theory and findings emphasize that any understanding of the decision to emigrate must appreciate the role of political conditions in migrant-sending countries.

WHY DO PEOPLE LEAVE?

International migration occurs when an individual leaves their country of origin and moves across a national border for the purpose of permanent or semi-permanent residence. Excluding those who are forced to migrate due to political repression, violent conflict, or natural disaster, we focus on *voluntary* migration decisions made at the individual or household unit level. The decision to emigrate, or to stay, is complicated. An individual's home – their geographic location – has a variety of social, economic, political, and cultural characteristics embedded within it. How can we better understand the decision to emigrate?

To answer this question, we begin by foregrounding a framework that centers on the intersection of emigration *aspirations* and *ability* (Carling 2002). This approach provides a simple conceptualization of mobility and immobility. Aspiration refers to whether an individual decides that emigration is preferable to non-emigration. Ability, meanwhile, refers to whether an individual faces binding barriers or constraints to their mobility.[1] These two concepts create a simple 2-by-2 matrix depicted in Figure 2.2. When individuals simultaneously aspire and are able to emigrate, they do so – these individuals are represented in the top-left cell as voluntary migrants. This book's focus is, for the most part, on this category: those who voluntarily decide to undertake international migration.

The remaining cells represent different classes of *non*-migrants – those who remain in place, despite conditions that might make us predict otherwise. In this sense, the aspiration-and-ability framework highlights the fact that most people do not emigrate over their lifetimes (Schewel 2020). Those who aspire to migrate but are unable to do so are represented in

---

[1] While we draw on migration studies for these concepts, note that they are in principle the same as willingness and ability to pay for a good or asset in a more economic conception of the decision to emigrate.

Aspiration

Ability	Aspire to migrate	Do not aspire to migrate
Able to migrate	Voluntary migrants	Voluntary non-migrants
Unable to migrate	Involuntary non-migrants	Acquiescent non-migrants

FIGURE 2.2 Aspiration-and-ability framework.
Adapted from Schewel (2020).

the bottom-left as involuntary non-migrants – those who have decided emigration is attractive, but who face some binding constraint to their mobility. Those who do not aspire to migrate despite having the ability to do so are represented in the top-right as voluntary non-migrants. Finally, those who neither aspire nor are able to migrate are represented in the bottom-left corner as voluntary, or acquiescent, non-migrants.[2] A wealth of polling data suggests that a substantial majority of the global population falls in the right-side cells of Figure 2.2 – that is, they have no aspiration to migrate, regardless of ability. This empirical fact is represented in Figure 2.1. Only a minority of individuals even expresses an intention to emigrate, and regardless of region, a tiny fraction of people is actively preparing to move internationally.

This framework suggests that it is necessary to identify the factors that shape both the *aspiration* and *ability* of potential migrants to explain why people migrate or remain in place. What characteristics or conditions influence whether individuals decide they prefer migration to non-migration? Accordingly, what characteristics or conditions shape individuals' ability to undertake international migration? Recent contributions broadly identify two classes of factors that operate on different levels of analysis: individual-level characteristics and social characteristics, the environment in which individuals currently live (Carling and Schewel 2018). Demographic characteristics such as age, gender, and marital status consistently predict the likelihood that individuals aspire to emigrate, along with individual socioeconomic status. Meanwhile, local and national factors such as level of economic development, violence, and social attachments and norms consistently shape aspirations and abilities (Aslany et al. 2021).

---

[2] Schewel (2015) discusses at length the concept of acquiescent immobility and the potential distinction between true voluntary and acquiescent immobility.

Economic Explanations for Emigration

Perhaps the most influential theories of emigration originate from economic thinking. These models discuss how economic considerations shape the benefits and costs of emigration and fit neatly within an aspiration–ability framework. Neoclassical economic models posit that, like all rational economic behavior, the primary driver of whether individuals emigrate is whether doing so would result in an expected increase in wages, after accounting for emigration costs (Lewis 1954; Sjaastad 1962; Todaro 1976). All else equal, when the difference between the expected wage a person can earn abroad and the wage received at home is positive, after accounting for the costs of moving, neoclassical models predict that person would emigrate. These models suggest a simple reason for emigration: rational maximization of personal economic self-interest (Massey et al. 1993; Constant and Massey 2002).

While parsimonious, these models massively overpredict emigration. Wages are near-uniformly higher abroad for those living outside the wealthiest countries. This suggests that nearly all people who live in low- and middle-income countries should want to emigrate.[3] Yet we know this is not the case. Around the world, most people do not express a desire to leave their current country, as illustrated in Figure 2.1. The only factor that constrains emigration in neoclassical models is cost: When moving is costlier than expected wage gains, emigration does not occur.

More sophisticated models in this tradition incorporate the idea of financial constraints. Emigration is only an option for those who have sufficient material resources, those for whom financial costs are not a binding constraint. People living in developing countries for whom the expected net wage gain is large may fail to emigrate because they do not possess the requisite financial resources to cover the costs of travel, file necessary applications for entry, and support oneself while searching for employment in a new destination (Dustmann and Okatenko 2014; Angelucci 2015). We note that while this explains why people do not move despite desiring to do so, it fails to explain why some who can emigrate and would benefit from doing so prefer to remain at home.

---

[3] We focus here on intentions to emigrate. Neoclassical models of migration suggest that wage differentials, absent barriers in destination countries and accounting for transportation costs, would drive immigration until wages in home countries equal those in host countries.

An alternative tradition, termed the New Economics of Labor Migration (NELM), rests on fundamentally different assumptions. NELM models propose that the household, not the individual, is the appropriate unit for analyzing the emigration decision (Stark and Levhari 1982). Households, especially those in countries of the Global South, face a variety of economic risks that potentially endanger their prospect for stable and reliable income. Labor markets are often weak and volatile, and households engaged in agricultural production face the risk of a poor harvest that can threaten their whole-year income. Underdeveloped private insurance markets, as well as the lack of a strong public social safety net, mean that managing these economic risks often proves difficult (Massey et al. 1993; Massey 2009).

NELM theories posit that emigration is part of a household's strategy to diversify its economic risk and insure itself against domestic economic volatility. In the canonical NELM model, household members migrate to different labor markets to smooth income in the hopes that labor market risks across the home and destination labor markets are uncorrelated. The optimal way to decrease the correlation between home and destination labor markets is for a household member to migrate internationally. Once in the destination labor market, the migrant sends money back to the household, in the form of remittances, to help decrease the volatility of consumption and reduce local credit constraints faced by the household (Taylor 1999). Whether invested or used for additional consumption, NELM scholars view remittances as an essential mechanism allowing households to use emigration as a household risk diversification strategy.[4]

Proponents of NELM theories suggest that this household-level model is more reflective of international migration from countries in the Global South to the Global North than the neoclassical approach, which may be more reflective of wage maximization behavior among migrants that circulate between countries in the Global North (Massey 2009). This distinction is important, as most international migrants originate in the Global South. However, mobility costs may still limit this strategy of risk diversification as some households are unable to finance the migration of a household member, just as in the neoclassical approach.

Yet those who leave are not part of a homogeneous group that faces an identical economic calculus. Perhaps the most salient feature in economic models is the migrant's education or skill level. Economic models typically treat each additional increment of education as an investment in human

---

[4] We discuss the causes and consequences of migrant remittances in greater detail in Chapter 5.

capital on which an individual expects a return. Emigration is a mechanism to achieve that return – once abroad, highly educated migrants receive wages that are orders of magnitude larger than they would receive at home (Gibson and McKenzie 2012). Emigration costs are also lower for the highly skilled because most major destination countries have policies that explicitly favor them and natives have more positive views of them (Hainmueller and Hiscox 2010; Papademetriou and Sumption 2011). This means that we expect individuals' emigration predispositions to vary systematically with educational attainment. Indeed, Figure 2.3 illustrates that relatively more educated people are more likely to express an intention, and to be actively engaged in preparation, to emigrate – a trend also borne out in realized emigration (Gibson and McKenzie 2011). Accounting for the lens of education and skill is essential in models of emigration.

Neoclassical and NELM approaches are useful starting points in economic models of emigration. Note that these theories focus on different units of analysis (individuals versus households) and utilize divergent economic logics for emigration (wage maximization versus risk diversification). These models also generate fundamentally different observable implications: While neoclassical models suggest that people choose to migrate to a destination country that maximizes their wage, NELM models instead suggest that individuals who belong to household units may not always seek a destination with high wages, but rather one that satisfices their desire to manage household risk. That said, both models posit that improved economic well-being, depending on how the unit of analysis is defined, is the primary driver of migration.

Sociological Explanations for Migration

Migration has a sociological dimension in addition to an economic one. Sociological theories give pride of place to the role of transnational social networks in the emigration process. Regardless of approach, the primary insight is that a person is more likely to emigrate when she has friends and family who have previously migrated.[5] Transnational social networks reduce the non-economic costs of relocation. The prospect of migrating internationally can be psychologically costly, leading to the severing of social ties at home while also requiring significant social adjustment once abroad. Having a network of friends and family in a destination country

[5] See Aslany et al. (2021) for a comprehensive overview of over thirty studies which confirm the importance of social networks in determining whether or not people emigrate.

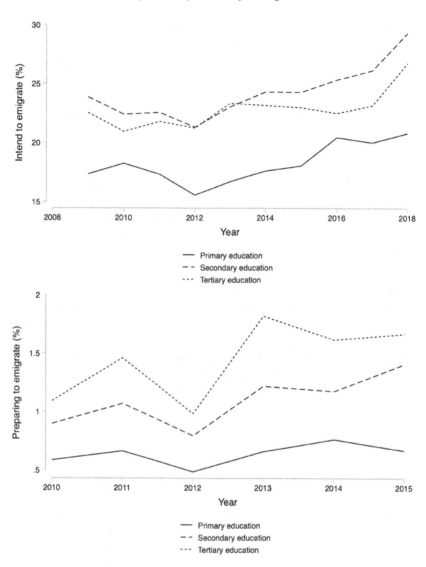

FIGURE 2.3 Potential emigration by educational attainment. Top panel: percentage of respondents who intend to emigrate by educational attainment, 2009–18. Bottom panel: percentage of respondents who are actively preparing to emigrate by educational attainment, 2010–15.
Source: Gallup World Poll.

can significantly reduce these costs. A pre-existing social network eases adjustment to lost connections at home and fosters social integration abroad (Massey and España 1987). Having friends and family who previously emigrated simultaneously increases aspirations to leave and makes emigration more psychologically possible.

Social networks also transmit crucial information, facilitating migration and economic integration. Transnational social networks inform potential migrants about the process of traveling and applying for necessary legal documentation in the host country (Massey et al. 1993). These networks also provide invaluable information about employment opportunities that are critical to the wage maximization goal of emigration; this kind of information, provided because of social obligations like kinship and friendship, is difficult to acquire by other means for most migrants (Massey and España 1987; Palloni et al. 2001). Finally, migrant networks serve as a social safety net that reduces the risks of emigration. Migrant networks often help new arrivals find housing, learn the local language of business, and more broadly integrate into the local economy (Portes and Böröcz 1989; Light, Bernard, and Kim 1999). Again, these are valuable resources that substantially increase the ability of many individuals to migrate.

Sociological theories point out that transnational social networks can produce a "cumulative causation" loop. The first emigrants from an origin country face psychological and information costs as they are pioneers, with no social ties on which to draw. However, once they establish initial roots, the act of subsequent migration becomes marginally less costly and risky for new potential migrants in their social networks, fostering mobility. This further expands migrant networks in destination countries, further decreasing risks and costs for future waves of migrants (Massey 1990; Fussell 2010). This cumulative process creates sustained migration flows due to the cost-reducing effects of each additional migrant, sometimes to the point that migration costs are so low that it overshadows the wage maximization equation (Massey et al. 1993). However, evidence suggests that social networks have diminishing effects with the size of the migrant population (Clark, Hatton, and Williamson 2007), policies that limit migration channels and family reunification can constrain the effects of migrant networks (Böcker 1994; Collyer 2005), and social ties at home can limit the attractiveness of migrant networks abroad (Manchin and Orazbayev 2018).

Sociological theories at the same time challenge and complement economic theories. On the one hand, they highlight that the modal individual has no aspiration to emigrate regardless of ability or potential payoffs, that there are significant non-economic costs of migration, and that transnational social networks overshadow other considerations like wage maximization. In this sense, they suggest a separate logic explaining emigration. On the other hand, migrant networks fit neatly within economic models: Economists conceive of networks as resources that decrease information and search costs at the destination, make obtaining employment abroad easier, and provide prospective migrants with a built-in social safety net. Regardless, social network-based theories are among the most well-supported by the empirical record. Quantitative cross-national analyses repeatedly confirm the social network hypothesis, making the inclusion of social network variables essential in any model of international migration (Clark, Hatton, and Williamson 2007; Hatton and Williamson 2011; Fitzgerald, Leblang, and Teets 2014).

Political Explanations for Emigration

Economic and sociological explanations for emigration are compelling. Wage maximization, household economic risk reduction, and trans-national social ties undoubtedly underlie emigration. We add to these contributions by focusing on the *political* roots of emigration, arguing that individual beliefs about the quality of domestic governance and political institutions fundamentally shape mobility and immobility dynamics alongside economic and social forces.

We are by no means the first to make this argument. Hirschman's (1970) exit, voice, and loyalty framework links dissatisfaction with the political status quo to the decision to emigrate. A political economy tradition following Hirschman explores the political roots of migration (Dowding et al. 2000; Dowding and John 2008; Warren 2011), highlighting that "voting with one's feet" is an individual-level response to unsatisfying political conditions (Somin 2020). We extend this literature by building and testing a micro-level theory that links politics to voluntary *immobility*. Our central claim is that when individuals perceive that they enjoy quality local governance, responsive political institutions, and physical safety, they are less likely to emigrate. In other words, our focus is on how perceptions of quality governance foster voluntary immobility.

Our argument has a simple starting point: Like economic models of emigration, people seek to invest in their own well-being, desiring a state of the world in which they have sufficient resources to meet their own life challenges, whether psychological, social, or material (Dodge et al. 2012). When mobility is well-being-enhancing and feasible, an individual will emigrate. Conversely, when an individual has a high degree of well-being at home, emigration proves unnecessary and does not occur.

Yet personal assessment of well-being is not based solely on economic calculation. Political institutions and conditions are particularly salient as they provide individuals with, or deprive them of, resources to help overcome life challenges. We focus on three primary ways that local and national politics influence well-being. First, governments are responsible for providing local governance and the delivery of public goods. The provision of welfare-enhancing services like healthcare, education, and transport infrastructure primarily falls on local and national governments. When these goods are high-quality and accessible, well-being increases; when they are of poor quality and inaccessible to many citizens, well-being falls (Halleröd et al. 2013).

This proposition is well-supported by empirical research. Provision of quality public goods matters as much, or more, to the well-being of ordinary people as their economic conditions (Helliwell and Huang 2008; Helliwell et al. 2018). Relatedly, individuals who live in societies with more progressive taxation report higher life satisfaction; the main mechanism connecting these two variables is greater satisfaction with public goods (Oishi, Schimmack, and Diener 2012). This means that even when wages and economic risk remain constant, provision of quality public goods can meaningfully increase well-being by providing new resources to meet life challenges.

Second, political institutions are responsible for translating and transmitting citizen preferences to officeholders and for holding policy makers accountable. Citizens benefit when political institutions more accurately reflect their own interests and are harmed when those institutions instead represent the preferences of a narrower population. Personal experience with corruption, which can be a significant life challenge, is also strongly associated with declining well-being (Sulemana, Iddrisu, and Kyoore, 2017). More accountable political institutions are associated with less welfare-reducing corruption because they allow citizens to better punish politicians who engage in malfeasance (Lederman, Loayza, and Soares 2005; Ferraz and Finan 2011). More representative and accountable governments result in greater well-being for citizens more generally (Tavits 2008).

Finally, and perhaps most fundamentally, the provision of physical safety is a key well-being-enhancing duty of governments. Whether experienced directly or indirectly, crime has high individual costs: It has significant deleterious effects on mental health and overall well-being, and significantly changes how people rate their own life satisfaction (Lorenc et al. 2012; Dustmann and Fasani 2016). When governments effectively provide physical safety to their citizens and prevent widespread crime victimization, the perceived physical challenges that individuals face fall, and well-being subsequently increases.

In short, political conditions shape mobility and immobility because they are intimately related to individual well-being. Political institutions can extend material resources to individuals, augmenting their ability to meet life challenges. When political institutions foster greater well-being, emigration provides a relatively lower return, and people remain voluntarily immobile. But governments can also withhold vital resources when they fail to adequately provide public goods, and political conditions like corruption and a lack of safety can present new life challenges that are well-being-reducing. When these dynamics lead to falling well-being, they can raise aspirations to exit and increase emigration. Through these pathways, politics independently shapes micro-level decisions to emigrate.

Education, Politics, and Emigration Intentions

We also argue that, as in the case of economic conditions, an important moderator of the relationship between political conditions and emigration is human capital. Specifically, we hypothesize that perceptions of quality governance matter most for the emigration decisions of those who have more education. We highlight recent research demonstrating a conditional relationship between education, institutional quality, and political engagement. When educated citizens perceive that political institutions at home are strong, their willingness to use political voice to pursue greater well-being increases, fostering voluntary immobility. But when institutional quality is lacking, the highly educated are likely to see emigration as an attractive alternative to political action.

A wealth of research illustrates that education shapes individual-level political preferences and behaviors. Modernization theory argues that education is essential to the democratization process (Dahl 1971). Education is most directly associated with increased attention paid to politics, as well as augmented political knowledge (Verba, Schlozman, and Brady 1995; Larreguy and Marshall 2017). Education also enhances citizens' ability to evaluate policies and hold politicians accountable (Ocantos, Jonge, and Nickerson 2014). Education increases political sophistication – voters are better at discerning the credibility of different forms of information surrounding issues like corruption (Weitz-Shapiro and Winters 2017). In general, more educated people are more politically aware and better understand the impacts of policies and politicians on their well-being.

Yet political awareness and cognitive ability do not always translate into political engagement. Especially in developing country contexts, whether education leads to the use of political voice is strongly conditioned by the institutional environment in which citizens live. For instance, in electoral authoritarian regimes, more educated citizens often deliberately disengage from political participation despite expressing higher interest in politics (Croke et al. 2016). Even in democratic contexts, corruption significantly mitigates the relationship between education and political participation. When national corruption is high, highly educated people are no more likely to engage formally with the political process than relatively less-educated people (Agerberg 2019), perceiving that such engagement is not well-being-enhancing.

In short, research shows that increasing education only translates into political engagement in conditions of institutional strength. When educated citizens already perceive that political conditions are poor, the exercise of voice is unlikely. We extend this insight to argue that emigration is likely to be an attractive exit option for the highly educated in these contexts. When educated people disengage at home due to weak political conditions, they look to alternative means by which they can improve their own well-being besides political action. International migration is an attractive exit option for politically disengaged, highly educated citizens who have decided that the exercise of voice is not feasible in a context of weak political institutions.

For highly educated citizens, emigration is a credible exit option. Advanced economies, which experience shortages of high-skilled labor, explicitly design their immigration policies to attract highly educated immigrants (Kahanec and Zimmermann 2010; Czaika and Parsons 2017). These policies privilege those who hold in-demand educational qualifications, and they often ease the naturalization process for this subset of immigrants. As a result, more educated people have a credible outside option in the form of emigration when they find the exercise of voice non-viable.

Our argument suggests a negative interactive relationship between perceptions of political conditions and education when explaining emigration behavior. When more educated citizens perceive that the institutional context in which they live is conducive to the exercise of voice, they are more likely to feel more politically efficacious and remain voluntarily immobile. On the other hand, in the presence of weak political conditions, those same citizens are more likely to exercise the exit option of emigration.

MODELING THE DECISION TO EMIGRATE

We explore the political roots of (im)mobility by building a micro-level empirical model of emigration intentions. We test our expectations alongside prominent economic and sociological theories. To do this, we use a relatively novel, globally representative survey of individuals: the Gallup World Poll (GWP). The GWP has conducted a yearly survey of at least 1,000 individuals from approximately 180 countries every year since 2005. The result is a wealth of data that is representative of more than 99 percent of the global population. The GWP is widely regarded as a high-quality survey and is used in research across a range of disciplines, including political science, economics, and migration studies (Dustmann and Okatenko 2014; Docquier, Tansel, and Turati 2020; Kustov 2020). Our sample includes data from roughly 130 countries.[6]

The GWP has asked respondents consistent questions about potential emigration for more than a decade. While the survey does not measure realized emigration (which proves difficult in any survey context), its data on potential emigration have been widely used as they are strongly correlated with observed emigration rates (Tjaden, Auer, and Laczko 2019; Clemens and Mendola 2020).[7] We discuss the migration-related survey questions in more detail below. Importantly, the GWP also includes a wide range of information about a respondent's level of education, employment, income, family status, and gender. Of particular importance, it includes questions related to an individual's assessment of their home country's political conditions, including (a) satisfaction with local governance and public goods, (b) confidence in national political institutions, and (c) perceptions of physical safety. We use responses to these questions to create individual-level measures of political perceptions.

Measuring Emigration Intentions and Behaviors

The GWP contains the most extensive micro-level data on emigration decision-making of any survey instrument and is widely used to study

---

[6] See Appendix Table A2.1 for a list of sample countries.

[7] Tjaden, Auer, and Laczko (2019) in particular find that potential emigration as measured by concrete emigration preparations in the Gallup World Poll is strongly correlated with actual macro-level migration flows at around 0.8.

migration behavior.[8] Each respondent is asked three nested questions about emigration. The first question asks about emigration *intentions*: "Ideally, if you had the opportunity, would you like to move permanently to another country, or would you prefer to continue living in this country?" Respondents can answer "yes," "no," "don't know," or refuse to answer.[9] Those who answer "yes" are asked about concrete *plans* to emigrate: "Are you planning to move permanently to another country in the next 12 months, or not?" Those who answer that they both intend and plan to emigrate are asked about active *preparations* to emigrate: "Have you done any preparation for this move (for example, applied for residency or visa, purchased the ticket, etc.)?" We use the questions about emigration *intentions* and *preparations* to proxy for both preferences and behaviors surrounding emigration.

Figure 2.4 maps the percentage of individuals for each country who state that they *intend* or are *preparing* to emigrate in two panels. These emigration intention and preparations rates are calculated by pooling all survey waves from 2009–2020 for each country. The map illustrates that major regions of emigration during the time period – Central America, Africa, and Eastern Europe – also have the highest percentage of individuals who state that they intend or are preparing to leave. The United States and Western European countries see much lower potential emigration rates by comparison.

Our theoretical framework focuses primarily on explaining *voluntary* choices to emigrate or remain at home. The GWP data do not allow us to cleanly distinguish between those who leave voluntarily and those "forced" to do so. The questions we employ primarily frame emigration as a voluntary choice, asking respondents if they would like to emigrate, and we follow much existing literature by focusing on the choice to emigrate. Recent research problematizes "forced" migration, instead characterizing emigration decisions on a spectrum of choice and constraints (Schewel 2020). Some who are able to emigrate remain in place despite repressive political conditions, natural disasters, or civil conflict – events that we often associate with forced migration (Holland and Peters 2020; Schon 2020). Our approach continues in this tradition by analyzing mobility as a micro-level choice, albeit a choice subject to varying constraints. We also note that the GWP does not allow us to distinguish between *channels* of emigration (for example, authorized and unauthorized migration pathways).

---

[8] See, for instance, Dustmann and Okatenko (2014); Dao et al. (2018); Manchin and Orazbayev (2018); and Clemens and Mendola (2020).
[9] Less than 3 percent of respondents either respond that they don't know or refused to answer.

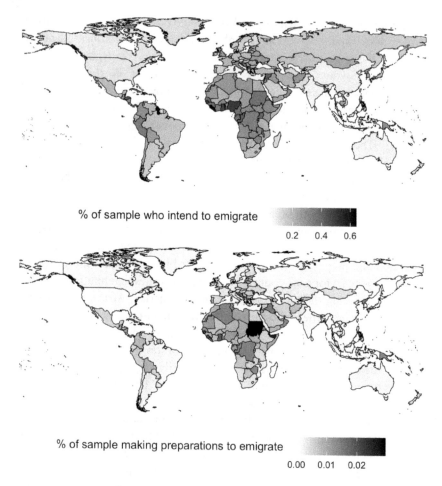

FIGURE 2.4 Emigration intentions and plans by country. Top panel: percentage of respondents who intend to emigrate by country. Bottom panel: percentage of respondents who are actively preparing to emigrate by country. Percentages calculated by pooling all survey waves from 2009 to 2020 for each country. Source: Gallup World Poll.

Measuring Satisfaction with Political Conditions

The GWP provides a trove of questions that we use to construct indices measuring the three dimensions of political conditions we discussed above: satisfaction with public goods, confidence in political institutions, and perceptions of physical safety. For each index, we take responses to clusters of perception-related questions and combine them into a single

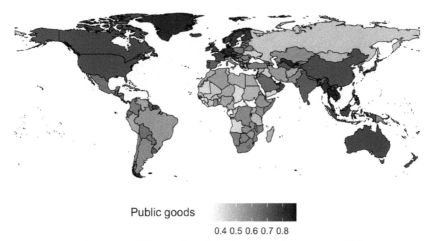

Public goods

0.4 0.5 0.6 0.7 0.8

FIGURE 2.5 Average public goods satisfaction score by country. Higher scores indicate greater satisfaction. Scores calculated by pooling all survey waves from 2009 to 2020 for each country. Scores derived using polychoric principal components analysis (PCA).
Source: Gallup World Poll.

index using polychoric principal components analysis (PCA). Polychoric PCA allows for the aggregation of information from multiple discrete numeric measures into a single index that grants a fine-grained measure of an underlying concept (Kolenikov and Angeles 2009) and is useful in this context, as it allows us to operationalize the most important political conditions that shape emigration in a parsimonious fashion.[10]

Our first index measures individual satisfaction with local public goods. We use binary responses to questions about satisfaction with the following categories of public goods: healthcare, education, affordable housing, air quality, water quality, roads, and transit. Respondents state whether they are either satisfied or dissatisfied with each of these categories. We combine these responses using polychoric PCA and take the first component to generate a continuous measure of satisfaction with local public goods. We standardize this measure so that all values lie between 0 and 1; higher values represent greater satisfaction with public goods. Figure 2.5 illustrates cross-national variation in satisfaction with public goods across the sample period.

We next construct an index that measures individuals' confidence in national political institutions. We employ binary responses to questions

[10] Our implementation of polychoric PCA is similar to that of Dustmann and Okatenko (2014).

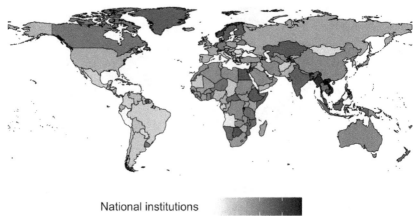

National institutions

0.2   0.4   0.6   0.8

FIGURE 2.6 Average confidence in national institutions score by country. Higher scores indicate greater confidence. Scores calculated by pooling all survey waves from 2009 to 2020 for each country. Scores derived using polychoric principal components analysis (PCA).
Source: Gallup World Poll.

about confidence in and approval of a range of political institutions: confidence in the honesty of elections, confidence in the courts, confidence in the national government, and approval of the country's current leadership. Respondents state whether they are confident in or approve of each of these institutions. We again use PCA to combine these responses and take the first component to generate a continuous measure of confidence in political institutions. We also standardize this measure so that all values lie between 0 and 1; higher values represent greater confidence in political institutions. Figure 2.6 illustrates cross-national variation in confidence in political institutions across the sample period.

Finally, we create an index that measures individuals' perceptions of physical safety. We employ binary responses to questions about experience with crime and perceptions of safety in the local environment: whether the respondent has had money stolen from them in the past 12 months, whether the respondent has been assaulted in the past 12 months, and whether the respondent feels safe walking alone at night. We again combine these responses using polychoric PCA and take the first component to generate a continuous measure of perceptions of physical safety. We also standardize this measure so that all values lie between 0 and 1; higher values represent greater perceptions of safety. Figure 2.7 illustrates cross-national variation in perceptions of physical safety across the sample period. These three indices represent our political variables of interest in the empirical models that follow.

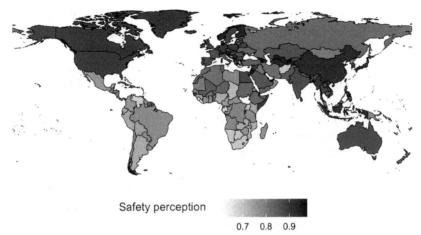

Safety perception

0.7 0.8 0.9

FIGURE 2.7 Average safety perception score by country. Higher scores indicate greater safety perceptions. Scores calculated by pooling all survey waves from 2009 to 2020 for each country. Scores derived using polychoric principal components analysis (PCA).
Source: Gallup World Poll.

Empirical Model

We use a linear probability model to estimate Equation (1):[11]

$$IntendMigrate_{ijt} = \beta_1 PublicGoods_{ijt} + \beta_2 Institutions_{ijt} \qquad (2.1)$$
$$+ \beta_3 Safety_{ijt} + \phi X_i + \alpha_{jt} + \varepsilon_i$$

where $IntendMigrate_{ijt}$ is an indicator equal to 1 if individual i living in country j in year t expresses an intention to emigrate and 0 otherwise, $PublicGoods_{ijt}$ represents our measure of satisfaction with local public goods, $Institutions_{ijt}$ is our measure of confidence in national political institutions, $Safety_{ijt}$ is our measure of perceptions of physical safety, X_{ijt} is a vector of individual-level control variables, and α_{jt} is a complete set of country*year combination fixed effects. The use of country*year fixed effects means that we account for macro-level factors that are constant within a given country-year, allowing us to focus on variation between

---

[11] We use linear probability models for a few reasons: They are easy and efficient to compute, especially with the large samples that we can use; coefficients are readily interpretable; and the fixed effects strategy that we employ does not complicate estimation. However, we also estimate these models using logistic regression in results not reported here. The results that follow are all substantially similar and are available upon request.

individuals within that country-year. This strategy obviates the need to control for any potential confounding variables that are fixed for all individuals in the same country and in the same year, such as economic performance, natural disasters, civil conflict, or political institutions. We cluster standard errors by country-years and use the GWP's sample weights in all estimations.

Our battery of individual-level control variables, X_i, captures a number of salient demographic characteristics informed by existing theory that may influence both political perceptions and emigration intentions: gender, age, educational attainment (primary, secondary, and tertiary), household size, within-country income quintile, employment status, and whether or not an individual has family or friends who live abroad. We also include an additional measure of emigration intentions capturing domestic movement that proxies for an individual's underlying mobility propensity. We include responses to the following question: "In the next 12 months, are you likely or unlikely to move away from the city or area where you live?" Respondents can answer likely, unlikely, or don't know. We exclude all respondents who do not respond by saying likely or unlikely, leaving a binary measure of domestic mobility intentions.[12]

Baseline Results

We present our baseline results in Figure 2.8, which shows a coefficient plot from our fully specified model of emigration intentions.[13] For continuous variables, we depict the estimated effect of a one-standard-deviation increase; for indicator variables, we depict the estimated effect of a change from zero to one. These results demonstrate the explanatory power of existing economic and sociological explanations. Individuals with more education are more likely to express an intention to emigrate, while women and older individuals are less likely to do so. Those who fall in higher income quintiles are slightly less likely to state that they intend to emigrate, though not at conventional levels of statistical significance, while the unemployed are far more likely to prefer exit. Perhaps the most powerful predictor of emigration intention is being part of a transnational social network: Knowing someone who lives

---

[12] Appendix Table A2.2 displays summary statistics for all variables.

[13] In Appendix Table A2.3, we also present models without the inclusion of political conditions, as well as models that include each measure of political conditions separately.

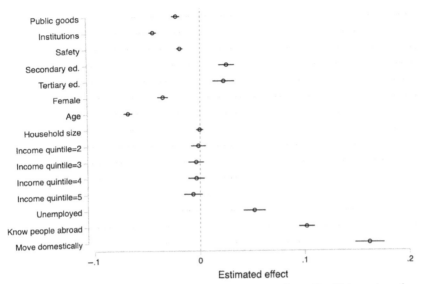

FIGURE 2.8 Political conditions and emigration intentions. Coefficient plot of main model of emigration intentions. Point estimates for continuous variables reflect one-standard-deviation increases. Indicator variables reflect moving from zero to one. 95% confidence intervals included. Estimates from Model (5) of Appendix Table A2.3.

abroad is, on average, associated with a 9-percentage point increase in the probability of intending to emigrate.

How do political conditions shape emigration intentions? For all measures of political conditions, higher values represent more favorable perceptions. All three political dimensions prove salient to emigration intentions. Increased satisfaction with local public goods, higher confidence in national institutions, and perceptions of greater safety are associated with a decreased probability of intending to emigrate. The estimated effects of political conditions are not only statistically significant, but substantively important. A one-standard-deviation increase in satisfaction with public goods is associated with a 2.3-percentage point decrease in the probability of expressing an emigration intention. For confidence in national political institutions, the same estimated effect is negative 4.5 percentage points, while for perceptions of physical safety the estimated effect is negative 1.9 percentage points. All are statistically significant at conventional levels. These magnitudes suggest that perceptions of political conditions are at least as important as economic and sociological drivers of emigration intentions, such as personal economic conditions or transnational social networks.

Our results demonstrate that perceptions of political conditions meaningfully shape *intentions* to emigrate. We corroborate these baseline findings using a more restrictive measure: whether individuals state that they are making costly *preparations* to emigrate within the next 12 months. Far fewer individuals respond affirmatively to this alternative question, as displayed in Figure 2.4. We replicate our baseline findings in Appendix Table A2.4 using this alternative measure. The relative magnitudes of all variables are diminished in accordance with the lower baseline probability, but the three political dimensions on which we focus consistently decrease the probability that one is making costly preparations to emigrate. This suggests that political conditions not only drive emigration desires, but also actual emigration behavior.

The Role of Education

Our results so far establish that political conditions shape emigration intentions. More favorable perceptions of public goods, national institutions, and physical safety are associated with a decreased probability of emigration intentions and preparations, even when accounting for prominent alternative explanations. Yet we also argue that more highly educated people are particularly sensitive to political conditions when considering emigration. To test this extension of our argument, we re-estimate our baseline empirical models, adding interaction terms between our indices of political conditions and individual-level educational attainment. The rest of the empirical specification remains identical to Equation (1).

Figure 2.9 summarizes our main findings with a set of three marginal effects plots. The figure shows the predicted probability of intending to emigrate for tertiary-educated and non-tertiary-educated respondents across the range of our three measures of political conditions. We also present underlying interactive models in Appendix Table A2.5. The figure shows that perceptions of public goods and confidence in political institutions are most important to highly educated people. When tertiary-educated respondents are extremely dissatisfied with public goods and political institutions, they are far more likely to intend to emigrate than less-educated respondents. However, at high levels of satisfaction with political conditions, high- and low-educated people have a statistically indistinguishable probability of intending to emigrate.

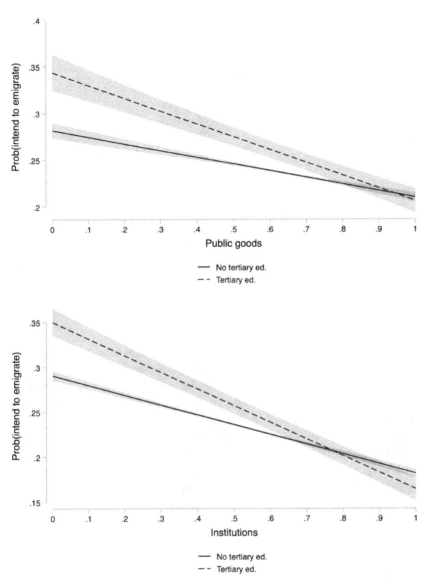

FIGURE 2.9 Political conditions, education, and emigration intentions. Predicted probability of intending to emigrate across range of political conditions by level of education. Top panel: public goods. Middle panel: confidence in institutions. Bottom panel: safety perceptions. Estimates from Model (4) of Appendix Table A2.5.

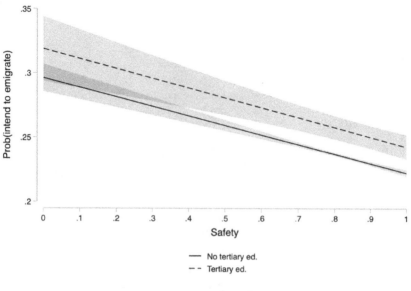

FIGURE 2.9 (*cont.*)

We note that in our model specifications, political conditions continue to matter regardless of educational attainment, but that they are particularly important for those with secondary or tertiary education. For respondents with a primary education only, a one-standard-deviation increase in satisfaction with public goods is associated with about a 1.2-percentage point decline in the probability of expressing an emigration intention. This effect more than doubles for secondary and tertiary education respondents, to about a 3-percentage point decline. The results suggest there is little distinguishable difference between these two groups of relatively more educated people. The interactive effect of education is also stark when it comes to confidence in political institutions. While a one-standard-deviation increase in confidence is associated with a roughly 3.4-percentage point decline in the probability of expressing an intention to emigrate for primary-educated people, this effect grows significantly with education. For secondary-educated people, this increase in confidence corresponds to a roughly 5-percentage point decline, and for tertiary-educated respondents, the decline grows to about 6.3 percentage points.

The fact that education significantly augments the mobility-reducing effects of confidence in political institutions aligns with our basic argument. When institutions are relatively stronger, the exercise of voice is seen as more viable by educated people and emigration become less attractive. Finally, there is weaker evidence to suggest an interactive effect of education and perceptions of physical safety. Feelings of safety appear to matter roughly equally regardless of educational attainment.

As with our baseline results, we analyze how the interactive effect of education and political conditions affects the probability of making costly *preparations* to emigrate, a much more restrictive measure of mobility. These results are available in Appendix Table A2.6. While the coefficient sizes again diminish due to the relatively lower baseline probability, education continues to augment the mobility-reducing effects of confidence in national institutions and perceptions of physical safety. This suggests again that education significantly conditions how political factors shape not only emigration preferences, but also concrete emigration behaviors.

POLITICS AS A MODERATOR

How might political conditions and other drivers of emigration interact with each other? While we empirically analyze factors like political perceptions, individual economic conditions, and social networks independently, we know that these variables all exist jointly in a single context. In the analysis that follows, we explore the possibility that satisfaction with political conditions at home mitigates these alternative drivers of emigration. This analysis grants a fuller picture of how political, economic, and social factors can work together to foster voluntary immobility – or encourage exit.

Economic Conditions

Does satisfaction with political conditions reduce the effect of deteriorating economic conditions on emigration intentions? To test this possibility, we draw on another question that asks respondents whether they feel their current standard of living is increasing, decreasing, or staying the same. From this question, we create an indicator variable that measures whether an individual's standard of living is declining to proxy for individual-level economic conditions. We include this indicator and interact it with our measures of satisfaction with political conditions.

Table 2.1 displays the results of these models. They provide some evidence for the proposition that political conditions blunt the relationship between deteriorating economic conditions and emigration intentions. Across the board, perceiving that one's standard of living is declining

TABLE 2.1 *Political conditions, declining standard of living, and emigration intentions*

	Dependent variable: $IntendMigrate_{ijt}$			
	(1)	(2)	(3)	(4)
$PublicGoods_{ijt}$* $DecliningStandard_{ijt}$	−0.018*** (0.006)			−0.014 (0.011)
$PublicGoods_{ijt}$	−0.114*** (0.005)			−0.068*** (0.007)
$Institutions_{ijt}$* $DecliningStandard_{ijt}$		−0.022*** (0.005)		−0.015* (0.007)
$Institutions_{ijt}$		−0.129*** (0.004)		−0.108*** (0.005)
$Safety_{ijt}$* $DecliningStandard_{ijt}$			−0.033*** (0.009)	−0.029*** (0.011)
$Safety_{ijt}$			−0.104*** (0.006)	−0.066*** (0.007)
$DecliningStandard_{ijt}$	0.059*** (0.004)	0.054*** (0.003)	0.086*** (0.008)	0.078*** (0.011)
Constant	0.361*** (0.007)	0.372*** (0.006)	0.398*** (0.010)	0.470*** (0.013)
Observations	627,061	543,849	373,656	245,227
Country * year FEs	Yes	Yes	Yes	Yes
Controls	Yes	Yes	Yes	Yes

Note: ***$p < 0.01$, **$p < 0.05$, *$p < 0.1$. All models estimated using ordinary least squares (OLS) with country*year fixed effects. Robust standard errors clustered by country-year combination in parentheses. Control variables included: education, gender, age, household size, within-country income quintile, employment status, know people abroad, and propensity to move domestically.

has a strong, positive relationship with the probability of intending to emigrate. But when each measure of political conditions is included separately in Models (1), (2), and (3), the interaction between declining standard of living and satisfaction with public goods, confidence in political institutions, and perceptions of safety are all negative and statistically significant.

When included jointly in Model (4), confidence in national institutions and perception of physical safety continue to blunt the effect of worsening standard of living on the probability of expressing an emigration intention, while the effect of public goods is not statistically significant at conventional levels.[14] We take this as evidence that while political conditions do not totally dominate economic considerations, they meaningfully mitigate the effects of economic adversity on the decision to emigrate. The results are consistent with the proposition that the provision of quality public goods and responsiveness of political institutions can be a bulwark against increasing economic hardship. In other words, the provision of quality governance can act as a "safety net" that tamps down emigration desires when economic conditions deteriorate.

Social Networks

We also explore the intersection of political factors and transnational social networks by interacting our measures of political conditions with whether a respondent knows someone who lives abroad. The results of these models are presented in Table 2.2. Across the board, increasing satisfaction with political conditions mitigates the positive effect of transnational social networks on emigration intentions. A one-standard-deviation increase in satisfaction with public goods is associated with a 3-percentage point decline in the probability of expressing an intention to emigrate for those who have social networks abroad. For confidence in national political institutions, the estimated effect is larger at about negative 6 percentage points, while it is smaller for perceptions of physical safety (negative 2.4 percentage points).[15]

Taken together, these results suggest that increasing satisfaction with political conditions not only shapes the decision to emigrate, but also mitigates other emigration drivers. While deteriorating economic conditions and transnational social networks are strongly associated with an increased probability of emigration, satisfaction with public goods, confidence in national institutions, and perceptions of safety dull their effects. The main takeaway is that quality governance is crucial in its own right, and in conjunction with other social and economic dynamics, in explaining why people emigrate.

---

[14] We replicate these findings using emigration preparations as the dependent variable; these results are available in Appendix Table A2.7.

[15] We replicate these findings using emigration preparations as the dependent variable; these results are available in Appendix Table A2.8.

TABLE 2.2 *Political conditions, social networks, and emigration intentions*

| | Dependent variable: IntendMigrate$_{ijt}$ | | | |
	(1)	(2)	(3)	(4)
PublicGoods$_{ijt}$* PeopleAbroad$_{ijt}$	−0.072*** (0.007)			−0.040*** (0.010)
PublicGoods$_{ijt}$	−0.104*** (0.005)			−0.065*** (0.008)
Institutions$_{ijt}$* PeopleAbroad$_{ijt}$		−0.075*** (0.005)		−0.061*** (0.008)
Institutions$_{ijt}$		−0.115*** (0.004)		−0.093*** (0.006)
Safety$_{ijt}$* PeopleAbroad$_{ijt}$			−0.060*** (0.010)	−0.034*** (0.011)
Safety$_{ijt}$			−0.096*** (0.007)	−0.061*** (0.008)
PeopleAbroad$_{ijt}$	0.135*** (0.005)	0.127*** (0.004)	0.148*** (0.009)	0.185*** (0.012)
Constant	0.368*** (0.007)	0.376*** (0.006)	0.404*** (0.011)	0.466*** (0.014)
Observations	627,061	543,849	373,656	245,227
Country * year FEs	Yes	Yes	Yes	Yes
Controls	Yes	Yes	Yes	Yes

Note: ***$p < 0.01$, **$p < 0.05$, *$p < 0.1$. All models estimated using OLS with country*year fixed effects. Robust standard errors clustered by country-year combination in parentheses. Control variables included: education, gender, age, household size, within-country income quintile, employment status, know people abroad, and propensity to move domestically.

CONCLUSION

In this chapter, we review major economic and sociological theories that explain why people emigrate. We add to these theories, arguing that political conditions in origin countries broadly shape international migration because they are intimately related to individual-level well-being. When potential emigrants are satisfied with the provision of public goods, are confident in their country's political institutions, and feel physically safe, they are far less likely to want to emigrate, and to make active preparations to do so. On the other hand, when potential emigrants perceive that political conditions are poor, emigration becomes much more attractive.

We find evidence in support of this argument using globally representative, micro-level survey data on emigration intentions and behaviors. Our findings broadly show that politics matter for free, voluntary, authorized international migration around the world, extending an existing political science literature that focuses primarily on human displacement and refugees. We already know that large, disruptive political events like civil wars or regime transitions drive forced out-migration (Adhikari 2012). We instead argue and show that more ordinary, "day-to-day" political conditions also shape mobility and immobility decisions of ordinary people. Our findings imply that politicians, by virtue of their control over policy and the provision of public goods, meaningfully shape the expectations of potential emigrants, who are actively deciding whether to invest socially and economically at home or to exit.

We also find that political conditions matter most for those with higher levels of education. Like economic models of emigration, human capital proves essential to understanding the relationship between politics and emigration, but by a distinct mechanism. Our findings are consistent with the logic that more educated citizens become disengaged in the presence of weak political institutions, and instead seek out exit options like emigration. This suggests that so-called brain drain – the disproportionate emigration of highly educated people from developing countries – could be driven in part by poor political conditions in migrant-sending countries (Gibson and McKenzie 2012). While the economic draw of higher wages abroad may pull educated migrants toward advanced economies, we suggest that weak political conditions at home are also a significant push factor for those who hold human capital.

Finally, we explore the potential moderating effects of political conditions on other major drivers of emigration, such as poor economic conditions and transnational social networks. We find evidence that satisfaction with political conditions at home can moderate the push of declining economic conditions and the pull of friends and family living abroad. While these factors continue to matter for explaining emigration intentions and behavior, we contend that satisfaction with political conditions can act as a "glue" that encourages some potential emigrants to remain immobile even in the face of economic and social factors that would otherwise favor emigration.

In short, when it comes to the decision to emigrate, politics matters. In the chapters that follow, we build on these micro-level findings to further explore the political economy of international migration, moving from whether people emigrate to where they go and how they re-engage with their home once abroad.

APPENDIX TABLE A2.1 *List of sample countries*

Afghanistan	Dominican Rep.	Latvia	Russia
Albania	Ecuador	Lebanon	Rwanda
Argentina	Egypt	Lithuania	Senegal
Armenia	El Salvador	Luxembourg	Serbia
Australia	Estonia	Madagascar	Singapore
Austria	Ethiopia	Malawi	Slovakia
Azerbaijan	Finland	Malaysia	Slovenia
Bangladesh	France	Mali	Somalia
Belarus	Gabon	Malta	South Africa
Belgium	Georgia	Mexico	South Korea
Benin	Germany	Moldova	South Sudan
Bhutan	Ghana	Mongolia	Spain
Bolivia	Greece	Montenegro	Sri Lanka
Bosnia & Herzegovina	Guatemala	Mozambique	Suriname
Botswana	Guinea	Myanmar	Sweden
Brazil	Haiti	Nepal	Switzerland
Bulgaria	Honduras	Netherlands	Taiwan
Burkina Faso	Hong Kong	New Zealand	Tajikistan
Burundi	Hungary	Nicaragua	Tanzania
Cambodia	Iceland	Niger	Thailand
Cameroon	India	Nigeria	Togo
Canada	Indonesia	North Macedonia	Tunisia
Central African Rep.	Iraq	Northern Cyprus	Turkey
Chad	Ireland	Norway	Uganda
Chile	Israel	Pakistan	Ukraine
Colombia	Italy	Palestine	United Kingdom
Dem. Rep. of Congo	Ivory Coast	Panama	United States
Rep. of Congo	Jamaica	Paraguay	Uruguay
Costa Rica	Japan	Peru	Venezuela
Croatia	Kazakhstan	Philippines	Vietnam
Cyprus	Kenya	Poland	Yemen
Czech Republic	Kosovo	Portugal	Zambia
Denmark	Kyrgyzstan	Romania	Zimbabwe

Note: list based on Model (5) of Appendix Table A.3.

APPENDIX TABLE A2.2 *Summary statistics*

Variable	Mean	St. Dev.	Minimum	Maximum
Intend to emigrate	0.233	0.422	0	1
Preparing to emigrate	0.009	0.096	0	1
Public goods	0.629	0.292	0	1
Nat. institutions	0.503	0.383	0	1
Safety perception	0.812	0.252	0	1
Secondary ed.	0.515	0.500	0	1
Tertiary ed.	0.144	0.351	0	1
Female	0.530	0.499	0	1
Age	39.863	17.088	15	99
Household size	4.418	2.813	1	31
Income quint.	3.240	1.414	1	5
Unemployed	0.066	0.248	0	1
Know people abroad	0.381	0.486	0	1
Move domestically	0.167	0.373	0	1
Standard of living worsening	0.239	0.427	0	1

Note: summary statistics based on sample of Model (5) in Appendix Table A.3

APPENDIX TABLE A2.3 *Political conditions and emigration intentions*

		Dependent variable: $IntendMigrate_{ijt}$			
	(1)	(2)	(3)	(4)	(5)
$PublicGoods_{ijt}$		-0.129***			-0.079***
		(0.005)			(0.007)
$Institutions_{ijt}$			-0.143***		-0.117***
			(0.004)		(0.005)
$Safety_{ijt}$				-0.120***	-0.076***
				(0.006)	(0.006)
$SecondaryEd_{ijt}$	0.028***	0.030***	0.025***	0.028***	0.025***
	(0.002)	(0.002)	(0.003)	(0.003)	(0.004)
$TertiaryEd_{ijt}$	0.037***	0.031***	0.025***	0.032***	0.022***
	(0.003)	(0.003)	(0.004)	(0.004)	(0.005)
$Female_{ijt}$	-0.035***	-0.033***	-0.031***	-0.038***	-0.035***
	(0.002)	(0.002)	(0.002)	(0.002)	(0.003)
Age_{ijt}	-0.004***	-0.004***	-0.004***	-0.004***	-0.004***
	(0.000)	(0.000)	(0.000)	(0.000)	(0.000)
$HHSize_{ijt}$	0.000	0.000	0.001*	-0.000	-0.000
	(0.000)	(0.000)	(0.000)	(0.001)	(0.001)
$IncomeQuintile_{ijt}$	-0.006***	-0.003	-0.002	-0.004	-0.002
	(0.002)	(0.002)	(0.002)	(0.003)	(0.004)

	(1)	(2)	(3)	(4)	(5)
IncomeQuintile3$_{ijt}$	-0.009***	-0.006**	-0.006**	-0.005	-0.004
	(0.002)	(0.002)	(0.002)	(0.003)	(0.004)
IncomeQuintile4$_{ijt}$	-0.009***	-0.003	-0.004	-0.005*	-0.003
	(0.002)	(0.002)	(0.003)	(0.003)	(0.004)
IncomeQuintile5$_{ijt}$	-0.012***	-0.005	-0.008***	-0.010**	-0.007
	(0.003)	(0.003)	(0.003)	(0.004)	(0.004)
Unemployed$_{ijt}$	0.061***	0.055***	0.053***	0.061***	0.052***
	(0.003)	(0.004)	(0.004)	(0.005)	(0.005)
PeopleAbroad$_{ijt}$	0.090***	0.091***	0.090***	0.099***	0.102***
	(0.002)	(0.003)	(0.003)	(0.003)	(0.004)
MoveDomestic$_{ijt}$	0.190***	0.186***	0.192***	0.166***	0.162***
	(0.005)	(0.006)	(0.006)	(0.007)	(0.007)
Constant	0.312***	0.382***	0.390***	0.424***	0.498***
	(0.005)	(0.007)	(0.006)	(0.010)	(0.013)
Observations	805,712	627,061	543,849	373,656	245,227
Country * year FEs	Yes	Yes	Yes	Yes	Yes

Note: ***$p < 0.01$, **$p < 0.05$, *$p < 0.1$. All models estimated using OLS with county*year fixed effects. Robust standard errors clustered by country–year combination.

APPENDIX TABLE A2.4 *Political conditions and emigration preparations*

	Dependent variable: PrepareMigrate_ijt				
	(1)	(2)	(3)	(4)	(5)
PublicGoods_ijt		-0.006*** (0.001)			-0.002* (0.001)
Institutions_ijt			-0.007*** (0.001)		-0.005*** (0.001)
Safety_ijt				-0.009*** (0.001)	-0.007*** (0.001)
SecondaryEd_ijt	0.002*** (0.000)	0.002*** (0.000)	0.002*** (0.000)	0.002*** (0.001)	0.002*** (0.001)
TertiaryEd_ijt	0.007*** (0.001)	0.006*** (0.001)	0.006*** (0.001)	0.006*** (0.001)	0.005*** (0.001)
Female_ijt	-0.003*** (0.000)	-0.003*** (0.000)	-0.003*** (0.000)	-0.002*** (0.000)	-0.003*** (0.001)
Age_ijt	-0.000*** (0.000)	-0.000*** (0.000)	-0.000*** (0.000)	-0.000*** (0.000)	-0.000*** (0.000)
HHSize_ijt	0.000 (0.000)	0.000* (0.000)	0.000* (0.000)	0.000 (0.000)	0.000 (0.000)

	(1)	(2)	(3)	(4)	(5)
IncomeQuintile2$_{ijt}$	-0.001	-0.000	-0.001	-0.001**	-0.002**
	(0.000)	(0.000)	(0.000)	(0.001)	(0.001)
IncomeQuintile3$_{ijt}$	-0.001	-0.000	-0.001	-0.001	-0.001*
	(0.000)	(0.000)	(0.001)	(0.001)	(0.001)
IncomeQuintile4$_{ijt}$	0.001**	0.001**	0.001*	0.001**	0.002*
	(0.000)	(0.001)	(0.001)	(0.001)	(0.001)
IncomeQuintile5$_{ijt}$	0.004***	0.004***	0.004***	0.004***	0.004***
	(0.001)	(0.001)	(0.001)	(0.001)	(0.001)
Unemployed$_{ijt}$	0.004***	0.004***	0.004***	0.003***	0.002*
	(0.001)	(0.001)	(0.001)	(0.001)	(0.001)
PeopleAbroad$_{ijt}$	0.014***	0.015***	0.015***	0.014***	0.013***
	(0.001)	(0.001)	(0.001)	(0.001)	(0.001)
MoveDomestic$_{ijt}$	0.031***	0.031***	0.033***	0.028***	0.026***
	(0.001)	(0.001)	(0.002)	(0.002)	(0.002)
Constant	0.001	0.004***	0.004***	0.007***	0.009***
	(0.001)	(0.001)	(0.001)	(0.002)	(0.002)
Observations	805,553	626,958	543,764	373,589	245,197
Country * year FEs	Yes	Yes	Yes	Yes	Yes

Note: ***$p < 0.01$, **$p < 0.05$, *$p < 0.1$. All models estimated using OLS with county*year fixed effects. Robust standard errors clustered by country–year combination.

APPENDIX TABLE A2.5 *Political conditions, education, and emigration intentions*

	Dependent variable: IntendMigrate$_{ijt}$			
	(1)	(2)	(3)	(4)
PublicGoods$_{ijt}$	-0.080*** (0.006)			-0.042*** (0.009)
PublicGoods$_{ijt}$ * SecondaryEd$_{ijt}$	-0.085*** (0.006)			-0.061*** (0.010)
PublicGoods$_{ijt}$ * TertiaryEd$_{ijt}$	-0.119*** (0.009)			-0.066*** (0.014)
Institutions$_{ijt}$		-0.104*** (0.005)		-0.088*** (0.006)
Institutions$_{ijt}$ * SecondaryEd$_{ijt}$		-0.063*** (0.005)		-0.043*** (0.007)
Institutions$_{ijt}$ * TertiaryEd$_{ijt}$		-0.100*** (0.007)		-0.077*** (0.011)
Safety$_{ijt}$			-0.090*** (0.010)	-0.060*** (0.010)

	(1)	(2)	(3)	(4)
$Safety_{ijt} * SecondaryEd_{ijt}$			-0.049***	-0.029**
			(0.010)	(0.011)
$Safety_{ijt} * TertiaryEd_{ijt}$			-0.055***	-0.002
			(0.013)	(0.016)
$SecondaryEd_{ijt}$	0.082***	0.056***	0.068***	0.108***
	(0.005)	(0.004)	(0.009)	(0.014)
$TertiaryEd_{ijt}$	0.105***	0.073***	0.077***	0.102***
	(0.007)	(0.006)	(0.012)	(0.017)
$Constant$	0.354***	0.369***	0.399***	0.447***
	(0.007)	(0.006)	(0.012)	(0.017)
Observations	627,061	543,849	373,656	245,227
Country * year FEs	Yes	Yes	Yes	Yes
Controls	Yes	Yes	Yes	Yes

Note: ***$p < 0.01$, **$p < 0.05$, *$p < 0.1$. All models estimated using OLS with country*year fixed effects. Robust standard errors clustered by country-year combination. Control variables included: education, gender, age, household size, within-country income quintile, employment status, know people abroad, and propensity to move domestically.

APPENDIX TABLE A2.6 Political conditions, education, and emigration preparations

	Dependent variable: $PrepareMigrate_{ijt}$			
	(1)	(2)	(3)	(4)
$PublicGoods_{ijt}$	-0.001			-0.000
	(0.001)			(0.001)
$PublicGoods_{ijt} * SecondaryEd_{ijt}$	-0.007***			-0.002
	(0.001)			(0.002)
$PublicGoods_{ijt} * TertiaryEd_{ijt}$	-0.017***			-0.004
	(0.003)			(0.004)
$Institutions_{ijt}$		-0.004***		-0.002**
		(0.001)		(0.001)
$Institutions_{ijt} * SecondaryEd_{ijt}$		-0.005***		-0.003***
		(0.001)		(0.001)
$Institutions_{ijt} * TertiaryEd_{ijt}$		-0.014***		-0.009***
		(0.002)		(0.003)
$Safety_{ijt}$			-0.003**	-0.002
			(0.001)	(0.002)
$Safety_{ijt} * SecondaryEd_{ijt}$			-0.007***	-0.005**
			(0.002)	(0.002)

	(1)	(2)	(3)	(4)
$Safety_{ijt} * TertiaryEd_{ijt}$			-0.022^{***}	-0.019^{***}
			(0.005)	(0.006)
$SecondaryEd_{ijt}$	0.007^{***}	0.004^{***}	0.008^{***}	0.010^{***}
	(0.001)	(0.001)	(0.002)	(0.002)
$TertiaryEd_{ijt}$	0.016^{***}	0.013^{***}	0.024^{***}	0.026^{***}
	(0.002)	(0.001)	(0.004)	(0.005)
$Constant$	0.001	0.002^{**}	0.002	0.003
	(0.001)	(0.001)	(0.002)	(0.002)
Observations	626,958	543,764	373,589	245,197
Country * year FEs	Yes	Yes	Yes	Yes
Controls	Yes	Yes	Yes	Yes

Note: $^{***}p < 0.01$, $^{**}p < 0.05$, $^{*}p < 0.1$. All models estimated using OLS with country*year fixed effects. Robust standard errors clustered by country-year combination in parentheses. Control variables included: education, gender, age, household size, within-country income quintile, employment status, know people abroad, and propensity to move domestically.

55

APPENDIX TABLE A2.7 *Political conditions, declining standard of living, and emigration preparations*

	Dependent variable: PrepareMigrate$_{ijt}$			
	(1)	(2)	(3)	(4)
PublicGoods$_{ijt}$*DecliningStandard$_{ijt}$	−0.003* (0.001)			−0.006** (0.002)
PublicGoods$_{ijt}$	−0.005*** (0.001)			−0.001 (0.001)
Institutions$_{ijt}$*DecliningStandard$_{ijt}$		−0.001 (0.001)		0.002 (0.001)
Institutions$_{ijt}$		−0.007*** (0.001)		−0.005*** (0.001)
Safety$_{ijt}$*DecliningStandard$_{ijt}$			−0.004 (0.002)	−0.002 (0.003)
Safety$_{ijt}$			−0.008*** (0.001)	−0.006*** (0.002)
DecliningStandard$_{ijt}$	0.003*** (0.001)	0.001* (0.001)	0.005** (0.002)	0.004 (0.003)
Constant	0.003*** (0.001)	0.004*** (0.001)	0.006*** (0.002)	0.008*** (0.002)
Observations	626,958	543,764	373,589	245,197
Country * year FEs	Yes	Yes	Yes	Yes
Controls	Yes	Yes	Yes	Yes

Note: ***$p < 0.01$, **$p < 0.05$, *$p < 0.1$. All models estimated using OLS with country*year fixed effects. Robust standard errors clustered by country–year combination in parentheses. Control variables included: education, gender, age, household size, within-country income quintile, employment status, know people abroad, and propensity to move domestically.

APPENDIX TABLE A2.8 *Political conditions, social networks, and emigration preparations*

	Dependent variable: PrepareMigrate$_{ijt}$			
	(1)	(2)	(3)	(4)
PublicGoods$_{ijt}$* PeopleAbroad$_{ijt}$	−0.021*** (0.002)			−0.008*** (0.003)
PublicGoods$_{ijt}$	0.001** (0.001)			0.001 (0.001)
Institutions$_{ijt}$* PeopleAbroad$_{ijt}$		−0.019*** (0.001)		−0.012*** (0.002)
Institutions$_{ijt}$		−0.000 (0.000)		−0.000 (0.001)
Safety$_{ijt}$* PeopleAbroad$_{ijt}$			−0.024*** (0.003)	−0.017*** (0.003)
Safety$_{ijt}$			0.000 (0.001)	0.001 (0.001)
PeopleAbroad$_{ijt}$	0.027*** (0.001)	0.024*** (0.001)	0.033*** (0.003)	0.038*** (0.003)
Constant	−0.000 (0.001)	0.001 (0.001)	−0.001 (0.002)	−0.001 (0.002)
Observations	626,958	543,764	373,589	245,197
Country * year FEs	Yes	Yes	Yes	Yes
Controls	Yes	Yes	Yes	Yes

Note: ***$p < 0.01$, **$p < 0.05$, *$p < 0.1$. All models estimated using OLS with country*year fixed effects. Robust standard errors clustered by country-year combination in parentheses. Control variables included: education, gender, age, household size, within-country income quintile, employment status, know people abroad, and propensity to move domestically.

3

Destinations

Where Do Migrants Go?

Clearly, conditions in an individual's home country influence the decision to emigrate. Lack of access to economic opportunity, dissatisfaction with political institutions, and the desire for a better life for one's family are part of the mobility calculus. Global migration, however, is a costly and risky enterprise: Moving across or to countries with different languages, religions, and cultures is challenging to say the least. In Chapter 2, we explored individual preferences and decisions to move abroad or remain at home; we ignored preferences over potential competing destinations. That is the task we take on here.[1]

We are, of course, not the first to ask this question. As early as 1885, German geographer E.G. Ravenstein proposed that the distance between an individual's home and potential destinations informs their decision over where to migrate. Physical distance is not the only determinant of migration location choice. In Chapter 2, we highlighted the contributions of economists such as Borjas (2000) and Hatton and Williamson (2005), who theorize that destination choice is a function of expected wages and moving costs, while sociologists, notably Massey (1990), argue that we can understand migration flows by analyzing the strength of social networks, as these provide information and security for new migrants.

What role do political factors play in informing the choice of destination? Clearly, a country's entry policies matter. Well before countries

---

[1] We focus solely on labor migrants in this chapter and exclude from our discussion flows of refugees, asylum seekers, or others who are forced to migrate. See Neumayer (2005) and Hatton (2020) for a discussion of refugees, who comprise approximately 20 percent of the global migrant stock as of 2019 (McAuliffe and Khadria 2020).

abruptly closed their borders in response to COVID-19, Freeman predicted that for advanced democracies, "the long-term trend is undeniably toward greater, not less, government effort and capacity to control international migration" (1994, p. 29). A government's decision whether to open or close its border, however, is not our focus in this chapter; the (in)effectiveness of those policies is discussed elsewhere (e.g., Helbling and Leblang 2019).[2] Rather, our focus is on a country's *internal* political environment; we hypothesize that migrant flows respond not just to geographic, economic, and social characteristics, but also to the bundle of citizenship rights offered by destinations to migrants. While wages and social networks matter for destination choice, we argue that political factors also condition these decisions.

The hypothesis that political conditions – especially tolerance for foreigners – matter for understanding migration flows is underscored by recent political dynamics in migrant destinations. Policymakers in the EU, worried about declining fertility rates, warned that growing ethnic and racial intolerance would decrease migration which, in turn, could result in Europe sliding "into marginalization, becoming an increasingly irrelevant western peninsula of the Asian continent" (Project Europe 2010, p. 40). The Project Europe report concluded that to keep Europe's economy competitive, there must be a concerted effort to increase political rights and enhance opportunities to facilitate the social and cultural integration of migrants within member states. We assess this claim within a general framework that allows us to measure a country's political environment and empirically account for other factors that drive migration decisions. We find – for a narrow sample of OECD destination countries and then a more global sample – that political factors exert a substantively important and statistically significant effect on migration flows from a wide array of sending countries.

This chapter proceeds as follows. In the next section, we develop the argument linking a destination's political environment to migrant inflows, accounting for other economic, social, and geographic factors. We test hypotheses derived from these arguments through an examination of migration flows from 203 countries of origin into 23 OECD destination

---

[2] There are a variety of efforts to measure the magnitude and intensity of border restrictions. Mayda (2010) codes changes in immigration and immigrant policies, Ortega and Peri (2009) code changes in entry, stay and asylum laws, while Grogger and Hanson (2011) focus on visa granting policies. As we argue below, these policy changes are correlated with the broader political environment that attracts or deters migrants to or from destinations.

countries between 1990–2015. We also explore whether education conditions the effect of the political environment. The penultimate section
extends our analysis to a global sample of destinations based on decennial
censuses to examine migration flows between 216 origins and 140 destinations between 1990–2010. The final section concludes.

DETERMINANTS OF BILATERAL MIGRATION

What factors drive bilateral flows of migrants? Some bilateral flows, such
as those between Mexico and the United States, Morocco and France, or
Turkey and Germany, may be simple to explain based on proximity or a
shared common history. But migration flows between these sets of countries change significantly over time. For example, countries of Southern
Europe – Italy, Greece, and Spain – were sources of intra-European
migrants through the 1990s. Political instability and sustained drought
in Africa, combined with North Africa's proximity to Southern Europe,
shifted these countries from *em*igration to *im*migration destinations at the
beginning of the twenty-first century. This change results, in part, from
increased labor market opportunities in Southern Europe, but also
because these countries made political integration an attractive part of
their political environments.

As discussed in Chapter 2, economic explanations of migration begin
with the assumption that individuals seek to maximize wages. All else
equal, an individual from origin country o will move to destination
country d if the expected wages in country o exceed expected wages in
country d, less the costs associated with moving (Borjas 1989; Clark,
Hatton, and Williamson 2007). While initially developed to explain
individual migration decisions, this framework has been extended such
that one can model migration flows from country o to country d as a
function of country characteristics and dyadic factors that may also influence cross-border mobility (Ortega and Peri 2009; Grogger and Hanson
2011). We discuss this framework – often called the gravity model – later
in this chapter.

Existing economic models are useful in that they generate plausible
observable implications. First, migrant inflows should increase as the
wage gap between countries o and d increases. Second, migration should
be lower between countries as the cost of moving increases. What factors
shape migration costs? As noted in the introduction, Ravenstein (1885)
suggested that geography is an important factor – greater travel distance
increases the costs associated with moving. While Ravenstein was

concerned with the role of geography, physical distance is not the only way to capture migration costs between origin and destination countries. Linguistic distance – or similarity – also matters, as there are economic benefits of language fluency for migrants (McManus, Gould, and Welch 1983; Chiswick and Miller 1995; Lazear 1995). Likewise, migration is greater between countries that share a common colonial history or border, as these factors help potential migrants collect information about possible opportunities in destinations (Hatton and Williamson 2003; Ortega and Peri 2009; Mayda 2010).

Chapter 2 also emphasized the role of social networks in decreasing migrants' expected risk and minimizing the costs associated with relocation (Portes and Böröcz 1989; Portes 1995; Massey et al. 1993). In general, social network models argue that co-ethnic networks help supply information, minimize uncertainty, reduce transaction costs, and generally decrease the relative importance of traditional economic barriers to migration.[3] The resulting empirical prediction is that migrants from country *o* will be more likely to choose a destination *d* if that destination contains relatively more people who previously migrated from country *o*.

How does the political environment of a destination country come into play? Anecdotal evidence suggests that potential migrants are aware of variation in political opportunities across destination countries and that they act on that information (Awases et al. 2004; Crawley 2010). But why might potential migrants privilege political conditions in potential destinations? While wage maximization and reconnection with fellow expatriates are of obvious importance, a destination's citizenship rules – what we refer to as the political environment – send potential migrants a signal about how open that country's social and economic system will be for foreign-born populations. Put differently, a country's willingness to offer permissive citizenship rights to migrants not only provides information about social and economic opportunities, but also signals the potential for immigrants to have political voice, labor market access, legal protection, and social service provision (Hansen 2009). These rights provide potential migrants with knowledge about long-term prospects for themselves and their families across potential destinations.

---

[3] Work in this tradition investigates how transnational networks of co-ethnics facilitate migration in general (Massey et al. 1993; Faist 2000); by helping migrants find work (Hily and Poinard 1987; Joly 1987; Massey and España 1987; Rex and Josephides 1987; Wilpert 1989), housing (Bailey and Waldinger 1991; Sassen 1995; Light, Bernard, and Kim 1999); and helping ease their integration into the host society (Boyd 1989; Hagan 1998; Fong and Ooka 2002).

Importantly, we posit that it is not only *de jure* policies that influence potential migrants, but also the perceived level of intolerance and hostility directed at existing immigrant populations. In the conclusion to her study, Prinz (2005) summarizes the attitude of Tanzanian students contemplating migration after graduation:

[T]he main drawback of Europe, however, was said to be racism, which, according to the students, stems from a lack of tolerance towards non-white people which is caused by the homogeneity of the European population...it was presumed that racial discrimination occurs on every social level and in all parts of society. According to the interviewees, it affects individuals, the work of organizations, social institutions, and the society as a whole or parts of it like the job market or the school system (p. 128).

The same concern was expressed by Albanians contemplating relocating from Greece (Iosifides et al. 2007), Romani considering migrating to the UK in the 1990s (Sobotka 2003), and African Americans relocating within the US at the advent of Jim Crow (Henry 2009).

We hypothesize that a destination's rights regime influences a migrant's location choice. Our focus is on rights associated with citizenship and residency, as these are key prerequisites to accessing other rights and opportunities, including health and educational benefits and employment. There are a variety of different approaches to conceptualizing citizenship policy: different indices, measures, and data.[4] Our approach focuses on three features of a country's citizenship regime that are observable and should influence the attractiveness of a particular destination: residency requirements for citizenship, dual citizenship provision, and language requirements. We discuss each of these in turn.

All else equal, potential migrants will evaluate the length of time they need to be present in a destination before they are able to access the same set of rights and privileges afforded to native-born citizens. A lengthy residency requirement, we hypothesize, is disadvantageous for potential migrants as it limits their participation in the political system and labor market. Bloemraad (2000) highlights how disenfranchised residents are scapegoated by politicians who align themselves with groups that are eligible to vote. A longer residency requirement also limits a migrant's access to labor markets (Fougère and Safi 2009) and decreases the likelihood of family reunification (Yang 1994). In addition to the number of years in a destination, some countries add a language requirement to their

---

[4] See Goodman (2015) for a systematic review.

residency. Austria, Belgium, Canada, the Netherlands, and Norway, for example, all require that migrants pass a language test to be eligible for citizenship. These tests are not just an additional hurdle for potential immigrants, but they may also contribute to anti-immigrant sentiment on the part of local populations (Alarian and Neureiter 2021).

Finally, we hypothesize that a destination country's willingness to provide citizenship rights without requiring that the immigrant abrogate or vacate citizenship in their home country will be attractive. In addition to the political dimensions of citizenship, this status confers rights in areas of land ownership, inheritance transfers, and investment. We posit that immigrants are reluctant to forfeit home-country citizenship because retaining citizenship in the country of origin entitles migrants to those material benefits, and easier temporary and permanent return should they decide to do so.[5]

While citizenship policies provide information about *de jure* opportunities in a particular destination, prospective migrants also make judgments about the *de facto* political environment (Fitzgerald, Leblang, and Teets 2014; Beine, Bourgeon, and Bricongne 2019). Broadly speaking, an immigrant's prospects for economic gains and integration are constrained in an environment that is hostile toward new arrivals. This hostility may be apparent in the *de jure* rules described above, or when anti-immigrant sentiment is high. Directly observing a country's latent level of intolerance is difficult. We leverage a measure of revealed intolerance of migrants: support for radical right-wing parties, which tend to take a restrictionist stand on immigration-related issues. The Swiss People's Party and France's National Front, for example, both propose to make family aid and other social services unavailable to immigrant families, while the Austrian Freedom Party has called for limits on the number of foreign students allowed in the country's classrooms (Fitzgerald, Leblang, and Teets 2014; Fitzgerald 2018). Public support for these platforms matters, in that it signals how relatively inhospitable different destinations are for prospective immigrants.

Furthermore, because success for the radical right represents politicized anti-immigrant sentiment, it can be interpreted as threatening to immigrants' legal rights and protections. Therefore, we see electoral support for radical right parties as a clear signal regarding prospective treatment of migrants and hypothesize that higher levels of support for these parties will be associated with lower migrant inflows.

---

[5] We further discuss the importance of retaining home country citizenship in Chapter 5.

In sum, we argue that along with economic, geographic, and social factors, the political context of a destination country matters when examining migration flows. We hypothesize that, all else equal, we will observe larger flows into countries that have shorter residency requirements, impose no language requirement, and allow dual citizenship. In addition, we expect that electoral support for radical right parties will be interpreted as a signal of a destination's hostility towards migrants and will thus be associated with smaller migration flows. These conjectures are tested in the next section.

MODELING BILATERAL MIGRATION

We test these hypotheses using data on migrant flows from 203 countries of origin into 23 destination countries over the period 1990–2015. Our sample of destination countries is constrained by available data on *annual* migration flows.[6] The destinations are homogeneous in that they are all democracies and OECD members.[7] They are, however, economically and geographically heterogeneous. The 203 origin countries in our sample comprise most of the world. We exclude countries that are protectorates, but otherwise include all countries for which data are available. Missing data means that our sample covers 4,596 out of 4,669 possible dyads.

Data on migration flows by country of origin are collected by national statistical offices of destination countries and aggregated by international organizations. The challenges in combining these data are twofold. First, there is substantial variation in the years when destinations begin collecting data. For example, Austria has collected migration data by country of origin since 1995 and Ireland since 2000, while the US and Germany have done so since 1960. Second, while most destinations define the migrant's country of origin based on country of birth, others (such as Austria and France) instead define it based on nationality.[8] We use consistent definitions of migrants (birth or nationality) as defined by destination countries based

---

[6] In the section that follows, we discuss the robustness of these results using a global sample of countries based on migrant *stocks* observed at ten-year intervals.

[7] The destination countries in our sample are: Australia, Austria, Belgium, Canada, Denmark, Finland, France, Germany, Greece, Iceland, Ireland, Italy, Japan, Luxembourg, the Netherlands, New Zealand, Norway, Portugal, Spain, Sweden, Switzerland, the United Kingdom, and the United States.

[8] A third, smaller, problem is that countries differ in how they collect immigration flow statistics. Some use data from national population registers, while others obtain data at border crossings, while others use data collected from the issuance of residency permits.

on which series have the largest cross-sectional coverage. Combining data from the OECD (2019), United Nations (2019a), and Eurostat (2020), we create an unbalanced panel dataset of 106,364 observations.

The canonical approach to modeling migration flows focuses on the utility that an individual residing in origin country o at time t derives from moving to destination country d at time $t + 1$.[9] Grogger and Hanson (2011) and Ortega and Peri (2013) show that under certain distributional assumptions, we can use a *gravity model* as an empirical framework within which to understand bilateral migration flows. Derived from Newton's law of gravitation, the gravity model holds that population flows between two countries will be in proportion to the size of the two countries and inversely proportional to the distance between those two countries.

Within this framework, scholars propose a variety of ways to measure size and distance. From Newton's gravitational perspective, particle attraction is based on the mass of other particles. Migrants, however, are not particles and have agency over where they go and what they wish to maximize, meaning that a range of political, economic, social, historical, and geographic factors are likely to matter. We discuss these factors in turn.

To measure characteristics of a destination country's political environment, we extend and update an original dataset created by Fitzgerald, Leblang, and Teets (2014). They use three variables to capture citizenship rights: dual citizenship provision, an indicator coded as one when a destination allows migrants to maintain home-country citizenship after naturalizing; language requirement, an indicator coded as one for countries that do *not* require a language test for residency; and length of residency requirement, which ranges from one (Australia) to fifteen (Germany) years.[10] Because these very short and long residency requirements are far from the mean, we construct a residency index, coded as zero when the residency requirement is between one and five years, one when it is between six and nine years, and two when it is ten years or longer.

---

[9] We need not go into formal derivations here. See Beine, Bertoli, and Moraga (2016) for a synthesis and review.

[10] Potential migrants are most assuredly attracted to countries that provide citizenship rights to children born in the host country. Bertocchi and Strozzi (2008) find that during the nineteenth century, *jus solis* was a prime driver of migrant destination choice. There is no temporal variation in this element of a country's citizenship regime over our sample period and, because we include destination fixed effects for reasons described below, we are unable to include this variable in our citizenship index.

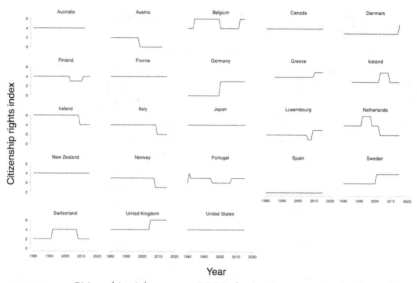

FIGURE 3.1 Citizenship rights across OECD destination countries. Higher values indicate more migrant rights.

In Figure 3.1, we show the evolution of citizenship rights in destination countries over time using a composite index of the preceding measures.[11] While most countries experience some change in their political environment over time, some, like the United States, Canada, Spain, Japan, and Australia, do not.[12] These changes can represent single discrete shifts along one dimension of citizenship rights, or a broader simultaneous change of multiple rights for migrants.

Our final measure of the domestic political environment focuses on support for radical right-wing parties. Fitzgerald, Leblang, and Teets (2014) base their coding of parties on Norris (2005) who, in turn, relies on expert surveys conducted by Lubbers (2000) and Huber and Inglehart (1995) to assess party ideology and immigration stances.[13] Any party that scores an eight or higher on their scale is categorized as belonging to the radical right party family. We collect data on the percentage of the vote

---

[11] This index is calculated as the inverse of the residency requirement + 2*no language requirement + 2*dual citizenship allowed, resulting in an index ranging between zero and six.

[12] Empirically, this means that these countries provide no identifying information for the estimation of the coefficients on the political variables, as the political environment is collinear with included destination fixed effects.

[13] See Norris (2005, p. 46–49) for details on her classification process.

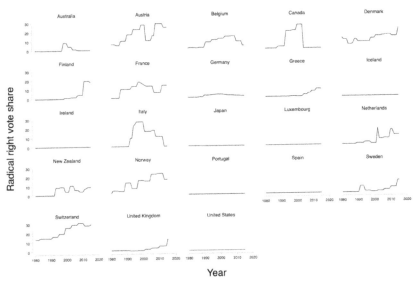

FIGURE 3.2 Radical right-wing party support across OECD
destination countries.

won by this group of parties in the most recent national legislative
election. In the case of bicameral legislatures, we focus on lower house
election results.[14] Figure 3.2 illustrates temporal trends of this variable for
the countries in our sample.

While our focus is on domestic policies that attract or deter migrants,
all countries regulate physical entry into their countries in a variety of
ways.[15] These regulations can seek to encourage labor migration (e.g.,
broaden visas or liberalize entry requirements) or discourage individuals
from seeking entry (e.g., blanket restrictions or quotas). Because immigration policies at the border vary quantitatively and qualitatively across
countries and over time, it is challenging to construct a comparable
measure across observations.[16] Our approach follows Mayda (2010)
and Ortega and Peri (2013), who construct chronologies capturing when
a country has liberalized or restricted entry policies. We utilize the
DEMIG POLICY database created by the University of Oxford's
International Migration Institute as the source of our chronologies,

[14] See Fitzgerald, Leblang, and Teets (2014) for details on data sources for these variables.
[15] See Helbling and Kalkum (2018) for an overview and discussion of various approaches
to measurement.
[16] See Helbling et al. (2017) for an effort in this direction and Helbling and Leblang (2019)
for an application.

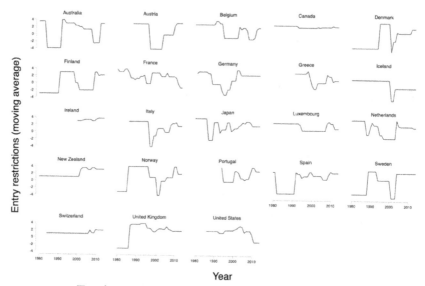

FIGURE 3.3 Trends in entry policy across OECD destination countries. Higher values indicate more permissive entry policy.

coding liberalizations as "1" and restrictions as "-1" (de Haas, Vezzoli, and Natter 2014).[17] Because policies may be announced before they are enacted and enforced, we use a three-year moving average to capture a country's migration policy. Figure 3.3 presents trends in entry restrictions.

A final policy-relevant variable is Schengen Area membership – an indicator variable coded one when countries o and d are both Schengen members at time t. The Schengen Area – currently comprised of twenty-six countries – allows for unrestricted movement of people. Our sample of destination countries contains many Schengen members; we anticipate that joint membership in this area will increase migration flows.

Prospective migrants assess economic opportunity when they consider different destinations. Economic expectations differ across individuals, as some are interested in higher wages while others are only interested in obtaining employment. We control for economic features of destination countries using three variables, all drawn from the World Bank's World Development Indicators (WDI). GDP per capita provides a proxy for expected wages in country d at time t; we log this variable to decrease

---

[17] The DEMIG POLICY database codes whether a change in entry policy is more permissive or restrictive than the prevailing policy. We rely on this coding in the construction of our indicators.

the influence of high-income destination countries. Country d's economic growth rate at time t proxies for economic expectations, as countries with higher rates of growth feature both increased wages and more employment opportunities. Finally, we control for country d's unemployment rate at time t, as this proxies for the likelihood that a prospective migrant will be able to find employment (Clark, Hatton, and Williamson 2007; Mayda 2010; Ortega and Peri 2013).

Geographic and historical factors also influence migration decisions. The gravity model posits that migration will decrease as the physical distance between countries o and d increases. Consequently, we control for logged bilateral distance and the existence of a shared border between countries o and d to proxy for moving costs. Gravity models of economic transactions, whether they are commodities, capital, or labor, also account for historical colonial relationships between countries and whether the countries were previously part of the same country. These factors proxy for greater familiarity and knowledge about the institutions, culture, and economy of the destination country, increasing the likelihood of migration.[18] Migration costs are also lower if countries o and d share a common language, as this eliminates a barrier to entry and increases the likelihood that a migrant will be able to secure employment and housing. Existing research documents the economic returns of language fluency for immigrants.[19] These variables are sourced from the CEPII gravity dataset and are time-invariant.

Finally, we measure social networks as the existing stock of migrants from country o residing in country d at time t. The stock of migrants represents the accumulated sum of prior migrant flows between countries o and d. We measure migrant stocks using data from the United Nations (2019) and linearly interpolate missing values.

EMPIRICAL MODEL

Migration flows are discrete, countable, and have a zero–lower bound. Approximately 20 percent of our origin-destination country pairs have zero migration flows. As we discuss below, we also include a large

---

[18] This effect is not unambiguous, as Riley and Emigh (2002) and Sharpe (2005) find that not all colonial relationships are alike for integrating immigrants into a destination society, and Neumayer (2005) finds that these historical ties are not always associated with greater flows of asylum seekers.

[19] See McManus, Gould, and Welch (1983) and Chiswick and Miller (1995) for more detail.

number of fixed effects in our empirical specifications. Consequently, we employ the pseudo-Poisson maximum likelihood (PPML) estimator developed by Santos Silva and Tenreyro (2006) as extended and implemented by Correia, Guimarães, and Zylkin (2020). Santos Silva and Tenreyro (2006) show that PPML is efficient and outperforms both ordinary least squares (OLS) and negative binomial models when there are a large number of fixed effects.[20] There are, as discussed in Chapter 2, a multitude of origin-country factors – political, economic, social, and environmental – associated with emigration intentions and rates. Because our focus here is on destination countries, we eliminate origin-country factors by including a set of 5,248 origin*year fixed effects. The inclusion of these fixed effects accounts for any variable that varies across origin countries over time and is associated with bilateral migration flows.

The baseline model we estimate takes the form:

$$\lambda_{odt} = e^{\delta\psi_{odt-1} + \mu x_{odt-1} + \xi\pi_{odt-1} + \rho v_{odt} + \alpha_o t_t + \gamma_d} \tag{3.1}$$

where λ_{odt} is the count of migrants from country o in destination d at time t and δ, μ, ξ, and ρ are vectors of coefficients related to the matrices of political (Ψ), economic (χ), social (π), and geographic/historical (v) variables. $\alpha_o t_t$ is a vector of origin*year fixed effects, and γ is a vector of destination fixed effects. The set of destination fixed effects is included for two reasons. First, there may be time-invariant features of destination countries that make them relatively more or less attractive to larger migration flows (e.g., Greece and Spain's proximity to North Africa) that are not captured by our set of geographic and historical covariates. Second, as highlighted by Bertoli and Moraga (2013), migrants choose among multiple destinations. The inclusion of a set of destination fixed effects – along with a time-varying measure of country d's immigration policy – helps account for multilateral resistance to migration (Beine, Bertoli, and Moraga 2016).

RESULTS

We summarize our baseline results in Figure 3.4. The plot displays the marginal effects of our primary variables of interest. These marginal effects are calculated from our fully specified model of Equation (1), with

---

[20] PPML is also consistent in the face of a dependent variable with a large proportion of zeros. Correia, Guimarães, and Zylkin (2020) develop a tractable approach to generate maximum likelihood estimates when there are high dimensional fixed effects.

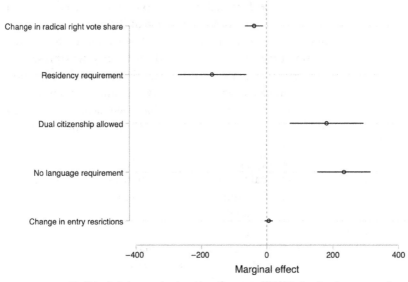

FIGURE 3.4 Political rights and migration flows to OECD destination countries. Marginal effects of primary variables of interest with 95 percent confidence intervals. Estimates from Model (1) of Appendix Table A3.1.

all measures of the political environment included jointly.[21] All variables are statistically significant and in the expected direction. All else equal, we observe larger migration flows into countries that have shorter residency requirements, do not require a language test for citizenship, and provide for home country dual citizenship. Migrants are also wary of potential changes in the political environment, as evidenced by the negative and statistically significant coefficient on the variable for radical right-wing party support. We also observe greater migration flows when a country's immigration policy regime becomes more permissive, though this association does not reach conventional levels of significance.

The marginal effects of the citizenship policy variables and radical right-wing party support likely underestimate the true effect of the political environment on bilateral migration flows, as these variables are theoretically and empirically related with one another. The Danish government, for example, has tightened its immigration policies (by curtailing family reunification) since the 1990s, and at the same time, the Danish People's Party – a radical right-wing party – has seen increased vote share.

[21] We present the complete results of this model in Appendix Table A3.1.

New Zealand has likewise curtailed immigration by making education a part of its entry requirements since 2002, while at the same time increasing the residency requirement for citizenship from three to five years. Notably, during this time, the New Zealand First Party was present in the legislature. Germany is also illustrative: though its immigration restrictions have tightened over time (family reunification laws have tightened since 2002), citizenship acquisition has been facilitated through a decreased residency requirement since 2000. Germany simultaneously legalized dual citizenship.

In Columns (2) through (5) of Appendix Table A3.1, we include the political variables individually. The individual political variables – radical right party support, language and residency requirement, and dual citizenship – are all statistically significant and in the expected direction. In Column (6), we replace the language requirement, residency requirement, and dual citizenship allowance with the summary citizenship index displayed in Figure 3.1. We do this because citizenship policies are highly collinear with one another. Australia, for example, has traditionally combined dual citizenship, short residency requirements (currently two years), and no language requirement. Italy, on the other hand, has a relatively high residency requirement (currently ten years), a language requirement, and did not allow dual citizenship until 1992. We again see that a more permissive political environment is associated with increased migration flows.

We recognize that the importance of political variables may vary systematically across migrant origin countries based on initial levels of income. To explore this possibility, we split origin countries into two subsamples based on whether they are OECD members. We include these models in Appendix Table A3.2 and summarize our findings in Figure 3.5. The results from non-OECD origin countries are largely in line with the pooled sample, though with different magnitudes. All variables remain statistically significant and in the anticipated direction for non-OECD origin countries. Migrant flows from OECD origins, however, are not responsive to the prospect of radical right success, nor are they deterred by the prospect of a language requirement. This may be because a larger proportion of flows between OECD countries are comprised of higher-educated migrants who already have language fluency; relatively more skilled, fluent migrants are less often the primary target of restrictionist political parties.[22]

---

[22] We further explore heterogeneous effects by education level later in this chapter.

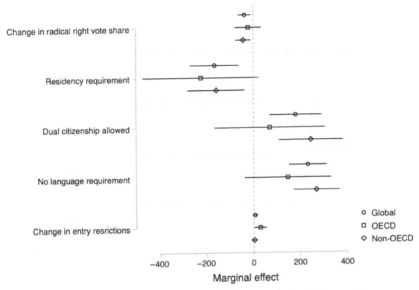

FIGURE 3.5 Robustness of results across different sets of origin countries. Marginal effects of primary variables of interest with 95 percent confidence intervals. Estimates from models in Appendix Tables A3.1 and A3.2.

We use our index measure of a destination's political environment to ask deeper questions about the importance of political rights to potential migrants. Are political rights sufficient to spur migration flows even when geographic or economic factors would suggest otherwise? We interact the indicator for the destination's political environment with the logged distance between countries o and d. We plot the marginal effect of the political environment on bilateral flows across the range of bilateral distance in Figure 3.6.[23] All else equal, the positive effect of a destination's political openness increases as the distance between origin and destination increases, with the largest effect observed at the maximum of bilateral distance, which is approximately 5,000 km (or 8.5 in log form). This suggests that political rights in a destination country compensate for higher moving costs – be they physical or psychological – between origin and destination.

The results thus far support the hypothesis offered at the beginning of this chapter: the political environment – both in terms of rights and public support for radical right-wing parties – influences migration decisions even

---

[23] We present the complete results of this model in Appendix Table A3.3.

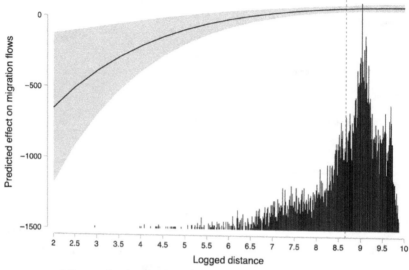

FIGURE 3.6 Interaction between political rights and bilateral distance. Marginal effect of political rights index on migration flows across range of bilateral distance. Estimates from Model (1) in Appendix Table A3.3.

after we account for economic, social, and geographic factors. In the remainder of this chapter, we extend our analysis by disaggregating migration flows by education, as well as analyzing a global panel of destination countries.

EDUCATION AND POLITICAL OPENNESS IN DESTINATION COUNTRIES

In Chapter 2, we showed that the effects of political institutions on the decision to emigrate vary with the individual's level of education. We found that political conditions in origin countries have the largest impact on the emigration decisions of highly educated people. We leverage additional data that disaggregates migration by education levels to explore whether the same is true of political conditions in destination countries. To measure migration by education level, we draw on the German Institute for Employment Research (IAB)'s Brain Drain Database (Brücker and Marfouk 2013). This database uses country censuses to measure migrant *stocks* disaggregated by country of origin and level of education. We code higher-educated migrants as those with an undergraduate college degree or higher, and lower-educated migrants as those with no higher than a high school degree. These data are collected at five-year intervals for 20 OECD destination countries between 1980–2010.[24] We create our two dependent variables – higher-educated and lower-educated migration *flows* – by differencing migration *stocks* at time t and time $t-5$, replacing negative values with zeroes.[25] We lag all independent variables by five years to match the structure of the data.

Table 3.1 contains the results of estimating Equation (1) on bilateral flows of lower- and high-educated migrants separately using PPML. In Column (1), the dependent variable is lower-educated migration flows, while in Column (2), the dependent variable is higher-educated migration flows. The results suggest that while level of education matters, it does so heterogeneously for different features of a destination's political environment. Longer residency requirements are associated with reduced flows of both lower- and higher-educated migrants, though more so for those with lower education. This result is consistent with the idea that higher-educated migrants may enjoy faster effective routes to residency than their lower-educated counterparts, given their attractiveness to destination countries (Czaika and Parsons 2017). Higher-educated migrants are also more likely to migrate to destinations where they have already secured employment, so attaining residency is not necessary for accessing the labor market.

Similarly, the lack of language requirement is associated with increased flows of lower-educated, but not higher-educated, migrants. This result is consistent with the proposition that higher-educated migrants – those with college degrees – already have the requisite linguistic capacity to fulfill language requirements. We also note that the role of common language is relatively larger for higher- than lower-educated migrants, suggesting that higher-educated migrants are more likely to come from origin countries where language familiarity already exists. Yet the allowance of dual citizenship, while statistically insignificant for lower-educated migration, is positive and statistically significant for higher-educated migration. We tentatively suggest that those who possess human capital have the resources to engage in more return migration and are more likely to do so for purposes of family or business interests, so they

[24] These countries are: Australia, Austria, Canada, Chile, Denmark, Finland, France, Germany, Greece, Ireland, Luxembourg, the Netherlands, New Zealand, Norway, Portugal, Spain, Sweden, Switzerland, United Kingdom, and the United States.

[25] This approach – inferring migration flows from over-time differences in migration stocks – is common to gravity models of international migration where flow data is unavailable (e.g., Beine and Parsons 2015; Dao et al. 2018).

TABLE 3.1 *Political rights and higher- versus lower-educated migration flows*

Dependent variable:	LowEdMigrants$_{odt}$	HighEdMigrants$_{odt}$
	(1)	(2)
ResidencyRequirement$_{dt-5}$	−1.25**	−0.47**
	(0.34)	(0.15)
NoLanguageRequirement$_{dt-5}$	0.74**	0.04
	(0.20)	(0.11)
DualCitizenship$_{dt-5}$	−0.27	0.26**
	(0.25)	(0.11)
RadicalRightChange$_{dt-5}$	−0.96**	0.35*
	(0.34)	(0.21)
log (MigrantStock$_{odt-5}$)	0.92**	0.71**
	(0.04)	(0.03)
log (Distance$_{od}$)	−0.06	−0.10
	(0.08)	(0.06)
CommonColony$_{od}$	−0.02	0.07
	(0.18)	(0.13)
CommonBorder$_{od}$	0.13	−0.14
	(0.19)	(0.15)
CommonLanguage$_{od}$	−0.12	0.49**
	(0.13)	(0.10)
SameCountry$_{od}$	0.94**	0.26
	(0.31)	(0.26)
Schengen$_{od}$	0.83**	0.40**
	(0.32)	(0.16)
CommonReligion$_{od}$	−0.84**	−0.56**
	(0.32)	(0.22)
log (GDPPC$_{dt-5}$)	−0.98	3.96**
	(1.61)	(0.85)
Unemployment$_{dt-5}$	0.02	−0.04**
	(0.03)	(0.01)
EconomicGrowth$_{dt-5}$	0.03	0.17**
	(0.04)	(0.03)
EntryRestrictions$_{dt-5}$	−0.03	−0.02*
	(0.03)	(0.01)
Constant	4.54	−12.52**
	(6.14)	(3.44)
Observations	13,269	13,249
Destination FEs	Yes	Yes
Origin * year FEs	Yes	Yes

Note: * $p < 0.10$, ** $p < 0.05$. All models estimated using PPML with robust standard errors clustered by dyad in parentheses. All models include destination and origin*year fixed effects.

value the provision of dual citizenship relatively more (Cohen and Haberfeld 2001; Makina 2012).

Finally, increasing support for radical right-wing parties is associated with lower inflows of lower-educated migrants, but not for higher-educated migration flows. We regard this finding as plausible, driven by the fact that restrictionist parties often construct nativist pitches around concerns of labor market competition, positing that lower-educated migrants are more likely to harm blue-collar workers (Hainmueller and Hopkins 2014). Taken together, these results suggest that education does condition how a destination's political environment shapes migration flows, yet not consistently so for lower- or higher-educated migrants. Rather, different facets of the political environment matter relatively more to these two groups.

POLITICAL RIGHTS AND MIGRATION IN GLOBAL PERSPECTIVE

Our findings so far are based on panel data that tracks migration flows into a small and homogeneous sample of OECD destination countries. These destinations are overrepresented in studies of international migration, and studies of migration between countries in the Global South are lacking (Helms and Leblang 2019). We expand our empirical analysis to include a global set of destination countries. While global data on migration *flows* are not available, like our analyses of migration by education level, we leverage available data on bilateral migrant *stocks*. We draw these data from the United Nations (2019a), which are available at ten-year intervals from 1980 to 2010. We create our dependent variable – migration *flows* – by differencing migration *stocks* at time *t* and time *t*-10, replacing negative values with zeroes. This yields a bilateral panel dataset of migration flows for a matrix of 220 countries at three time points.

We discuss how we collect analogous data for our political variables for this global sample in Appendix 3.B. Due to data limitations, we can gather complete data on the political environment for 139 destination countries, but only through 2010, after which data for many African and Asian countries become less reliable. Using these data, we again construct an index measuring the political environment for migrants using measures of dual citizenship, residency requirements, and lack of language requirement.

Measuring hostility to migrants via electoral support for radical right anti-immigrant parties proves more difficult for a global context. As a proxy, we rely on Grzymala-Busse et al. (2020), who collect data on votes for populist parties that "both make the claim that the status quo elites are corrupt or malevolent, and that the people need representation as such." This data does not map directly onto the party platforms of European radical right-wing parties. In fact, many populist parties and leaders, especially in Latin America, voice explicit pro-immigrant language even when restricting migration (e.g., Nestor Kirchner in Argentina or Rafael Correa in Ecuador). Consequently, our priors regarding the sign on this variable will differ based on the set of destination countries under consideration.

Unlike our previous analyses, where all host countries are democratic, in the global sample we have a mix of democratic and autocratic destinations. We control for regime type using the polyarchy measure from V-Dem (Coppedge et al. 2021). As with the measure of political institutions, our priors on the effect of democracy on attracting migrants is mixed. All else equal, we expect that migrants are attracted by open political systems where they can enjoy myriad political rights. This sample and data, however, force us to qualify that expectation. Since the data are based on foreign-born populations – not migrant flows – they include both labor migrants and refugees. We know that most refugee flows are local: Most refugees move to geographically proximate countries. We also know that democracies – and autocracies – cluster spatially. This means that forced displacement likely results in more mobility from autocracies into other autocracies. Consequently, our priors are mixed.

In the global context, we add an additional feature of a destination's political environment that may shape migration decisions: corruption. We demonstrated in Chapter 2 that individuals are more likely to express an intention to emigrate when they have low confidence in their country's political institutions. Several macro-level studies also demonstrate that corruption is an important migration push factor (Dimant, Krieger, and Meierrieks 2013; Poprawe 2015; Cooray and Schneider 2016). Other micro-level research finds that corruption-concerned emigrants express an intention to move to less corrupt countries than their compatriots who do not perceive high corruption (Helms 2022). Because corruption imposes significant economic costs on individuals via its negative effects on economic growth, inequality and poverty, and the provision of public goods, we hypothesize that more corrupt destination countries will receive fewer migrants, all else equal (Olken and Pande 2012; Dimant and Tosato 2018). To test this proposition, we include V-Dem's measure of regime corruption, which codes a country's level of corruption on a continuous scale bounded by zero and one; higher values indicate greater corruption.

Finally, to deal with increased heterogeneity when we pool all countries, we include a logged measure of the destination country's population measured in millions; these data come from the WDI. All variables are lagged by ten years to match the decadal structure of our migration flow data, while support for populist parties is measured in terms of the most recent election.[26]

In Table 3.2, we use the PPML estimator with destination fixed effects and origin*decade fixed effects to account for factors in countries of origin that generate migrant outflows over time. Column (1) of Table 3.2 includes all origins and destinations. The coefficient on the destination's political environment is positive and statistically significant, indicating that, in general, migrants globally flow to destinations that offer greater opportunities for political incorporation. Other measures of the political environment are mixed. Electoral support for populist parties is not statistically significant; this may reflect the heterogeneity of populist parties in the world, with some of these parties in the Global South supporting labor migration, while those in the Global North favor migration restrictions. However, corruption proves vital to understanding migration flows. More corrupt destination countries experience far less migration on average, suggesting that migrants avoid places that do not protect the rule of law and impose large corruption-related costs on their residents.

All else equal, we observe more migration to less democratic countries. This may be because more autocratic states make it easier for migrants to gain citizenship rights; those rights may be less meaningful or threatening to incumbent political leaders. It may also result from spatial clustering of autocracies: mobility within Africa, which is dominated by autocratic countries, is (relatively) easy given common cultural and linguistic origins and shorter bilateral distances. Likewise, because refugees tend to remain close to home, the fact that we observe more migration to autocracies is consistent with descriptive accounts. The economic variable we include – logged GDP per capita – is positive and statistically significant, indicating that migrants, as anticipated, move to destinations with greater economic prospects.[27]

---

[26] To be clear, we calculate the bilateral flow of migrants from country *o* into country *d* over a ten-year period (e.g., 1980–1990) and regress it on covariates observed ten years earlier.

[27] Due to the lack of comparable global data on unemployment, we do not include that variable in these specifications.

TABLE 3.2 Political rights and migration in global perspective

	Dependent variable: $Migrants_{odt}$				
	All Dyads (1)	South–North (2)	South–South (3)	North–South (4)	North–North (5)
$RightsIndex_{dt-10}$	0.024* (0.015)	0.050* (0.030)	0.043* (0.022)	0.431*** (0.069)	0.100** (0.040)
$PopulistParty_{dt-}$	-0.011 (0.076)	-0.771*** (0.124)	0.220 (0.137)	0.764*** (0.247)	-0.120 (0.230)
$Corruption_{dt-10}$	-1.459*** (0.109)	-1.511** (0.610)	-1.440*** (0.142)	7.628*** (1.814)	-1.103*** (0.242)
$\log(MigrantStock_{odt-10})$	0.140*** (0.004)	0.007 (0.005)	0.203*** (0.005)	0.055*** (0.013)	0.052*** (0.013)
$\log(GDPPC_{dt-10})$	0.284*** (0.045)	-1.187*** (0.181)	0.291*** (0.059)	0.952*** (0.350)	0.211* (0.110)
$\log(Population_{dt-10})$	-0.000*** (0.000)	-0.000*** (0.000)	-0.000*** (0.000)	-0.000* (0.000)	-0.000*** (0.000)
$Democracy_{dt-10}$	-0.837*** (0.062)	0.354 (0.323)	-0.412*** (0.084)	-1.994*** (0.739)	0.359** (0.161)
$\log(Distance_{od})$	-0.216*** (0.011)	-0.345*** (0.020)	-0.281*** (0.016)	0.065* (0.037)	-0.307*** (0.041)

CommonLanguage$_{od}$	0.293***	0.265***	0.313***	0.224***	0.245***
	(0.019)	(0.027)	(0.028)	(0.081)	(0.059)
CommonColony$_{od}$	-0.075	0.317***	-0.072	-0.026	0.149*
	(0.049)	(0.050)	(0.204)	(0.109)	(0.084)
CommonBorder$_{od}$	-0.027	-0.280	-0.127***	-0.003	-0.360
	(0.051)	(0.196)	(0.049)	(0.095)	(0.249)
Constant	0.642	16.943***	0.713	-9.143**	2.104**
	(0.441)	(1.880)	(0.516)	(3.625)	(0.993)
Observations	74,385	12,464	52,540	1,794	6,942
Observations	74,385	12,464	52,540	1,794	6,942
Destination FEs	Yes	Yes	Yes	Yes	Yes
Origin * decade FEs	Yes	Yes	Yes	Yes	Yes

Note: * $p < 0.10$, ** $p < 0.05$. All models estimated using pseudo-Poisson maximum likelihood (PPML) with robust standard errors clustered by dyad in parentheses. All models include destination and origin*year fixed effects.

In the remaining columns of Table 3.2, we split the sample by migration corridor. Comparing magnitudes is not possible due to vast differences in sample sizes and the variance of the dependent variable. That said, for all corridors, the destination's political environment has a positive and statistically significant effect on migration flows. Support for populist parties, however, is statistically significant and negative in the South–North Corridor, as shown in Column (2), a result consistent with our earlier results. In Column (4), the North–North Corridor, the coefficient is positive and statistically significant – likely driven by large flows of migrants into Hungary, Poland, Austria, and Japan, the four destinations with the strongest support for populist parties. Corruption continues to exert a negative and statistically significant effect on migrant inflows across all corridors along which significant human mobility occurs.[28]

Column (2) also shows an initially curious result: The coefficient on logged GDP per capita is negative and statistically significant in this sample. A closer look at the data – and a reflection on the current state of immigration politics – provides a plausible explanation. The bulk of African migration flows to Southern Europe (Italy, Greece, Malta, Spain), relatively lower income within the Global North. Taken together, these results broadly support the proposition that a destination's political environment matters *globally* for migrants' immigration decisions.

Overall, we find that migration patterns across the globe are influenced by political factors. In all cases, the nature of the political environment – the extent to which it is inclusive and provides potential migrants with opportunities for political expression and empowerment – matters when it comes to understanding the distribution of global migrants. Migrants also move toward countries with less corrupt environments, suggesting that they are sensitive to the costs of weak governance and poor protection of the rule of law. Regime type also matters for migration flows, but in ways that are context- and destination-specific.

---

[28] The coefficient on corruption is positive and statistically significant for migration from the Global North to the Global South, but very little migration occurs along this corridor. This result is primarily driven by migration not just to Southern Europe, but also within Eastern Europe (namely Poland and Hungary) after the fall of the Soviet Union.

CONCLUSION

The conventional approach to understanding international labor migration comes from economic and sociological explanations that emphasize wage maximization and the importance of social networks. We argue that individuals not only want to live but thrive in an environment that affords migrants political rights, providing opportunities for both economic and political engagement in the host country. Countries that are perceived as hostile to migrants – those whose electorate supports radical right-wing political parties – will see fewer migrants, as potential immigrants seek out more inclusive destinations.

Our focus – along with our consistent findings – on the importance of the political environment in a destination country echoes those of Chapter 2, which finds similar support for the importance of the political environment in the migrant's homeland. Political and economic inclusion, along with quality provision of public goods, plays a primary role in keeping migrants at home; political opportunities in destination countries are likewise an important pull factor. This is especially important as destination countries compete for high-skilled workers. Bloemraad (2004) argued, and our results confirm, that high-skilled workers want to take advantage of dual citizenship. For those with less education, the political environment – especially perceived threats from radical right parties – plays a particularly important role.

This suggests an important set of policy implications. If politicians want to attract migrants, both high- and low-skilled, then they should examine not just the kinds of immigration control policies that exist, but also the set of rights that comprise the political environment. This is important not just for attracting migrants, but because migrants, once they arrive, play an important role in connecting their host country with their homeland, spurring trade and investment. The nexus between migration and economic flows is the subject of the two chapters that follow.

APPENDIX TABLE A3.1 *Political rights and migration flows to OECD countries*

	Dependent variable: Migrants$_{odt}$					
	(1)	(2)	(3)	(4)	(5)	(6)
ResidencyRequirement$_{dt-1}$	-0.16** (0.05)			-0.06 (0.05)		
NoLanguageRequirement$_{dt-1}$	0.22** (0.04)		0.22** (0.04)			
DualCitizenship$_{dt-1}$	0.17** (0.05)				0.13** (0.06)	
RadicalRightChange$_{dt-1}$	-0.04** (0.01)	-0.03** (0.01)				-0.03** (0.01)
RightsIndex$_{dt-1}$						0.04** (0.01)
log(MigrantStock$_{odt-1}$)	0.64** (0.02)	0.65** (0.02)	0.65** (0.02)	0.65** (0.02)	0.65** (0.02)	0.65** (0.02)
log(Distance$_{od}$)	-0.23** (0.04)	-0.23** (0.04)	-0.23** (0.04)	-0.23** (0.04)	-0.23** (0.04)	-0.23** (0.04)
CommonColony$_{od}$	0.04 (0.12)	0.04 (0.12)	0.04 (0.12)	0.04 (0.12)	0.04 (0.12)	0.03 (0.11)
CommonBorder$_{od}$	-0.13 (0.13)	-0.13 (0.13)	-0.13 (0.13)	-0.13 (0.13)	-0.13 (0.13)	-0.13 (0.12)

	(1)	(2)	(3)	(4)	(5)	(6)
$CommonLanguage_{od}$	0.30**	0.30**	0.30**	0.30**	0.30**	0.30**
	(0.07)	(0.07)	(0.07)	(0.07)	(0.07)	(0.07)
$SameCountry_{od}$	0.25*	0.28**	0.26*	0.28**	0.27**	0.26
	(0.14)	(0.14)	(0.14)	(0.14)	(0.14)	(0.14)
$Schengen_{od}$	0.46**	0.41**	0.46**	0.42**	0.40**	0.41**
	(0.10)	(0.10)	(0.10)	(0.10)	(0.10)	(0.10)
$CommonReligion_{od}$	0.04	0.04	0.03	0.04	0.04	0.04
	(0.14)	(0.14)	(0.14)	(0.14)	(0.14)	(0.13)
$\log(GDPPC_{dt-1})$	0.96**	1.12**	0.77*	1.10**	1.18**	1.08**
	(0.45)	(0.43)	(0.44)	(0.43)	(0.43)	(0.43)
$Unemployment_{dt-1}$	-0.03**	-0.03**	-0.04**	-0.03**	-0.03**	-0.03**
	(0.01)	(0.01)	(0.01)	(0.01)	(0.01)	(0.00)
$EconomicGrowth_{dt-1}$	0.02**	0.02**	0.02**	0.02**	0.02**	0.02**
	(0.01)	(0.01)	(0.01)	(0.01)	(0.01)	(0.00)
$EntryRestrictions_{dt-1}$	0.01	0.00	0.00	0.00	-0.00	-0.00
	(0.01)	(0.01)	(0.01)	(0.01)	(0.01)	(0.00)
$Constant$	0.15	-0.47	0.75	-0.30	-0.78	-0.57
	(1.75)	(1.68)	(1.71)	(1.68)	(1.70)	(1.66)
Observations	106,364	106,364	106,364	106,364	106,364	106,364
Destination FEs	Yes	Yes	Yes	Yes	Yes	Yes
Origin * year FEs	Yes	Yes	Yes	Yes	Yes	Yes

Note: * $p < 0.10$, ** $p < 0.05$. All models estimated using pseudo-Poisson maximum likelihood (PPML) with robust standard errors clustered by dyad in parentheses. All models include destination and origin*year fixed effects.

APPENDIX TABLE A3.2 *Political rights and migration flows to OECD countries by corridor*

	Dependent variable: Migrants$_{odt}$	
	Non-OECD to OECD (1)	OECD to OECD (2)
ResidencyRequirement$_{dt-1}$	−0.18** (0.07)	−0.13* (0.07)
NoLanguageRequirement$_{dt-1}$	0.30** (0.06)	0.08 (0.05)
DualCitizenship$_{dt-1}$	0.27** (0.08)	0.04 (0.07)
RadicalRightChange$_{dt-1}$	−0.05** (0.02)	−0.01 (0.02)
log (MigrantStock$_{odt-1}$)	0.64** (0.02)	0.59** (0.04)
log (Distance$_{od}$)	−0.31** (0.05)	−0.28** (0.04)
CommonColony$_{od}$	−0.16 (0.12)	0.37** (0.14)
CommonBorder$_{od}$	−0.16 (0.19)	−0.14 (0.12)
CommonLanguage$_{od}$	0.31** (0.08)	0.29** (0.12)
SameCountry$_{od}$	0.47** (0.21)	0.05 (0.20)
Schengen$_{od}$		0.26** (0.11)
CommonReligion$_{od}$	0.46** (0.17)	0.12 (0.20)
log (GDPPC$_{dt-1}$)	0.82 (0.60)	0.75 (0.62)
Unemployment$_{dt-1}$	−0.04** (0.01)	−0.03** (0.01)
EconomicGrowth$_{dt-1}$	0.02** (0.01)	0.03** (0.01)
EntryRestrictions$_{dt-1}$	0.00 (0.01)	0.02** (0.01)
Constant	1.43 (2.36)	1.59 (2.46)
Observations	89,448	16,916
Origin*year FEs	Yes	Yes
Destination FEs	Yes	Yes

Note: * $p < 0.10$, ** $p < 0.05$. All models estimated using pseudo–Poisson maximum likelihood (PPML) with robust standard errors clustered by dyad in parentheses. All models include destination and origin*year fixed effects.

APPENDIX TABLE A3.3 *Political environment, distance, and migration flows*

	Dependent variable: Migrants$_{odt}$
	(1)
log (Distance$_{od}$)*RightsIndex$_{dt-1}$	0.03**
	(0.01)
RightsIndex$_{dt-1}$	−0.20**
	(0.05)
log (Distance$_{od}$)	−0.39**
	(0.05)
RadicalRightChange$_{dt-1}$	−0.03**
	(0.01)
log (MigrantStock$_{odt-1}$)	0.64**
	(0.02)
CommonColony$_{od}$	0.03
	(0.12)
CommonBorder$_{od}$	−0.13
	(0.13)
CommonLanguage$_{od}$	0.32**
	(0.07)
SameCountry$_{od}$	0.12
	(0.16)
CommonReligion$_{od}$	0.04
	(0.14)
log (GDPPC$_{dt-1}$)	1.00**
	(0.43)
Unemployment$_{dt-1}$	−0.04**
	(0.01)
EconomicGrowth$_{dt-1}$	0.02**
	(0.01)
EntryRestrictions$_{dt-1}$	−0.00
	(0.01)
Constant	0.95
	(1.72)
Observations	106,364
Destination FEs	Yes
Origin * year FEs	Yes

Note: * $p < 0.10$, ** $p < 0.05$. All models estimated using pseudo-Poisson maximum likelihood (PPML) with robust standard errors clustered by dyad in parentheses. All models include destination and origin*year fixed effects.

APPENDIX 3.B: SOURCES FOR CITIZENSHIP RIGHTS VARIABLES

General Sources

Boll, A. M. 2007. *Multiple Nationality and International Law.* Netherlands: M. Nijhoff.

de Groot, Gerard-Rene. 2003. "Loss of Nationality: A Critical Inventory." David Margin and Kay Hailbronner (eds) *Rights and Duties of Dual Nationals.* The Hague: Kluwer Law International. Table 1 (p.279).

Martin, David. 2005. "Dual Nationality," in Matthew Gibney and Randall Hansen (eds). *Immigration and Asylum.* Santa Barbara CA: ABC CLIO

United States Office of Personnel Management. 2001. *Citizenship Laws of the World.* United States: American Immigration Lawyers Association.

Country-specific sources

Algeria	www.voyage.gc.ca/countries_pays/report_rapport-eng.asp?id=5000
Armenia	www.legislationline.org/documents/action/popup/id/6638
Austria	www.coe.int/t/e/legal_affairs/legal_co%2Doperation/foreigners_and_citizens/nationality/documents/national_legislation/AUSTRIA-En.pdf
Azerbaijan	www.coe.int/t/e/legal_affairs/legal_co-operation/foreigners_and_citizens/nationality/documents/national_legislation/AZERBAIJAN%20Law%20Citizenship_ENG.pdf
Bahamas	www.unhcr.org/cgi-bin/texis/vtx/refworld/rwmain?docid=3ae6b4fc10
Bahrain	www.arabicnews.com/ansub/Daily/Day/020611/2002061115.html
Belarus	www.unhcr.org/refworld/country,,,LEGISLATION,BLR,4562d8b62,49c75c6c2,0.html
Bolivia	http://muse.jhu.edu/journals/latin_american_research_review/v042/42.3escobar.html
Bulgaria	http://international.ibox.bg/news/id_690983922
Burundi	www.unhcr.org/refworld/country,,IRBC,,BDI,456d621e2,3f7d4d591c,0.html
Cameroon	www.dibussi.com/2006/05/dual_citizenshi.html
Canada	www.cic.gc.ca/english/resources/publications/dual-citizenship.asp

Czech Republic	http://en.wikipedia.org/wiki/Czech_nationality_law
Egypt	http://en.wikipedia.org/wiki/Egyptian_Nationality_Law#Dual_Citizenship
Estonia	www.globalpolicy.org/component/content/article/173/30382.html
Fiji	http://en.wikipedia.org/wiki/Constitution_of_Fiji:_Chapter_3
Germany	www.lrct-tz.org/PositionPaperOnDualCitizenship.pdf
Ghana	www.modernghana.com/news/209842/1/the-benefits-of-dual-citizenship-to-the-socio-econ.html
Greece	www.geocities.com/nationalite/greek-eng.txt
Guatemala	http://muse.jhu.edu/journals/latin_american_research_review/v042/42.3escobar.html
Guyana	www.unhcr.org/refworld/topic,4565c2252,4565c25f5f,492ac7c9c,0.html
Honduras	http://muse.jhu.edu/journals/latin_american_research_review/v042/42.3escobar.html
Indonesia	www.indonesiamatters.com/733/citizenship-law/
Iraq	http://news.bbc.co.uk/2/hi/middle_east/3119020.stm
Ireland	www.answers.com/topic/irish-nationality-law#Loss_of_citizenship
Italy	www.coe.int/t/e/legal_affairs/legal_co-operation/foreigners_and_citizens/nationality/documents/bulletin/Italy%202004%20E.pdf
Jordan	www.indonesiamatters.com/733/citizenship-law/
Kuwait	www.kuwaittimes.net/read_news.php?newsid=MTkzNTU2Mzk=
Kyrgyz Republic	www.coe.int/t/e/legal_affairs/legal_co-operation/foreigners_and_citizens/nationality/documents/bulletin/Kyrgyzstan%20E.pdf
Laos	www.unhcr.org/refworld/category,LEGAL,,,LAO,3ae6b4f014,0.html
Latvia	www.cic.gc.ca/english/resources/publications/dual-citizenship.asp
Lithuania	www.warsawvoice.pl/view/862/
Mali	www.lrct-tz.org/PositionPaperOnDualCitizenship.pdf

(*continued*)

(continued)

Mauritius	www.culture.gouv.fr/entreelibre/Laurette/country/mauritiustext.html
Moldavia	www.law.ed.ac.uk/citmodes/files/moldovancitizenshipreport19march09.pdf
Nigeria	http://books.google.com/books?id=eZ8MBYRrXoEC&pg=PA268&lpg=PA268&dq=nigeria+nationality+law&source=bl&ots=QDQuH7Mn-o&sig=vA1UFiB4sT2GE7tf7–oPACbF93c&hl=en&ei=NMseSrWjIp7UlQfyoPnFBQ&sa=X&oi=book_result&ct=result&resnum=4
Pakistan	www.pakistan.gov.pk/divisions/ContentInfo.jsp?DivID=23&cPath=221_227&ContentID=754
Philippines	http://en.wikipedia.org/wiki/Philippine_nationality_law
Romania	www.romanianpassport.co.il/english/romanian-citizenship-law/
Russia	http://en.wikipedia.org/wiki/Russian_nationality_law#Citizenship_act_of_1991
Senegal	www.unhcr.org/refworld/country,,IRBC,,SEN,456d621e2,469cd69a8,0.html
South Korea	http://joongangdaily.joins.com/article/view.asp?aid=2890640
Tanzania	www.lrct-tz.org/PositionPaperOnDualCitizenship.pdf
Spain	http://books.google.com/books?id=nFmjkTnXNQAC&pg=PA334&lpg=PA334&dq=spain+dual+nationality&source=bl&ots=vXQIilNCoT&sig=yFSQ-AZwiGvGMbevJrkAnwhFhNk&hl=en&ei=vfAjSvjHNYzEMe-w5KEJ&sa=X&oi=book_result&ct=result&resnum=8
Uganda	http://allafrica.com/stories/200905180234.html
Venezuela	http://muse.jhu.edu/journals/latin_american_research_review/v042/42.3escobar.html

4

Diaspora Bonds

Global Migration and International Investment

Globalization, as we discuss in Chapter 1, refers to complex connections between individuals, firms, markets, and states. Migration, we argue, is an essential component of globalization. Individuals forge connections with co-ethnics both at home and abroad, helping to build social networks. In this chapter and the next, we argue that a perspective focusing on migrant-based networks is essential to understand patterns of *financial* globalization. Why is migration essential for unpacking global capital markets? Aren't international institutions like the World Trade Organizaton (WTO) and/or the International Monetary Fund (IMF), combined with domestic central banks, sufficient to provide the regulatory environment for international capital mobility?

Capital is necessary for investment and to finance trade – behaviors that drive economic growth. Access to capital, whether from public or private sources, is essential. Investment is all about risk and return: Investors are willing to lend to a household, corporation, or government if they believe that the risk-adjusted return exceeds the potential loss of investment. Capital, like commodity trade, ebbs and flows based on supply and demand. Yet, unlike commodity trade, there is no equivalent to the WTO for cross-border investment that provides information and a semblance of contract enforcement.

We argue that the growth and spread of capital investment across the world is, in part, due to migration. As investment opportunities become more complex – from portfolio equities, to venture capital, to mergers and acquisitions, to greenfield investment – the information required to ensure an adequate return and acceptable level of risk increases. Migrants, we demonstrate, are essential in providing potential investors with information about investment opportunities and the contracting environment. Just as migrant networks provide information to potential émigrés regarding opportunities across destinations, we argue that migrant networks provide potential investors with information vital to decisions of global capital allocation.

Our point of departure is a stylized model of capital allocation. Textbook models suggest that capital should, all else equal, flow from capital-rich to capital-poor countries, as this would allocate capital to where it yields the highest rate of return. While elegant in theory, this neoclassical model performs poorly in practice, as very little capital flows from rich to poor countries. Lucas (1990) refers to this puzzle as the "central question for economic development" (p. 92).

Political economists have spent decades addressing the Lucas Paradox, developing a broad set of approaches focusing on a country's economic "fundamentals," such as the country's economic structure of production and access to technology, policies and institutions related to credible contracting, and asymmetries of information as they pertain to sovereign risk. Some of the most powerful explanations focus on a country's political and institutional environment: The extent to which a government signals to international investors that policymakers are credibly committed to protecting property rights, enforcing contracts, and are willing to forgo policies that would lead the investment to lose value (e.g., Alfaro, Kalemli-Ozcan, and Volosovych 2008). This work explores domestic (e.g., Henisz 2000; Jensen 2003; Pandya 2014) and international (e.g., Büthe and Milner 2008) institutions as signals of a policymaker's commitment.

Institutional commitments – whether domestic or international – provide a transparent way for investors to form expectations regarding political and economic risk in a given country. But transparent institutions do not always exist and are often difficult to design. Does this mean that countries without transparent and credible institutions are absent from global capital markets? Figure 4.1 shows that the answer to this question is clearly no, as we observe countries with differing levels of democracy and corruption – indicators used to proxy for credible commitments – that have equal access to both foreign direct and portfolio investment.[1] Countries such as Laos (Qatar) and Costa Rica (Estonia), for example, receive roughly equivalent amounts of foreign direct (portfolio) investment as a share of their GDP, despite having very different levels of democracy. Similarly, these measures

---

[1] We use the V-Dem measures of polyarchy and corruption; those measures are defined below.

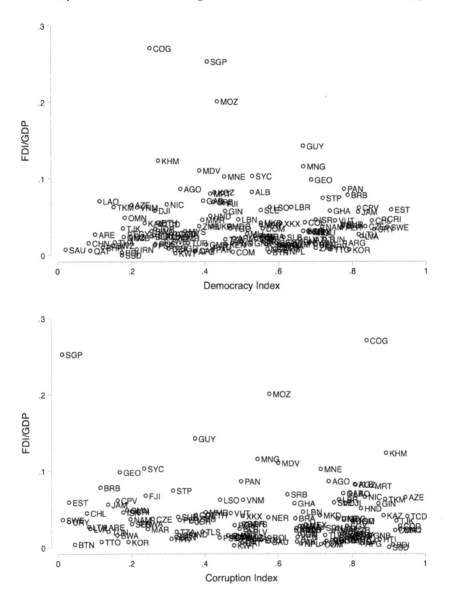

FIGURE 4.1 Political institutions and investment. FDI/GDP is average FDI as a share of GDP from 2015 to 2019. Source: World Development Indicators. Portfolio/GDP is average portfolio investment as a share of GDP from 2015 to 2019.
Source: World Development Indicators. Democracy is the V-Dem polyarchy measure and corruption is the V-Dem regime corruption index.

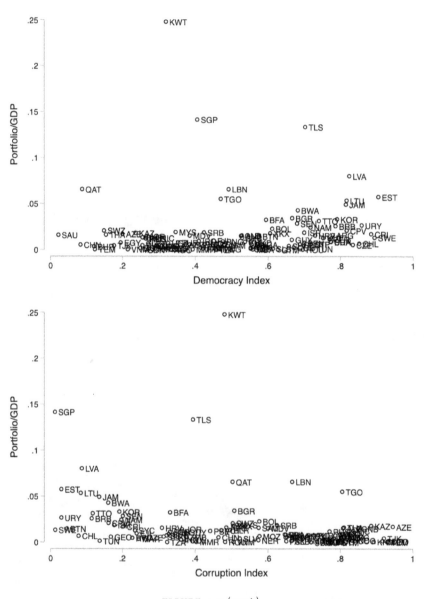

FIGURE 4.1 *(cont.)*

of institutional commitments do not explain why, despite identical levels of democracy or corruption, Botswana receives more portfolio investment as a share of GDP than Israel, and Cambodia receives more FDI than Ethiopia.

This is not to say that focusing on institutions is unwarranted. Indeed, it is hard to question the importance of credible commitments, especially when considering cross-border patterns of investment. But institutional design is only one part of the contracting environment and does not help us understand information asymmetries that plague global markets. Investors may have incomplete or imperfect information about investment opportunities, lack knowledge about the structure of markets, and misinterpret the ways that policymakers use institutions to signal their commitments. In this chapter, we argue that migrant, diaspora, or co-ethnic networks decrease problems of information asymmetries and increase contract-specific knowledge essential for international investment.

Our argument that migrant networks are an important component of international economic exchange is not novel. Greif (1989, 1993) illustrated the role that the Maghrebi traders of the eleventh century played in providing informal institutional guarantees that facilitated trade. Cohen's (1997) historical survey identifies not only the Phoenicians but also the "Spanish Jews [who] were indispensable for international commerce in the Middle Ages. The Armenians controlled the overland route between the Orient and Europe as late as the nineteenth century. Lebanese Christians developed trade between the various parts of the Ottoman Empire" (p. 170). Rauch and Trindade (2002) provide robust empirical evidence linking the Chinese diaspora to patterns of imports and exports with their home country. And in related work, Leblang (2010), Javorcik et al. (2011), Pandya and Leblang (2017), Kugler, Levintal, and Rapoport (2018), Graham (2019), and Zeitz and Leblang (2021) apply this argument to flows of portfolio investment and FDI, as well as to bank lending.

Migrant networks facilitate the cross-border flow of capital in several ways. Fundamentally, migrant networks reduce information asymmetries that may, all else equal, result in less investment than textbook models of capital allocation suggest. This reduction in information asymmetries operates in two different ways. First, migrant communities embedded in host countries provide investors with information about their homeland – information related to the tastes of consumers in their country of origin – that can influence the decision of entrepreneurs to invest there. Second, migrants may have asymmetric, specialized information about investment opportunities, information about regulations and procedures, and familiarity with language and customs, which decreases the transactions costs associated with cross-border investment. In addition to the reduction of information asymmetries, co-ethnic ties may influence the direction of investment based on attachment. If migrants are the entrepreneur and can direct some of their company's investment portfolio, they may prefer investing in their homeland.

This chapter proceeds as follows. We first develop a theory linking diaspora networks to cross-border capital flows. We derive hypotheses from that theory and test them using a large panel of country dyads. The use of panel data allows us to generalize from the results of Leblang (2010), Javorcik et al. (2011), and Kugler, Levintal, and Rapoport (2018), who base their conclusions on static, cross-sectional samples. We examine the effect of educated migrants as well as migrants employed in the finance, investment, and real estate (FIRE) sector. The chapter concludes by asking whether migrant networks are substitutes or complements for existing institutional arrangements.

DETERMINANTS OF GLOBAL INVESTMENT

How can we understand the effect of co-ethnic networks on cross-border flows of capital? Consider an investor in country o deciding whether to purchase stocks or bonds in two foreign countries, d_1 and d_2. The investor compares the expected return on investment in country d_1 to the expected return in country o as well as the expected return in country d_2. How does an investor decide where to invest? What factors influence their preferences over markets o, d_1, and d_2?

One approach uses the international capital asset pricing model (ICAPM) to understand international portfolio diversification. ICAPM models posit that a portfolio should contain domestic assets in proportion to its country's share of global market capitalization.[2] The intuition behind this result is that overall portfolio risk can be reduced by including assets that are negatively correlated with home-country returns. This allows an investor to achieve average expected returns while minimizing overall portfolio risk. While theoretically appealing, empirical work consistently finds little support for the ICAPM, concluding that portfolio investors exhibit "home bias" – a systematic preference for assets issued in their home country (Lewis 1999). This result is puzzling, as it means that investors forgo higher returns and risk larger losses due to lack of diversification.

Home bias is, however, consistent with standard models of information asymmetries.[3] The dominant explanation for home bias is that

---

[2] See Lane (2006) and Lane and Milesi-Ferretti (2008) for studies of bilateral investment that are explicitly derived from the ICAPM model. Elton et al. (2003) give a textbook exposition of capital asset pricing models.

[3] See French and Poterba (1991) and Tesar and Werner (1995). Lewis (1999) reviews the relevant literature.

information-gathering costs are substantial, and a large literature finds that information costs limit international capital flows (e.g., Portes, Rey, and Oh (2001); Portes and Rey (2005)). Kang and Stulz (1997), for example, document that foreign investors in Japan disproportionally own more shares of those firms whose information is more readily available. More generally, Tesar and Werner (1995, p. 479) argue that taste factors such as "language, institutional, and regulatory difference" explain the propensity of investors to invest at home rather than abroad. Likewise, French and Poterba (1991) account for home bias with reference to a set of factors they broadly categorize as "familiarity" effects, while Coval and Moskowitz (2001) attribute home bias to information asymmetries, arguing that investors have better information about assets sold in geographically closer markets.[4]

In a global context, it is difficult (if not impossible) to separate familiarity with, and cultural preferences for, home-country assets from decisions based on information asymmetries. To minimize problems of model misspecification associated with omitted variable bias, empirical studies of cross-border investment often exploit gravity-type models of international transactions. Like the models discussed in Chapter 3, gravity models of financial transactions hold that bilateral transactions are a positive function of the size of the two economies (their mass) and a negative function of the distance between them. In dealing with the empirical fact that investors exhibit a home bias, scholars augment these gravity models with a variety of variables. Eichengreen and Luengnaruemitchai (2006), Lane and Milesi-Ferretti (2008), and Rose and Spiegel (2009), for example, include variables that measure whether the country pair shares a common language, border, or colonial heritage. These measures of commonality are interpreted in the context of greater familiarity, better information, lower barriers to entry, and lower transactions costs.

Scholars also interpret negative coefficients on physical distance in gravity models of international investment as a proxy for information asymmetries. The greater the distance from a market, so the argument

---

[4] Huberman (2001), Grinblatt and Keloharju (2001), and Portes and Rey (2005) also find that investors tend to purchase assets sold in more proximate markets. These papers attribute this behavior to the idea that investors have more complete information as distance between markets decreases. Coval and Moskowitz (1999, 2001) attempt to distinguish between familiarity and information asymmetries. Their 1999 study documents that investors prefer to invest in the "familiar" while their 2001 paper provides evidence in favor of the information asymmetry hypothesis. It is worth noting that their earlier paper does not distinguish between the two explanations.

goes, the greater the information costs and the lower the level of investment. Arguing that distance proxies for information costs, however, is
theoretically unsatisfying and, in a series of papers, Portes, Rey, and Oh
(2001) and Portes and Rey (2005) employ a more direct measure of
information asymmetries and transactions costs by including a measure
of bilateral telephone traffic. They find that telephone traffic is associated
with higher levels of bilateral portfolio investment.[5]

These approaches remain incomplete. Even models that include measures of communication flows and costs find that investors retain a home
bias (e.g., Loungani, Mody, and Razin 2002). Taking this as its point of
departure, a growing literature argues that investment across countries
may be driven not by familiarity but rather by "cultural affinity", whereby
individuals have more trust in individuals and institutions from countries
that share common cultural characteristics (e.g., Guiso, Sapienza, and
Zingales 2009; Siegel, Licht, and Schwartz 2011). Cultural similarity,
viewed within the context of ICAPM models, would constitute a more
direct measure of information costs and should be correlated with lower
transactions costs and greater ease of doing business across borders.

THE ROLE OF MIGRANT NETWORKS[6]

Scholars have long recognized the importance of social networks as a
mechanism to facilitate economic exchange when formal institutions are
absent or incomplete (e.g., Greif 1989; North 2005).[7] Migrant networks
facilitate investment both directly and indirectly.[8] The direct mechanism
arises when migrants themselves are investors, driving global capital
flows. In his study of the Korean diaspora, Choi (2003) documents how
Shin Kyuk-ho and Masayoshi Son, Korean entrepreneurs living in Japan,
helped accelerate Korea's role as a destination for FDI. But foreign investment does not only come from wealthy expatriates: Schüttler (2007) and

---

[5] Loungani, Mody, and Razin (2002) reach similar conclusions regarding the relationship
between telephone traffic and FDI.

[6] This section draws on Leblang (2010).

[7] The relational approach to economic sociology focuses on relations between parties to a
transaction rather than on the transaction itself. This view, that economic processes are
"embedded" in social relations, has been used to study labor markets (Granovetter 1973),
business transactions (Uzzi 1996), and FDI (Bandelj 2002, 2007).

[8] There is a voluminous literature focusing on one dimension of direct immigrant financial
flows: migrant remittances – financial transfers from a host country back to family and
friends in the homeland. We return to an examination of remittances in Chapter 5.

Schulte (2008), respectively, tell the story of investment decisions made by Moroccan and Turkish migrants living in Germany. Combining a wealth of ethnographic information, survey data, and qualitative case studies, these scholars conclude that Moroccan and Turkish investments are driven by cultural ties and linguistic familiarity.[9] Scholars reach similar conclusions about the importance of ethnic, cultural, and linguistic ties for diaspora-connected investment in studies of Armenia (Freinkman 2002), India (Kapur 2001; Saxenian 2002), Israel (Kleinman 1996), and China (Weidenbaum and Hughes 1996; Rauch and Casella 2003).

From a research design perspective, it is difficult to generalize from these cases in a convincing fashion. Elite investor surveys are one option, but it is unlikely that they would admit to either making an investment based on their heart and not their head or possessing private information. Because we want to understand broad patterns of global capital allocation, we embed empirical measures of co-ethnic networks in a well-established empirical framework; our inferences and conclusions are statements about average effects conditional on a set of covariates.

How do we understand the role of co-ethnic networks in facilitating cross-border investment? As noted in the introduction, there are two mechanisms: Migrant networks foster (1) increased familiarity and (2) reduction in information asymmetries.

The "familiarity" effect occurs when investors in a source country become familiar with characteristics of and opportunities in a migrant's homeland via the investor's connections with, and observation of, migrant communities in their own homeland. Migrants provide a *signal* that allows the investor to form expectations about labor quality, work ethic, and the culture of doing business in that destination. In his study of Indian communities in the United States, Kapur (2001, p. 273) observes that the mere presence of that community enhances investment opportunities in India:

Companies like Yahoo, Hewlett Packard and General Electric have opened R&D centers in India largely because of the confidence engendered by the presence of many Indians working in their US operations. This points to the cognitive effects arising from the projection of a coherent, appealing, and progressive identity on

---

[9] Migrants are aware of this advantage as Schulte (2008) documents with a quote from one of her interviewees: "Logically, one has advantages as a Turk when approaching business partners [in Turkey]. One speaks the same language, one is aware that small talk is required and one is on the same level of understanding, one socializes, one has the same humour, one shares interest in specific topics. That is a major advantage" (p. 8).

the part of the diaspora which signals an image of prosperity and progress to potential investors and consumers.

Kapur and McHale (2005) refer to this as "branding" and argue that the Indian diaspora has created a brand name by signaling the productivity and trustworthiness of their countrymen. This branding acts as a focal point for United States investors, allowing them to make forecasts about expected return on investment in India.

The second mechanism, reduction of information asymmetries, works first by decreasing transactions costs. Migrant communities facilitate cross-national portfolio investment by reducing barriers to entry – through knowledge of language, institutional rules, and regulatory hurdles – that may otherwise prevent a foreign investor from purchasing equities or bonds. Knowledge of on-the-ground conditions is costly and provides investors with the ability to "match" capital to potential investment opportunities. This matching function of migrant networks has been observed in studies of international trade, where Rauch and Trindade (2002) find that migrant-generated information helps match buyers with sellers, a function that becomes more important as goods become increasingly heterogeneous.[10]

Qualitative evidence is consistent with this mechanism. Weidenbaum and Hughes (1996), in their study of the "Bamboo Network", document the comparative advantage that overseas Chinese co-ethnics have when investing in China. They argue that ethnic Chinese have an advantage due to common language and dialect, knowledge of cultural and legal hurdles, and pre-existing familial connections. Schulte (2008) tells a similar story about ethnic Turks residing in Germany, arguing that Turkish migrants are more likely to invest in their homeland rather than in China, for example, because language and cultural knowledge more than compensate for what may be marginally lower returns. This informational advantage does not privilege just individual investors. Rather, it can work through the larger network effects of co-ethnics.

The dynamics of exploiting information asymmetries also exist when migrants possess information regarding investment opportunities in their home country. Bandelj (2002) provides some evidence concerning the investment behavior of Western European and North American investors

---

[10] A wealth of evidence documents the relationship between migration and international trade flows. In addition to Rauch and Trindade (2002), see Felbmermayr and Toubal (2012); Sangita (2013); Parsons and Winters (2014); Parsons and Vézina (2018); and Ottaviano, Peri, and Wright (2018) for additional information on theory and evidence linking migration and international trade.

after the opening of markets in Eastern Europe. Investment in Eastern European countries, she writes, was "often based on ethnic ties between sizable and relatively affluent expatriate communities and their home countries" (p. 421). There was an informational advantage as "firms amassed information about investment opportunities through their business or personal ties" (Bandelj 2002, p. 412).

This informational advantage can translate into higher-than-average expected returns if the migrant herself has a higher level of human capital. In his examination of the Armenian diaspora, Freinkman (2002) notes that,

> when compared to the average economic agent, diaspora businessmen and professionals face a lower risk of becoming the first movers. They benefit from a specific informational advantage: Common cultural background and established social links between diaspora and local entrepreneurs help them to reduce transaction costs of new entry and building new partnerships. (p .334)

We hypothesize, then, that all else equal, co-ethnic networks will increase cross-border capital flows. All capital flows, however, are not equivalent even if they have the same dollar value. FDI comes in a variety of flavors: *greenfield*, where investors in one country create a foreign subsidiary from the ground up, *mergers and acquisitions* (M&A), whereby the investor purchases an existing overseas operation, and *venture capital* (VC), where the investment is made in the start-up phase of a firm (Pandya and Leblang 2017). FDI, even within these different categories, is heterogeneous as investors require information regarding potential competition within the market, the structure of production for M&A investment, and the potential for sale if the VC investment is successful. Portfolio investment, on the other hand, is more homogeneous as it is generally limited to an established set of assets: debt or equity stakes in companies exchanged on organized markets.

Following Rauch and Trindade (2002), we also hypothesize that migrant networks are more important for investment in heterogeneous (as compared with homogeneous) assets. This is because the information costs – both asymmetries and transactions costs – associated with heterogeneous assets are substantially larger than those associated with homogeneous assets. When it comes to cross-border investment, we argue that FDI is more heterogeneous than portfolio investment. Whereas portfolio investors choose debt or equity stakes that are offered by an issuing agency on an organized market, foreign direct investors can take innumerable different ownership stakes across a countless number of commodity classes. Because migrant networks provide information about investment opportunities and may have asymmetric knowledge about the quality of home-country assets, we hypothesize that migrant networks have a larger substantive effect on FDI than on portfolio investment.

RESEARCH DESIGN

We first examine portfolio investment flows in a global sample of 8,364 country pairs (63 investing and 155 recipient countries) over the period 2000–2017. We also examine FDI flows over a shorter period (2009–2017) due to data constraints. Albeit shorter, the FDI sample is broad, with 7,687 country pairs (71 investing and 154 recipient countries). Both samples are unbalanced panels, as there is substantial missing data on cross-border investment, with inconsistencies in country reporting of portfolio investment and FDI statistics. As in Eichengreen and Luengnaruemitchai (2006), Lane and Milesi-Ferretti (2008), and Leblang (2010), we remove off-shore financial centers from our sample.

We embed our hypotheses in a gravity model of international transactions. The motivation for using the gravity model is similar to our discussion in Chapter 3; the gravity model can be derived from established models of international transactions and provides a framework within which we can make reasonable inferences. Because we focus on the flow of financial assets and not people, our empirical specification is different.[11] Within the context of capital flows, we hypothesize that economic transactions between two countries will be positively associated with their two masses (as measured by the size of their economies) and negatively associated with the distance between them. Economic size should be positive as larger economies have more opportunities to engage in economic exchange. Distance, on the other hand, proxies for the cost of transporting goods between two countries. Empirical implementations of gravity models modify this basic model to include other measures associated with transportation, transactions, and information costs. Studies of bilateral trade find, for example, that countries sharing a common language (a proxy for transactions costs) trade more with each other, as do countries that have a common colonial history (a proxy for information

---

[11] Studies of FDI employing a gravity model include Wei (2000) and Loungani, Modi, and Razin (2002). Portes, Rey, and Oh (2001), Portes and Rey (2005), Lane (2006), Eichengreen and Luengnaruemitchai (2006), and Lane and Milesi-Ferretti (2008) use a gravity model to examine bilateral investment in equities and bonds.

costs) (Portes and Rey 2005; Eichengreen and Luengnaruemitchai 2006; Okawa and van Wincoop 2012).

To examine the link between migrant networks and international investment, we use data from the IMF's Coordinated Portfolio Investment Survey (CPIS), which collects information on the stock of cross-border investments in equities broken down by issuer's country of residence. Similarly, we source FDI data from the IMF's Coordinated Direct Investment Survey (CDIS). This source is relatively new; we use it because it provides consistent data on inward FDI positions for a global sample of countries.

Our key independent variable – migrant networks – measures the stock (or total number) of migrants from investment destination country d residing in investment origin country o at time t. The UNPD provides a 225×225 matrix of countries every five years between 1990 and 2015, along with estimates for 2017 and 2019. We use linear interpolation to fill missing values; this provides a complete, balanced panel of migrant stocks for over 50,000 country pairs. Because these data have many zeros and outliers, we add one and take the log transformation.

Following the gravity approach to trade, we account for physical distance between origin and destination countries as well as whether they share a common border, have a common colonial heritage, and if, by law, they have the same official language. These four variables are from the CEPII bilateral gravity dataset (Head, Mayer, and Ries 2010).

Trade in financial assets may be influenced by shared policy variables. As in Lane and Milesi-Ferretti (2008), we include an indicator variable, also from CEPII, indicating the existence of a common currency, which decreases costs associated with exchange across markets and should, all else equal, increase investment. ICAPM models are based on the importance of portfolio diversification, so we proxy for exposure to common economic shocks by including the lagged correlation of the two countries' growth rates. We measure this via a three-year moving correlation of GDP growth rates based on data from the World Bank's WDI. Common membership in international institutions may also proxy for either shared preferences or the ease of sharing information. We use two measures: an indicator variable coded one if the two countries have a dual taxation treaty in place and a count of the number of preferential trade agreements (PTAs) that the countries have in common.

One challenge to making inferences about the effect of migrant networks on global investment is that it is difficult, if not impossible, to separate homeland affinity, market familiarity, and informational asymmetries. Empirically, our approach is to exploit a conservative estimation strategy and do our best to account for other measures of cultural familiarity and affinity. We include several measures capturing cultural similarities between the source and destination countries. The first – a measure of common legal origin – is more institutional than cultural, but it captures the ability of investors from country *o* to invest in country *d* with minimal transactions costs because they will be familiar with the rules and regulations that exist. We control for the existence of a common religion, which measures religious proximity. This variable, based on Disdier and Mayer (2007), is calculated as the sum of products of the shares of Catholics, Protestants, and Muslims in the origin and destination countries. The variable is bounded between zero and one. Both common legal origin and common religion come from CEPII. All else equal, we expect that country pairs with common legal origins and religion will experience higher levels of cross-border investment than those pairs that are legally and religiously dissimilar.

The third cultural control is grounded in cultural economics and is operationalized as a measure of genetic distance between countries. Based on the work of Cavalli-Sforza, Menozzi, and Piazza (1994), scholars have developed measures of genetic distance between indigenous populations based on DNA polymorphism.[12] This measure of genetic distance has been used to proxy for cultural difference in studies of international trade and FDI (Giuliano, Spilimbergo, and Tonon 2006; Guiso, Sapienza, and Zingales 2009), economic development (Spolaore and Wacziarg 2009), and state formation in Europe (Desmet et al. 2009). We hypothesize that more dissimilar countries – based on larger genetic distances – will have less bilateral investment. Data on genetic distance come from Spolaore and Wacziarg (2018).

Finally, we include a more direct measure of cultural similarity. Studies in international business find that greater cultural distance between countries is associated with larger transactions costs, more uncertainty about business practices, and overall greater unease regarding the prospects for doing business (Kogut and Singh 1988; Habib and Zurawicki 2002; Siegel, Licht, and Schwartz 2011). Some studies of international trade find that countries that are culturally closer engage in larger levels of transactions (White and Tadesse 2008; Guiso, Sapienza, and Zingales 2009; Siegel, Licht, and Schwartz 2011).

---

[12] The details involved in the derivation of these measures constitute a paper in and of themselves. The interested reader is directed to Spolaore and Wacziarg (2009) for a discussion and application; we are grateful to them for generously sharing their data.

We use all available waves of the World Values Survey[13] (WVS) and extract four questions that proxy for cultural similarity and distance: (1) Can most people can be **trusted**, (2) **Are tolerance** and **respect** for others important qualities for a child, (3) How much **freedom** and **control** should individuals have, and (4) Should important child qualities include **obedience**. The questions related to trust, respect, and obedience are dichotomous responses, while control is measured on a 100-point scale that we transform so that it is bounded between zero and one. We measure cultural distance between countries o and d as:

$$Cultural\, Distance_{od} = \sqrt{(trust_o - trust_d)^2 + (respect_o - respect_d)^2 + (control_o - control_d)^2 + (obedience_o - obedience_d)^2} \tag{4.1}$$

We use cultural distance as a robustness check. Because in each wave these surveys are only given in approximately 60 countries, this variable is missing for over half of our sample.

EMPIRICAL MODEL

Our estimation model can be written as:

$$log\,(y)_{odt} = \phi log(M)_{dot} + \beta X_{odt} + \gamma Z_{od} + \delta_{ot} + \delta_{dt} + \varepsilon_{odt} \tag{4.2}$$

where $log\,(y)_{odt}$ is logged investment (FDI or portfolio) from country of origin o to destination d at time t; $log\,(M)_{dot}$ represents the logged number of migrants from the destination of investment d residing in the country where the investment originates o at time t; X_{odt} is a vector of time-varying bilateral controls, including the correlation of growth rates in countries o and d at time t and number of PTAs between country o and d; and Z_{od} is a vector of time-invariant bilateral controls including geographic, cultural, and genetic distance and common language and colonial origin.

We estimate Equation (4.2) using ordinary least squares (OLS). Note that this equation includes two sets of δ terms. The first, δ_{ot}, is a full set of origin*year fixed effects, while the second, δ_{dt}, is a full set of destination*year fixed effects. These fixed effects act as statistical controls for any origin- or destination-specific factors that may influence

---

[13] Desmet et al. (2009) provide evidence that European countries that are genetically alike have populations that provide similar answers to World Values Survey questions about cultural, religious, and moral issues.

cross-border investment. The inclusion of these fixed effects also accounts for the size of each country's economy in a given dyad-year.[14]

Inferences based on classical standard errors may be biased for at least two reasons. First, investment by source countries may cluster geographically; consequently, we need standard errors that are clustered by origin country o. Second, some destination countries, for a variety of reasons, receive more investment than other countries, a phenomenon that would call for clustering by destination country d. We address this potential bias by estimating standard errors that are robust to multiway clustering as developed by Cameron, Gelbach, and Miller (2011). Their approach allows for arbitrary correlations between errors that belong to "the same group (along either dimension)" (p. 241). They point out that this estimator is applicable in situations when errors exhibit spatial correlation. Consequently, we report standard errors that are clustered by both source and destination countries. Cameron, Gelbach, and Miller (2011) note that multiway clustering increases – by order of magnitude – the size of standard errors. The resulting standard errors reported below are conservative.[15]

RESULTS

Table 4.1 contains our baseline results for bilateral portfolio investment, with Column (1) being our benchmark specification. We have data for investment flows out of 62 countries of origin into 155 destination countries. Dyadic investment decreases with bilateral distance and increases between two countries that share a common border or language. This is consistent with the information interpretation of these variables – distance makes information gathering more challenging and helps explain why we observe a great deal of investment in geographically proximate locations. Measures of institutional and economic similarity are also positive and statistically significant, with both common exchange rate peg and the existence of a dual taxation treaty increasing bilateral investment. Interestingly, both the correlation of economic growth rates and the number of shared PTAs are statistically insignificant.[16]

---

[14] In regressions in which we are unable to include origin*year and destination*year fixed effects, we also control for joint economic size.

[15] We implement this model using the **reghdfe** command (version 5.7.3) developed in Correia (2017).

[16] If we remove the origin*year and destination*year fixed effects, both variables are statistically significant.

In Column (2), we add the measure of migrant networks, the logged count of migrants from investment destination country d living in investment origin country o at time t. The coefficient on migrant networks is positive and statistically significant. Note that this variable is statistically significant even after controlling for physical distance, common language, and common border, which we know from Chapter 3 are important determinants of migrant networks. Substantively, this indicates that a 10 percent increase in the size of migrant networks is associated with a more than 2 percent increase in bilateral portfolio investment. Evaluated at their means, we can interpret this as suggesting that each additional migrant helps channel a little over $450 in portfolio investment to their homeland on average.

Our measure of migrant networks could be measuring affinity or cultural similarity. In Column (3) of Table 4.1, we include variables measuring common legal heritage and common religion. Both variables are positive and statistically significant at $p < .10$, but their inclusion only marginally reduces the effect of migrant networks on portfolio investment; that coefficient decreases by less than 10 percent. In Column (4), we add genetic distance as an additional proxy for cultural affinity. This variable increases in value as the two countries in the dyad have underlying populations that are more different in terms of their DNA polymorphism. Genetic distance is negative and statistically significant, suggesting that country pairs with underlying genetic differences see smaller investment flows. We again note that the inclusion of this variable does not diminish the substantive effect of migrant networks on portfolio investment.

Column (5) uses our measure of cultural distance based on the WVS instead of genetic distance. Note that the use of this variable decreases our sample size by more than 50 percent. That said, the results in Column (5) are almost identical to those in Column (4): Cultural differences, all else equal, decrease portfolio investment, and inclusion of this variable does not mitigate the relationship between migrant stocks and investment.

Finally, it is likely that bilateral investment patterns reflect other existing economic relationships. Rauch and Trindade (2002) demonstrated the existence of an empirical relationship between the Chinese diaspora and China's global trade network. If trade follows investment – as discussed in the introduction – then the inclusion of bilateral trade should render our variable for co-ethnic networks statistically insignificant or diminish its impact. In Column (6), we account for this possibility and include a measure of total trade between countries o and d at time t-1. The results indicate, first, that trade and investment are complements, as the coefficient

TABLE 4.1 *Migrant networks and portfolio investment*

		Dependent variable: $\log(PortfolioInvestment_{odt})$				
	(1)	(2)	(3)	(4)	(5)	(6)
$\log(MigrantStock_{odt-1})$		0.230**	0.215**	0.205**	0.208**	0.186**
		(0.0452)	(0.0447)	(0.0453)	(0.0427)	(0.041)
$\log(Distance_{od})$	−1.490**	−1.182**	−1.128**	−1.116**	−0.992**	−0.898**
	(0.171)	(0.178)	(0.176)	(0.177)	(0.218)	(0.187)
$Contiguous_{od}$	0.791**	0.454*	0.340	0.175	−0.061	−0.111
	(0.284)	(0.259)	(0.266)	(0.257)	(0.356)	(0.259)
$CommonLanguage_{od}$	1.451**	1.098**	0.891**	0.862**	1.218**	0.872**
	(0.344)	(0.317)	(0.336)	(0.336)	(0.323)	(0.326)
$GrowthCorr_{odt-1}$	0.016	0.0152	0.0137	0.0000690	0.036	0.010
	(0.0490)	(0.0468)	(0.0461)	(0.0459)	(0.064)	(0.047)
$CommonPeg_{odt-1}$	0.767**	0.876**	0.877**	0.900**	1.221**	0.899**
	(0.254)	(0.257)	(0.253)	(0.251)	(0.330)	(0.267)
$TaxTreaty_{odt-1}$	2.369**	2.130**	2.060**	2.026**	1.919**	1.743**
	(0.292)	(0.303)	(0.307)	(0.303)	(0.382)	(0.288)
$PTAs_{odt-1}$	−0.066	−0.0962	−0.0992	−0.102	0.0850	−0.051
	(0.106)	(0.106)	(0.105)	(0.106)	(0.118)	(0.098)

	(1)	(2)	(3)	(4)	(5)	(6)
$CommonReligion_{od}$			1.186^{**}	1.173^{**}	0.876	1.281^{**}
			(0.537)	(0.520)	(0.775)	(0.549)
$CommonLegal_{od}$			0.392^{*}	0.404^{*}	0.592^{**}	0.383^{*}
			(0.218)	(0.221)	(0.262)	(0.209)
$\log(GeneticDistance_{od})$				-0.127^{*}		-0.115^{*}
				(0.0654)		(0.062)
$CulturalDistance_{od}$					-1.564^{*}	
					(0.839)	
$\log(Trade_{odt-1})$						0.250^{**}
						(0.074)
$Constant$	20.099^{**}	16.45^{**}	15.78^{**}	16.67^{**}	16.972^{**}	10.942^{**}
	(1.537)	(1.657)	(1.638)	(1.692)	(2.037)	(2.623)
Observations	94,995	94,995	94,995	92,478	40,275	80,910
Origin * year FEs	Yes	Yes	Yes	Yes	Yes	Yes
Destination * year FEs	Yes	Yes	Yes	Yes	Yes	Yes

Note: $* p < 0.10$, $** p < 0.05$. Models estimated with OLS. All models include origin $*$ year and destination $*$ year fixed effects. All time-varying variables lagged by one year. Robust standard errors clustered by both origin and destination countries in parentheses.

on bilateral trade is positive and statistically significant. Second, the inclusion of bilateral trade decreases the effect of co-ethnic networks by approximately 10 percent from our baseline specification, but the effect of these networks remains both substantively and statistically significant.

In Table 4.2, we substitute FDI for portfolio investment as the dependent variable. Our sample for this analysis is substantially smaller than for portfolio investment, so caution must be exercised in attempting to compare results between Tables 4.1 and 4.2. To summarize the findings, migrant networks have a positive and statistically significant effect on FDI flows. A 10 percent increase in the size of the migrant network is associated with a roughly 4 percent increase in FDI. The impact of co-ethnic networks on FDI flows is robust: including measures of legal, religious, and cultural similarity do little to decrease the effect of co-ethnic ties. Interestingly, we also find that co-ethnic networks and trade flows are complements rather than substitutes, and, as with portfolio investment, the inclusion of trade does decrease, but does not eliminate, the substantive effect of migrant ties on FDI.

Robustness

We evaluate the robustness of these results by examining the effect of co-ethnic networks on portfolio investment and FDI across different subsamples. This is motivated, in part, by Blonigen and Wang (2004), who document problems from what they term "inappropriate" pooling of high and low income countries in studies of FDI. We define a set of Global North countries as those who are OECD members except for Chile, Colombia, Mexico, and South Korea. All other countries are defined as part of the Global South. This allows us to examine investment between North–North, North–South, South–North, and South–South combinations of countries. We estimate Equation (2) separately for each combination of countries and summarize the effect of migrant networks in Figures 4.2 and 4.3.[17]

Figure 4.2 summarizes the marginal effect of migrant networks on portfolio investment across the four corridors. Unsurprisingly, the largest effect of migrant networks is on portfolio flows from countries of the Global North to countries in the Global South, followed by South–South, and then North–North flows. Figure 4.3 repeats this for FDI flows. While

---

[17] Appendix Tables A4.1 and A4.2 present the underlying estimations.

TABLE 4.2 *Migrant networks and FDI*

	(1)	(2)	(3)	(4)	(5)	(6)
			Dependent variable: $\log(FDI_{odt})$			
$\log(MigrantStock_{odt-1})$		0.399**	0.386**	0.357**	0.365**	0.270**
		(0.0544)	(0.0541)	(0.0565)	(0.0794)	(0.049)
$\log(Distance_{od})$	-2.607**	-2.028**	-1.964**	-1.838**	-1.991**	-1.422**
	(0.230)	(0.225)	(0.224)	(0.229)	(0.364)	(0.258)
$Contiguous_{od}$	1.586**	0.792	0.636	0.509	0.128	0.152
	(0.521)	(0.498)	(0.503)	(0.498)	(0.652)	(0.459)
$CommonLanguage_{od}$	1.946**	1.327**	1.094**	1.195**	1.508**	1.131**
	(0.411)	(0.367)	(0.368)	(0.372)	(0.596)	(0.362)
$GrowthCorr_{odt-1}$	0.0694	0.0765	0.0682	0.0642	0.018	0.044
	(0.0841)	(0.0778)	(0.0777)	(0.0808)	(0.105)	(0.082)
$CommonPeg_{odt-1}$	0.208	0.382	0.369	0.379	0.275	0.322
	(0.256)	(0.233)	(0.236)	(0.244)	(0.386)	(0.258)
$TaxTreaty_{odt-1}$	4.855**	4.226**	4.151**	4.081**	4.053**	3.521**
	(0.467)	(0.428)	(0.425)	(0.407)	(0.531)	(0.352)
$PTAs_{odt-1}$	0.00718	-0.0422	-0.0491	-0.0497	0.090	-0.042
	(0.0913)	(0.0863)	(0.0876)	(0.0887)	(0.113)	(0.078)

(*continued*)

III

TABLE 4.2 *(continued)*

CommonReligion$_{od}$		1.667**	1.695**	2.101*	1.860**
		(0.712)	(0.762)	(1.104)	(0.750)
CommonLegal$_{od}$		0.457*	0.478**	0.505	0.380
		(0.233)	(0.236)	(0.316)	(0.230)
log(GeneticDistance$_{od}$)			−0.154**		−0.105
			(0.0683)		(0.070)
CulturalDistance$_{od}$				−1.463	
				(1.036)	
log(Trade$_{odt-1}$)					0.608**
					(0.106)
Constant	28.32**	21.97**	21.32**	23.71**	7.52**
	(2.076)	(2.076)	(2.125)	(3.484)	(3.767)
Observations	52,069	52,069	48,934	19,701	43,308
Origin * year FEs	Yes	Yes	Yes	Yes	Yes
Destination * year FEs	Yes	Yes	Yes	Yes	Yes

Note: * $p < 0.10$, ** $p < 0.05$. Models estimated with OLS. All models include origin * year and destination * year fixed effects. All time-varying variables lagged by one year. Robust standard errors clustered by both origin and destination countries in parentheses.

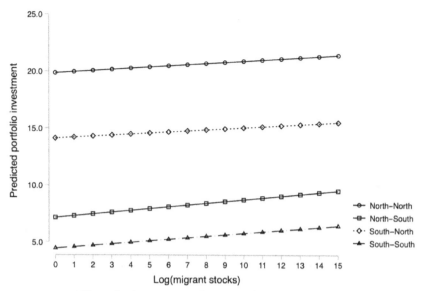

FIGURE 4.2 Effect of migrant networks on portfolio investment for country corridors. Predictive margins for different country pairs based on results in Appendix Table A4.1.

we do not report standard errors to keep the graph simple, and because these estimates are based on separate models, it is important to note that in the North–North sample, the effect of migrant networks on FDI is statistically insignificant. Some diagnostics reveal that most of the variance in North–North FDI flows is captured by the existence of a common currency; this explains a high amount of variation in FDI among members of the eurozone. Migrant networks have the largest effect on FDI in South–Northflows, followed by South–South and then North–South flows.

Migrant Networks and Heterogeneous Investment

The results in Tables 4.1 and 4.2 are not directly comparable, not only because they are estimated separately but because coefficient estimates are based on different sample sizes. A direct comparison is important, because we hypothesize that migrant networks should be more important – from an informational perspective – for FDI than for portfolio investment. The rationale is that FDI projects are heterogeneous, with investment opportunities ranging from greenfield investment to joint ownership to venture capital. Portfolio investments, on the other hand, can only be made in existing assets that are publicly issued by governmental or corporate

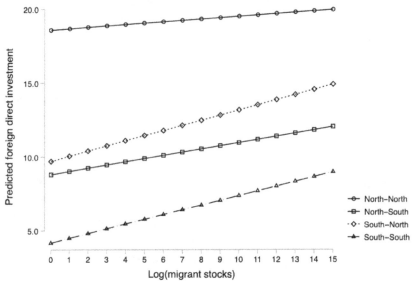

FIGURE 4.3 Effect of migrant networks on FDI for country corridors. Predictive margins for different country pairs based on results in Appendix Table A4.2.

entities. Consequently, the costs of acquiring information regarding the quality of FDI versus portfolio investment opportunities should be considerably different. FDI and portfolio investment also differ in their risk of expropriation. Because portfolio assets are liquid, they can more easily be moved from country to country. FDI, on the other hand, generally requires investment in capital and materials that are more difficult to move in response to anticipated government expropriation. Thus, we expect that migrant networks, because they provide asset-specific information, should be more important for FDI than for portfolio investment.

To test this hypothesis, we utilize a variant of Zellner's (1962) seemingly unrelated regression model. Consider a simplified version of Equation (4.2) with two dependent variables that are closely related conceptually:

$$Port_{odt,1} = X'\beta_1 + \varepsilon_{odt,1} \qquad (4.3)$$

$$FDI_{odt,2} = X'\beta_2 + \varepsilon_{odt,2} \qquad (4.4)$$

where $Port_{odt,1}$ and $FDI_{odt,2}$ refer to portfolio investment and FDI, respectively, X is a matrix of time-varying, time-invariant, and indicator variables discussed above, and ε_{odt} is the error term. The subscripts o and d index the origin and destination of investment, while the subscript t indexes the year. If $corr(\varepsilon_{odt,1}, \varepsilon_{odt,2}) = 0$, then estimating the two equations separately and making inferences based on independent hypothesis tests is not problematic. However, as Zellner (1962) shows, if the error terms are correlated, we can increase efficiency by estimating the two equations jointly, which allows for more reliable hypothesis tests.[18] A seemingly unrelated regression framework is appropriate as it allows for testing cross-equation restrictions – the null being that the effect of migrant stock on portfolio investment is equal to its effect on FDI. Rather than report standard errors, we provide 95% confidence intervals, which allow us to test the null hypothesis that a given variable has the same effect on portfolio and FDI.[19]

Appendix Table A4.3 contains the results from a seemingly unrelated regression estimation. The overlapping sample contains 50 countries of origin and 152 destinations of investment from 2009–2017. In both the portfolio and FDI models, migrant networks are positive and statistically significant. The effect of co-ethnic networks on FDI is almost twice as large as its effect on portfolio investment, as we observed in Tables 4.1 and 4.2. This is consistent with our expectation regarding the importance of migrant networks for heterogeneous investment opportunities and is consistent with the findings of Rauch and Trindade (2002) and Pandya and Leblang (2017). It suggests that co-ethnic networks, because of access to specialized information, play a particularly important role when valuable investment opportunities are heterogeneous.

Educated Migrants

Thus far, our results are consistent with the hypothesis that migrant networks provide information regarding investment opportunities in particular destinations. As with investment, we do not expect that immigrants are homogeneous. Both Leblang (2010) and Pandya and Leblang (2017) find that cross-border investment exhibits larger increases when migrant

[18] The intuition behind Zellner's (1962) contribution is similar to the logic underlying estimating a time series model containing serial correlation. If ε_t is correlated with ε_{t-1}, then knowledge of ε_{t-1} can help reduce the size of the error, ε_t. A formal discussion of Zellner's model is contained in Cameron and Trivedi (2005). The extension to non-normally distributed dependent variables – the model we deploy – is developed by Weesie (2000) and is implemented via the **suest** command in Stata.

[19] Hypothesis testing using seemingly unrelated regression assumes that the errors from both equations are asymptotically normal. We know that the large number of zeros in our sample generates non-normal residuals. We therefore calculate standard errors and associated confidence intervals using Huber/White standard errors. Unfortunately, Cameron, Gelbach, and Miller's (2011) approach for multiway clustering is not directly applicable to seemingly unrelated regression.

networks consist of highly educated people and when these networks include migrants employed in the FIRE sector. Unfortunately, we do not have access to time-varying data on the occupation of migrants across countries. To be consistent, we include results first reported in Leblang (2010), which rely on the OECD's Database on Immigrants in OECD Countries (DIOC). The DIOC only has occupational data on migrants residing in OECD countries for a single year – 2000. Consequently, those results are based on a restricted set of investment origin countries and cross-sectional data.[20]

Our variables of interest are the share of migrants from country d living in country o that are employed in the FIRE sector.[21] The DIOC also includes information on the education level of bilateral migrants, which we include along with the logged total number of migrants so that we do not conflate occupational sector with education.

The results in Column (1) of Table 4.3 are for portfolio investment using the share of migrants with tertiary education. Column (2) replaces tertiary education with the share of migrants employed in the FIRE sector, and Column (3) includes both measures. The results indicate that higher education, per se, does not have a statistically significant influence on portfolio investment, while the opposite is true for employment in the FIRE sector. In Columns (4), (5), and (6), we repeat this exercise using FDI as the dependent variable and reach the opposite conclusion, as the tertiary education variable is statistically significant and employment in the FIRE sector is not. While not consistent across all models, these results point to the importance of specific information when it comes to portfolio investment, something associated with training in the FIRE sector. The findings also support our inclination regarding different information requirements of heterogeneous versus homogeneous investments: Heterogeneous investment opportunities across many sectors – like those associated with FDI – do not necessarily privilege those with specific knowledge of banking or financial assets.

Migrant Networks as Substitutes for Quality Institutions

This chapter opened with a puzzle: What explains patterns of global investment? Existing explanations privilege the institutional environment

---

[20] While there are additional rounds of the DIOC in subsequent 5-year intervals, these data unfortunately do not consistently break down migrant stocks by education across all years.

[21] The DIOC includes occupational categories based on the standard classification of occupations (ISCO-88 codes). We use those codes to construct the measure of employment in FIRE.

TABLE 4.3 Educated migrants and international investment

Dependent variable:	$\log(PortfolioInvestment_{odt})$			$\log(FDI_{odt})$		
	(1)	(2)	(3)	(4)	(5)	(6)
$\log(MigrantStock_{odt-1})$	0.389**	0.344**	0.394**	0.439**	0.376**	0.439**
	(0.0986)	(0.0835)	(0.0996)	(0.130)	(0.126)	(0.131)
$TertiaryEd_{odt-1}$	1.376		1.414	2.087**		2.096**
	(0.901)		(0.909)	(0.840)		(0.846)
$FIRE_{odt-1}$		3.121**	3.696**		−0.413	0.462
		(1.485)	(1.496)		(1.458)	(1.499)
$(Economic\ Size_{od})$	0.0882	0.0949	0.0875	0.140**	0.155**	0.140**
	(0.0578)	(0.0583)	(0.0577)	(0.0539)	(0.0570)	(0.0538)
$\log(Distance_{od})$	−0.636**	−0.607**	−0.616**	−0.904**	−0.899**	−0.901**
	(0.310)	(0.309)	(0.310)	(0.384)	(0.393)	(0.386)
$Contiguous_{od}$	−0.636	−0.675	−0.629	0.140	0.0562	0.141
	(0.574)	(0.576)	(0.574)	(0.877)	(0.885)	(0.876)
$CommonLanguage_{od}$	0.0106	0.0847	0.00951	1.545**	1.621**	1.544**
	(0.397)	(0.394)	(0.399)	(0.686)	(0.682)	(0.685)
$GrowthCorr_{odt-1}$	−0.156	−0.143	−0.153	0.176	0.182	0.177
	(0.273)	(0.276)	(0.274)	(0.373)	(0.370)	(0.374)
$CommonPeg_{odt-1}$	1.017*	1.046*	1.006*	−0.0837	−0.0210	−0.0855
	(0.602)	(0.615)	(0.599)	(0.847)	(0.848)	(0.844)

(continued)

TABLE 4.3 (continued)

$TaxTreaty_{odt-1}$	0.754**	0.748**	0.750**	0.895*	0.877*	0.895*
	(0.354)	(0.361)	(0.355)	(0.467)	(0.466)	(0.467)
$PTAs_{odt-1}$	0.00046	0.106	0.0551	0.301	0.263	0.309
	(0.619)	(0.632)	(0.627)	(0.648)	(0.681)	(0.656)
$CommonReligion_{od}$	0.805**	0.821**	0.806**	0.275	0.295	0.275
	(0.306)	(0.312)	(0.311)	(0.448)	(0.454)	(0.449)
$CommonLegal_{od}$	−0.0787	−0.0869	−0.0788	0.643	0.606	0.644
	(0.219)	(0.225)	(0.221)	(0.409)	(0.413)	(0.409)
$\log(GeneticDistance_{od})$	0.00017	0.00008	0.00014	0.00004	−0.00013	0.00004
	(0.0006)	(0.0005)	(0.0006)	(0.0007)	(0.0007)	(0.0007)
$TelephoneTraffic_{odt-1}$	0.160	0.171*	0.163	0.220	0.231	0.220
	(0.102)	(0.0970)	(0.101)	(0.189)	(0.195)	(0.189)
$Constant$	−63.70	−68.74	−63.33	−116.2**	−127.4**	−116.0**
	(51.86)	(52.23)	(51.76)	(47.85)	(50.57)	(47.76)
Observations	1,993	1,993	1,993	1,365	1,365	1,365
Origin FEs	Yes	Yes	Yes	Yes	Yes	Yes
Destination FEs	Yes	Yes	Yes	Yes	Yes	Yes

Note: * $p < 0.10$, ** $p < 0.05$. All models include origin and destination fixed effects. Robust standard errors clustered by both origin and destination countries in parentheses.

118

that governs investment, arguing that a country's commitment to protecting property rights and enforcing contracts are essential for attracting foreign investment (Büthe and Milner 2008). Yet, as we see in Figure 4.1, countries with poor contracting environments receive substantial amounts of both portfolio and foreign direct investment. The evidence presented in this chapter supports the hypothesis that migrant networks explain patterns of global investment. The question that remains, however, is whether migrant networks complement existing institutional structures in the country of investment, or if they serve as substitutes.

The answer to this question is not straightforward in theory or practice. Migrant networks may serve as a substitute for transparent institutions because they provide "mutual trust" which, in turn, decreases the need to rely on formal contracting mechanisms. This is the finding of Weidenbaum and Hughes, who conclude that the Bamboo Network facilitated trade: "If a business owner violates an agreement, he is blacklisted. This is far worse than being sued, because the entire Chinese networks will refrain from doing business with the guilty party" (1996, p. 51). Wang similarly concludes that ethnic Chinese residing abroad provide a "linkage between China and the rest of the world [in that they] facilitate the understanding of and access to *guanxi* networks by other foreign investors. Without the agency of ethnic Chinese, it would have been much more difficult for foreign companies to use informal personal networks to complement and compensate for the weak formal legal institutions in China" (Wang 2000, p. 543).

On the other hand, migrant networks may provide information, in the aggregate, about the *lack* of opportunity, limited enforcement capacity, or high levels of corruption that will ultimately dissuade investors from seeking out opportunities in a specific country. In Chapter 2, we found that migrants often leave due to falling confidence in their home country's political institutions; they may be less willing to facilitate investment toward their home country as a result. The opacity of domestic political institutions is why some scholars argue that membership in international agreements is a critically powerful signal to investors about a policymaker's commitment to protect investment (Büthe and Milner 2008).

Whether migrant networks complement or substitute for political institutions is difficult to answer with aggregate data. Our approach is to augment Equation (4.2) by including an interaction between migrant networks and two different measures of a country's domestic institutional environment: one measuring corruption and the other capturing level of democracy. We use these two variables because some scholars argue that investment will be greater into those countries with greater respect for the rule of law, greater stability of property rights, and lower levels of corruption (e.g., Wei 2000). Other scholars focus on a country's political regime and argue that democracies are better able than autocracies to commit to the protection of private property rights and, consequently, are less likely to engage in expropriation (e.g., Henisz 2000; Jensen 2003). The key question is whether the interaction between these institutions and migrant networks is positive, suggesting that they are complementary, or negative, suggesting that they are substitutes.

Our measures of institutions – democracy and corruption – are measured in the migrant's homeland, the destination d of the investment. Democracy is measured using V-Dem's polyarchy index, which is scaled between zero and one with higher values indicating more democratic institutions (Coppedge et al. 2021). Corruption is similarly indexed between zero and one, with higher values reflecting greater corruption and is also drawn from V-Dem. Because these measures vary only across destination and over time, we exclude destination*year fixed effects.

We summarize our results with respect to portfolio investment in Figure 4.4 and present the estimates of underlying models in Appendix Table A4.4. We graph the predicted marginal effect of migrant networks across levels of corruption in Panel A. Regardless of whether we set corruption at its minimum observed value (0.007), its mean (0.51) or its maximum (0.97), increasing the size of the migrant network is associated with an increase in portfolio investment. Consider investment from Japan in 2015. That year, there were approximately 3,000 Italian and 3,100 Argentinian immigrants in Japan. We would expect more investment from Japan into Argentina than into Italy. However, corruption is more widespread in Argentina (0.64) than in Italy (0.164). Consequently, the net effect would be a sizable difference in portfolio investment between these two countries. This is what we observe, with an estimated $48 million flowing from Japan to Argentina and $260 million flowing to Italy.

In Panel B of Figure 4.4, we illustrate the marginal effects of these interactions. We broadly find that, due to collinearity between democracy and migrant networks, there is no independent effect of these variables on bilateral portfolio investment. When democracy is equal to zero, increasing the size of the migrant network has no statistically significant effect on portfolio investment – the standard error on that linear prediction expands such that there is no difference regardless of network size when democracy is equal to zero. This is not the case, however, for middle and high levels of democracy: Both have steep slopes, with the largest effect obtaining in consolidated democracies.

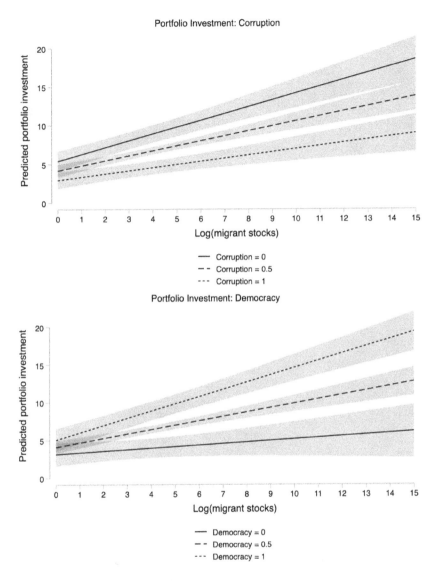

FIGURE 4.4 Institutions and portfolio investment. Results based on Columns (1) and (2) in Appendix Table A4.4.

We engage in the same exercise for FDI and summarize our results in Figure 4.5.[22] Here, we observe little separation between migrant networks and corruption or democracy; collinearity makes it impossible to identify

---

[22] Underlying estimates are available in Appendix Table A4.4.

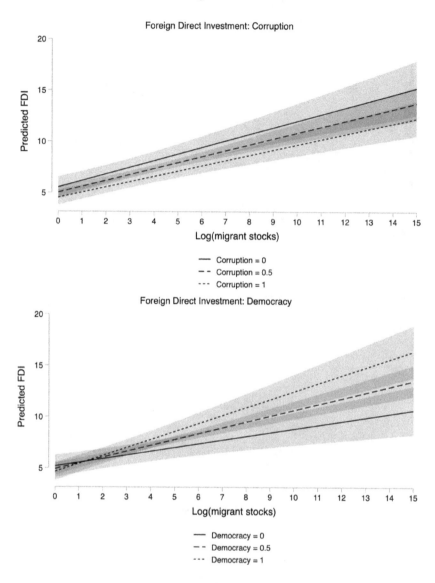

FIGURE 4.5 Institutions and FDI. Results based on Columns (3) and (4) in Appendix Table A4.4.

independent effects of these three variables. That said, we do observe similar patterns for FDI as we did for portfolio investment, as higher levels of co-ethnic networks correspond with higher levels of investment; those patterns are lower (higher) for countries that are more corrupt (democratic).

In sum, these results provide some clarity with regard to the ways in which institutions and migrant networks reinforce each other. Countries with institutions that provide investors with clear and transparent signals regarding their commitment to contract stability receive more investment. Migrant networks enhance this effect. What remains for future work is scholarship focusing on micro-level channels, which would allow us to observe whether migrant networks exploit informational advantages in helping investors understand systems of corruption or other ways to circumvent weak formal contracting systems.

CONCLUSION

The growth of international capital and commodity flows since the end of World War II has long been considered the sine qua non of globalization. We argue that migration should, at a minimum, be part of the story of financial globalization, as migrant networks help facilitate cross-border flows of both portfolio and foreign direct investment. This is not to say that institutions do not matter. Rather, we show that even in countries where credible, transparent institutions do not exist, capital can flow because migrants act as a mechanism for collecting and transmitting information, providing signals about institutional quality, and establishing trust (e.g., Greif 1989).

Giving pride of place to migrant networks in explaining global capital allocation allows us to speak to several seemingly disparate literatures. Broadly speaking, the emphasis on diaspora networks as a conduit for capital flows is a natural extension of Keohane and Nye's (1974) work on transnational – or nongovernmental – relations between states. While other scholarship from international relations fits within the category of transnationalism, it tends to focus on nongovernmental or inter-governmental organizations (e.g., Keck and Sikkink 1998; Slaughter 2004). Emphasizing the role of migrant networks in cross-national invest-ment provides another mechanism – this one non-institutional – by which we can understand the growing degree of interdependence that exists within the international system. From the perspective of international relations theory, our emphasis on migrant communities influencing their homelands allows us to speak to the growing interest in diaspora politics (e.g., Shain and Barth 2003; Sheffer 2003).

This last point is worth emphasizing. Homeland governments are aware of the key role that migrants play in facilitating investment and in further integrating their countries into the global economy. Gamlen

(2008) notes that even economically advanced countries such as New Zealand, Ireland, and Israel have well-developed diaspora engagement strategies designed to encourage active economic behavior on the part of their external citizens. In response to a question from a member of Parliament about how Scotland intends to engage their diaspora residing in Canada, the Scottish Executive Minister for Parliament declared, "The Scottish Executive intends to engage with and mobilize the Scottish diaspora to further Scotland's interests for the long-term benefit of our economy and society. We aim to encourage the diaspora's active participation and engagement in promoting Scotland as a great country to visit, live, learn, work, do business, and invest."[23]

Given this awareness, what do homelands do to attract migrant investment? In the next chapter, we examine migrant remittances – person-to-person transfers from family members abroad to family members remaining at home. Remittances are an essential part of global migration; as noted in Chapter 1, they far outstrip portfolio investment and foreign aid and have recently exceeded FDI flows to the Global South. In Chapter 5, we ask how home-country governments leverage their connections with expatriate populations to increase remittances, focusing on the set of policy tools that home country politicians have at their disposal.

[23] Accessed via https://web.archive.org/web/20120318034115/http://www.martinfrost.ws/htmlfiles/gazette/scot_diaspora.html.

APPENDIX TABLE A4.1 *Portfolio Investment by Corridor*

	Dependent variable: $\log(PortfolioInvestment_{odt})$			
	(1) North–North	(2) North–South	(3) South–North	(4) South–South
$\log(MigrantStock_{odt-1})$	0.102*	0.156***	0.092	0.131**
	(0.054)	(0.055)	(0.060)	(0.051)
$\log(Distance_{od})$	−0.800***	−1.218***	−1.164***	−1.269***
	(0.238)	(0.229)	(0.302)	(0.210)
$Contiguous_{od}$	−0.463**	0.801	0.086	0.620*
	(0.216)	(0.877)	(0.934)	(0.364)
$CommonLanguage_{od}$	0.063	1.689**	1.040*	1.263***
	(0.295)	(0.644)	(0.538)	(0.370)
$GrowthCorr_{odt-1}$	0.136*	−0.040	−0.231**	0.059
	(0.071)	(0.043)	(0.101)	(0.050)
$CommonPeg_{odt-1}$	1.146***	0.291	1.571***	0.793**
	(0.407)	(0.458)	(0.527)	(0.310)
$TaxTreaty_{odt-1}$	2.016***	1.201***	1.259**	1.788***
	(0.556)	(0.367)	(0.472)	(0.423)
$PTAs_{odt-1}$	−0.044	−0.168	0.511*	−0.018
	(0.055)	(0.133)	(0.288)	(0.255)
$CommonReligion_{od}$	0.734	0.364	−1.201	0.626
	(0.470)	(0.684)	(0.755)	(0.675)
$CommonReligion_{od}$	0.848***	0.203	0.923**	0.156
	(0.257)	(0.181)	(0.377)	(0.221)
$\log(GeneticDistance_{od})$	0.138**	−0.002	−0.042	−0.147***
	(0.050)	(0.148)	(0.067)	(0.050)
Constant	22.770***	17.153***	22.854***	15.347***
	(2.359)	(2.502)	(2.924)	(1.994)
Observations	9,187	38,793	9,942	34,538
Origin * year FEs	Yes	Yes	Yes	Yes
Destination * year FEs	Yes	Yes	Yes	Yes

Note: * $p < 0.10$, ** $p < 0.05$. Models estimated with OLS. All models include origin * year and destination * year fixed effects. All time-varying variables lagged by one year. Robust standard errors clustered by both origin and destination countries in parentheses.

APPENDIX TABLE A4.2 *FDI by Corridor*

	Dependent variable: $\log(FDI_{odt})$			
	(1) North– North	(2) North– South	(3) South– North	(4) South– South
$\log(MigrantStock_{odt-1})$	0.093 (0.119)	0.217*** (0.073)	0.347*** (0.107)	0.321*** (0.070)
$\log(Distance_{od})$	−0.898*** (0.317)	−2.550*** (0.631)	−1.913*** (0.398)	−2.016*** (0.354)
$Contiguous_{od}$	−0.190 (0.382)	2.717** (1.063)	2.023 (1.183)	0.479 (0.738)
$CommonLanguage_{od}$	0.502 (0.537)	1.621*** (0.377)	2.225** (1.043)	0.961* (0.534)
$GrowthCorr_{odt-1}$	−0.353* (0.200)	0.106 (0.156)	0.045 (0.178)	0.116** (0.051)
$CommonPeg_{odt-1}$	2.816** (1.021)	0.892 (0.779)	0.372 (0.794)	0.513* (0.304)
$TaxTreaty_{odt-1}$	3.795*** (1.337)	3.010*** (0.460)	2.091** (0.801)	4.107*** (0.487)
$PTAs_{odt-1}$	0.078 (0.104)	−0.091 (0.179)	0.142 (0.414)	0.234* (0.138)
$CommonReligion_{od}$	2.856*** (0.989)	−0.500 (1.192)	−0.960 (1.268)	2.073* (1.047)
$CommonReligion_{od}$	0.970*** (0.318)	0.183 (0.338)	0.424 (0.565)	0.460 (0.372)
$\log(GeneticDistance_{od})$	0.077 (0.093)	−0.059 (0.144)	−0.146 (0.221)	−0.097 (0.068)
Constant	19.083*** (3.484)	29.743*** (5.502)	24.755*** (3.004)	20.240*** (3.014)
Observations	4,218	16,546	5,224	22,923
Origin * year FEs	Yes	Yes	Yes	Yes
Destination * year FEs	Yes	Yes	Yes	Yes

Note: * $p < 0.10$, ** $p < 0.05$. Models estimated with OLS. All models include origin * year and destination * year fixed effects. All time-varying variables lagged by one year. Robust standard errors clustered by both origin and destination countries in parentheses.

APPENDIX TABLE A4.3 *Seemingly Unrelated Regression*

Dependent variable:	$\log(PortfolioInvestment_{odt})$	$\log(FDI_{odt})$
	(1)	(2)
$\log(MigrantStock_{odt-1})$	0.237**	0.408**
	[0.209, 0.265]	[0.377, 0.440]
$\log(Distance_{od})$	−1.109**	−1.872**
	[−1.229, −0.990]	[−2.011, −1.734]
$Contiguous_{od}$	0.221	0.305*
	[−0.0607, 0.503]	[−0.0285, 0.638]
$CommonLanguage_{od}$	1.384**	1.364**
	[1.160, 1.609]	[1.112, 1.617]
$GrowthCorr_{odt-1}$	−0.0694	0.0109
	[−0.164, 0.0250]	[−0.101, 0.123]
$CommonPeg_{odt-1}$	0.618**	0.516**
	[0.472, 0.764]	[0.351, 0.681]
$TaxTreaty_{odt-1}$	1.902**	3.800**
	[1.705, 2.100]	[3.573, 4.027]
$PTAs_{odt-1}$	−0.0478**	−0.0105
	[−0.0905, −0.00512]	[−0.0609, 0.0400]
$CommonReligion_{od}$	0.810**	2.165**
	[0.541, 1.078]	[1.852, 2.479]
$CommonLegal_{od}$	0.376**	0.354**
	[0.248, 0.504]	[0.211, 0.496]
$Economic\ Size_{odt-1}$	0.000	−2.39e-14**
	[−1.57e-15, 1.43e-14]	[−3.55e-14, −1.24e-14]
$\log(GeneticDistance_{od})$	−0.0944**	−0.0569**
	[−0.127, −0.0621]	[−0.0959, −0.0178]
Constant	11.08**	16.38**
	[7.764, 14.39]	[13.20, 19.57]
Observations	31,834	31,834
Origin * year FEs	Yes	Yes
Destination * year FEs	Yes	Yes

Note: * $p < 0.10$, ** $p < 0.05$. All models include origin * year and destination * year fixed effects. All time-varying variables lagged by one year. 95% confidence intervals based on robust standard errors in brackets.

APPENDIX TABLE A4.4 *Interactions with Political Institutions*

Dependent variable:	log (PortfolioInvestment$_{odt}$)		log (FDI$_{odt}$)	
	(1)	(2)	(3)	(4)
log (MigrantStock$_{odt-1}$)	0.880***	0.202	0.647***	0.364***
	(0.113)	(0.143)	(0.105)	(0.091)
Corruption$_{dt-1}$	−2.454***		−1.001	
	(0.914)		(0.670)	
log (MigrantStock$_{odt-1}$) *Corruption$_{dt-1}$	−0.473***		−0.132	
	(0.130)		(0.108)	
Democracy$_{dt-1}$		1.875		−0.531
		(1.308)		(0.813)
log (MigrantStock$_{odt-1}$) *Democracy$_{dt-1}$		0.753***		0.418***
		(0.188)		(0.130)
log (Distance$_{od}$)	0.730*	0.520	−0.859***	−0.875***
	(0.368)	(0.342)	(0.264)	(0.253)
Contiguous$_{od}$	1.165*	0.745	1.459*	1.402*
	(0.672)	(0.686)	(0.733)	(0.723)
CommonLanguage$_{od}$	0.824	0.938*	0.643	0.683
	(0.561)	(0.498)	(0.473)	(0.454)
EconomicSize$_{odt-1}$	0.000**	0.000***	0.000**	0.000**
	(0.000)	(0.000)	(0.000)	(0.000)
GrowthCorr$_{odt-1}$	0.348***	0.370***	0.322***	0.345***
	(0.081)	(0.087)	(0.072)	(0.081)
CommonPeg$_{odt-1}$	0.586*	0.340	0.445	0.361
	(0.325)	(0.305)	(0.307)	(0.293)
TaxTreaty$_{odt-1}$	4.663***	4.591***	5.139***	5.162***
	(0.588)	(0.579)	(0.527)	(0.525)
PTAs$_{odt-1}$	−0.311**	−0.316**	−0.217*	−0.220*
	(0.138)	(0.137)	(0.114)	(0.111)
CommonReligion$_{od}$	2.670***	1.468**	2.593***	2.267***
	(0.860)	(0.730)	(0.664)	(0.663)
CommonLegal$_{od}$	−0.219	−0.244	0.251	0.230
	(0.240)	(0.261)	(0.252)	(0.258)
log (GeneticDistance$_{od}$)	−0.333**	−0.363***	−0.161**	−0.159**
	(0.141)	(0.118)	(0.074)	(0.070)
Constant	−0.912	−0.814	11.646***	11.516***
	(3.537)	(3.530)	(2.524)	(2.440)
Observations	71,450	71,450	38,533	38,533
Origin * year FEs	Yes	Yes	Yes	Yes
Destination * year FEs	No	No	No	No

Note: * $p < 0.10$, ** $p < 0.05$. All models include origin * year fixed effects. All time-varying variables lagged by one year. Robust standard errors clustered by both origin and destination countries in parentheses.

5

Origin Statecraft

Remittances and Diaspora Engagement

Access to capital is essential for economic development, growth, and the provision of public goods. Leaders – in autocracies or democracies – are punished politically when they are unable to provide basic services to their constituents, losing office, being exiled, or even losing their heads (Chiozza and Goemans 2011). Global capital helps domestic firms hire and produce, households to earn and consume, and governments to tax and spend. Not all capital inflows, however, come from investors. Some countries, as we document in Figure 1.3, receive foreign aid, a financial flow that is small yet relatively stable. Flows of FDI are larger by orders of magnitude but are also far more volatile, fluctuating based on market returns in countries primarily located in the Global North. Remittances, financial flows directed to an émigré's household, are less volatile and have grown rapidly since the Great Recession.

The act of sending money to friends and families back home is as old as immigration itself, as is the development of governmental strategies designed to encourage migrants to send remittances. Zeitz and Leblang (2022) document how Luigi Luzzatti, a financier and future Prime Minister of Italy, helped the Banco di Napoli – an Italian bank originally chartered in the fifteenth century – establish banks across North and South America, Europe, and North Africa, in locations with sizable Italian populations. Luzzatti's rationale was instrumental: The existence of Italian banks would encourage Italian expatriates to send remittances back to their home communities.

The importance of remittances for a country's economic development has increased significantly over the last three decades. Remittances, as we discuss below, have become an indispensable source of capital that households use for investment and consumption. In some cases, remittances can reduce poverty and inequality and contribute to the provision of public goods. Policy makers understand that remittances afford them some "room to maneuver," especially when other sources of external capital dry up. What do policy makers do to increase remittance flows? Following Italy's example of setting up external banks, while interesting, is not feasible for many countries; a robust banking system requires liquidity, oversight, and rule of law that is nonexistent in some countries most in need of external capital.

In the first part of this chapter, we investigate the determinants of remittances, arguing that politicians use diaspora engagement strategies – specifically the provision of dual citizenship to expatriates – as mechanisms to provide external populations with a feeling of connection and inclusion in home-country politics and policies. The political incorporation of external populations, while increasingly widespread, is a relatively new phenomenon. The political practice du jour of the nineteenth and early twentieth centuries was to exclude expatriates from rights afforded to home-country residents, as countries tended to treat their expatriates "as prodigal sons and daughters who had abandoned their national family and who therefore should not be allowed to retain the original nationality" (Koslowski 2003, p. 7). This attitude has waned as countries increasingly see external citizens as important sources of financial and human capital.

But the reliance on external capital does not always trump other strategic political considerations. If all countries wanted – at least at the margin – to increase access to remittances, *all* nations would provide dual citizenship rights. But that is far from the case. In the second part of the chapter, we relax the assumption that policy makers want to harness expatriate resources. Building on seminal work by Hirschman (1970), Miller and Peters (2020) argue that depending on domestic conditions, policy makers are incentivized to encourage exit as a mechanism to rid their polity of political opponents. By contrast, we explore the conditions under which policy makers are likely to provide institutional arrangements that engage external populations.

MIGRATION AND REMITTANCES

While individual remittances are small in value, in aggregate they are economically consequential. Figure 1.3 shows growth over time in the value of global remittances. In 2019, total remittances exceeded $620

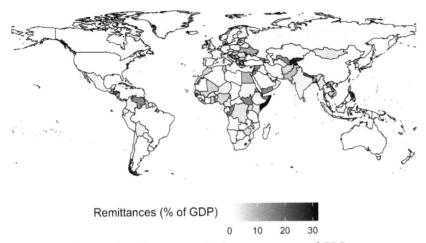

FIGURE 5.1 Personal remittances received as a percentage of GDP, 2019.
Source: World Bank World Development Indicators.

billion – higher than FDI inflows for low- and middle-income countries. Figure 5.1 maps remittances as a share of GDP in 2019 for the world. While developed economies do receive remittances, more than 75 percent of global remittances flow to low- and middle-income countries. For many countries, remittances are a critical source of external capital, especially for states that are not willing or able to attract FDI. In Figure 5.2, we show both remittances and FDI as shares of GDP for 2018, omitting labels for countries receiving less than 10% of GDP in both remittances and FDI for ease of presentation. We note that of the 115 low- and middle-income countries in this sample, only five exceeded 10% FDI as a percentage of GDP, while 30 received remittances more than this amount.

Remittances represent a crucial source of external capital because they allow households to finance consumption, insure against negative economic shocks, and invest in their family's future. Economics research consistently highlights that remittances have positive economic effects, including poverty alleviation, investment in human and productive capital, and long-run economic growth (Yang 2011). Political science scholarship, on the other hand, is more mixed, with some scholars arguing that remittances enable corruption, while others find that remittances increase democratic accountability (e.g., Ahmed 2012; Escribà-Folch, Meseguer, and Wright 2015). We return to a discussion of this literature below.

The rapid growth of remittances, as well as their potential political and economic effects, has drawn the interest of politicians in migrant origin countries. How can home-country governments reconnect with populations

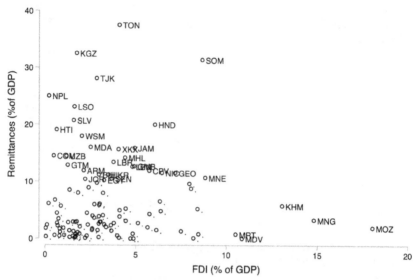

FIGURE 5.2 Remittances and FDI as a share of GDP, 2018.
Source: World Bank World Development Indicators.

who live, work, and study in another country? What mechanisms successfully leverage a migrant's feeling of connectedness to their family and country? In this chapter, we explore these mechanisms to understand how and why different policies encourage migrants to reconnect economically with their homeland. We focus on institutions that are designed to *engage* a country's diaspora. Our emphasis is on dual citizenship: the ability of migrants to naturalize in a host country without abrogating homeland citizenship. We compare dual citizenship with policies that grant expatriates the right to vote in home-country elections, as well as with diaspora-focused government ministries. The growth in dual citizenship and external voting rights has increased markedly in recent years (Wellman 2021), along with an increasing number of countries that create specific governmental institutions to support populations abroad (Gamlen 2019).

We argue that governments can build and use these diaspora engagement institutions to stimulate remittances. Though difficult to parse empirically, we also suggest that these institutions facilitate return migration, a phenomenon that can confer significant benefits on countries of origin (Wahba 2014). In short, we highlight that sending countries are not helpless with respect to harnessing their diaspora. Rather, they can leverage the economic potential of their expatriates by building institutions that meaningfully engage their diaspora.

In the section that follows, we review existing literature on the causes and consequences of remittances. We then develop our argument connecting dual citizenship and other diaspora engagement policies to increased remittances. We find that dual citizenship – but not external voting rights or diaspora ministries – has a positive and robust effect on remittances. If dual citizenship is so powerful in helping countries harness their diaspora, why do we observe cross-national and -temporal variation in its adoption? We provide a new answer to this question, developing and testing a principal-agent model that analyzes the relationship between a diaspora and its home country.

REMITTANCES: CAUSES AND CONSEQUENCES

Why do migrants send remittances? Existing scholarship suggests a wide range of potential reasons for sending money home. One self-evident motivation is altruism: Migrants remit because they derive positive utility – good feelings – from financially supporting friends and family (Chami et al. 2008). Remitting, however, may also be in a migrant's own material self-interest. Migrants who intend to return home may remit to maintain their own productive assets while absent, or to finance their own consumption upon return (Stark 1995). It is difficult, then, to separate altruism from the self-interest hypothesis. One perspective that combines elements of altruism and self-interest conceptualizes remittances as a loan repayment mechanism. From this view, remittances are a means of repaying the investment that friends and family made to facilitate the individual's initial migration (Poirine 1997). Migration and remittances may also be a mechanism to repay those who financed previous investments in human capital (Rapoport and Docquier 2006).[1] These perspectives fit into the broader NELM model discussed in Chapter 2 that conceives of migration – and remittances – as a risk diversification strategy that smooths consumption, alleviates credit constraints, and protects household members from shocks.

Regardless of motivation, remittances have political and economic consequences for receiving countries. Generally, empirical evidence suggests that remittances have positive economic impacts. Because wage

---

[1] Rapoport and Docquier (2006) and Yang (2011) provide a fuller description of these arguments. Chami et al. (2008) point out that it is often difficult, if not impossible, to empirically distinguish between these theories because they are not mutually exclusive concepts. Empirical studies may find support for multiple theories because independent variables attempting to operationalize these different theories often have multiple interpretations.

differentials between migrant origins and destinations are often stark, the economic value of remittances to those who stay home is large. An array of studies – across a range of different contexts – suggest that remittances help lift recipient households out of poverty, in some cases substantially reducing poverty rates in low-income countries (Adams and Page 2005; Yang and Martínez 2006; Acosta et al. 2008; Gupta, Pattillo, and Wagh 2009). Beyond these poverty-alleviating and consumption-enhancing effects, households use remittances to invest in productive and human capital. Empirical studies, many leveraging natural experiments and individual-level data, find that households receiving increased remittances often spend them on education, entrepreneurial activities, housing, and health, activities that they may otherwise be unable to finance (Yang 2008, 2011; Adams and Cuecuecha 2010, 2013).

These positive effects at the individual and household level push scholars to ask whether remittances increase macro-level, long-run economic growth. While cross-national analyses of the relationship between remittances and growth are inconclusive (Yang 2011), a range of recent evidence suggests that remittances likely have a positive effect on economic development (e.g., Catrinescu et al. 2009; Imai et al. 2014; Salahuddin and Gow 2015). Potential mechanisms include investment in human and physical capital, which contributes to development in low- and middle-income countries. Remittances help households in poor countries overcome access barriers to traditional financial institutions (Giuliano and Ruiz-Arranz 2009; Gupta, Pattillo, and Wagh 2009) and promote development of the local financial sector by increasing deposits and credit provided by banks (Aggarwal, Demirgüç-Kunt, and Pería 2011). Finally, remittances can also reduce economic inequality in low- and middle-income countries, providing benefits to social cohesion (Taylor et al. 2008; Koczan and Loyola 2018; Azizi 2021). Overall, the consensus is that remittances are economically beneficial for developing countries.

The political impacts of remittances are more disputed, though recent research suggests that they have the potential to improve governance. One widely supported proposition is that remittances allow households to privately access traditionally public goods like education, healthcare, and electricity (e.g., Abdih et al. 2012; Lee, Walter-Drop, and Wiesel 2014), shielding them from the consequences of poor governance. Some scholars argue that because citizens use remittances to finance these goods instead of engaging with the state, politicians are free to shift government spending away from public goods and toward the financing of patronage (Ahmed 2012). The clear result would be a decline in governance quality. Others instead argue that remittances allow for the private provision of goods that previously required clientelistic exchange (Diaz-Cayeros, Magaloni, and Weingast 2003; Pfutze 2012, 2014). As a result, clientelist networks weaken and citizens become more politically independent. These effects are hypothesized to increase the likelihood of democratization and embolden people to protest against autocratic rule (Escribà-Folch, Meseguer, and Wright 2015, 2018).

We do not parse the debate about the effect of remittances on public goods and governance outcomes.[2] From our perspective, what matters is that remittances positively influence individuals' perceptions of economic conditions in their homelands, making them more likely to believe that the national economy is doing well (Fiorina 1978) and increase their support for incumbents (Ahmed 2017). In the next section, we ask how policy makers use diaspora engagement strategies to connect with their expatriate populations and increase remittances.

ENGAGING THE DIASPORA[3]

Given that remittances can have beneficial economic and political effects, it is no surprise that politicians and policy makers in sending countries are increasingly interested in harnessing their diaspora. We argue that governments can build diaspora-centric institutions that incentivize emigrants to engage more with their homelands, fostering increased remittances and, perhaps, more return migration. Governments around the world have increasingly built these kinds of institutions in recent years. In this section, we discuss this backdrop and build our argument linking the creation of diaspora institutions to increased remittance inflows for origin countries.

The growth of institutions and practices seeking re-engagement with expatriate communities is a relatively new occurrence. The international norm of the nineteenth and twentieth centuries held that individuals should renounce home country citizenship rights before naturalizing in another country. Holding multiple citizenships was seen as a moral failing. US ambassador to Germany, George Bancroft (1849), famously remarked that states should "as soon tolerate a man with two wives as a man with two countries; as soon bear with polygamy as that state of double allegiance which common sense so repudiates that it has not even

---

[2] See Escriba-Folch Wright, and Meseguer (2022) for a definitive review.
[3] This section draws on Leblang (2017).

coined a word to express it." This idea was echoed by the dominant international organization of the day. A 1925 League of Nations conference produced the 1930 Hague *Convention on Certain Questions Relating to the Conflict of Nationality Laws*, a document stating, "it is in the interest of the international community to secure that all members should recognize that every person should have a nationality and should have one nationality only" (League of Nations 1930, as quoted in Koslowski 2003).

Excluding expatriates from rights afforded to home-country residents was consistent with the realpolitik view, popular in the nineteenth and early twentieth century, that dominated international affairs. Dual citizenship was rejected because it blurred the lines of diplomatic protection and military obligation (Koslowski 2003), potentially decreased the incentive for assimilation and participation in the host country (Renshon 2005), and was thought to promote "disloyalty and deceit, divided allegiances and torn psyches" (Spiro 2002, p. 22). The disdain for emigrant communities found expression in how countries treated these populations, often referring to them as "traitors" who turned their backs on their homelands.

This predominantly negative view of a country's diaspora changed as homelands began to see their external populations as a resource rather than a threat. In some cases, homelands viewed their external populations as a mechanism with which to influence the foreign policy behavior of host countries via lobbying, hoping to motivate foreign aid and Cold War policies (Shain 1999a; Sheffer 2003). In other cases, increases in international migration for work and education resulted in the loss of the "best and the brightest" for some Global South countries (e.g., Carrington and Detragiache 1998). In response, countries developed a variety of mechanisms to remain in contact or renew connections with populations who had moved abroad.

Scholars have proposed a variety of different political and economic dimensions of diaspora engagement policies (Calderón Chelius 2003; Lafleur and Calderón Chelius 2011; Escobar 2017). Pedroza, Palop-Garcia, and Hoffman (2016) eschew the political versus economic categorization, instead preferring to focus on administrative versus policy dimensions. These categories are based on the idea that while there are a variety of policy dimensions, the administrative capacity to implement policies must be present.[4]

---

[4] Palop-Garcia and Pedroza (2019) provide data on these different dimensions for twenty-two Latin American and Caribbean countries for 2015.

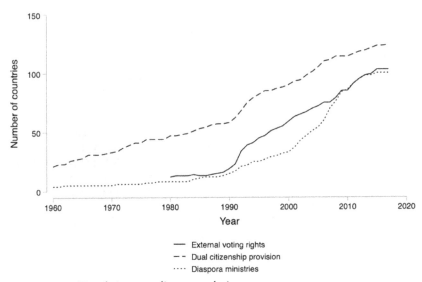

FIGURE 5.3 Trends in state–diaspora relations.
Source: Dual citizenship from Vink et al. (2019); external voting rights from Allen, Wellman, and Nyblade (2019); diaspora institutions from Gamlen (2019).

The UN, in its biennial *World Population Policies* (United Nations 2019b), likewise captures a country's efforts regarding its diaspora. Surveying policy makers in responding countries, the UN asks whether a country has institutions to engage their diaspora and whether there are specific policies to attract remittances or encourage return. The challenges in using these data are twofold: First, the data collection effort only began in 2015 and second, there are significant non-response rates across countries.[5]

While there are a variety of diaspora engagement strategies, we focus on three that are widespread, utilized for long periods of time, and easily observable: the allowance of dual citizenship – the provision that if an émigré naturalizes abroad, they do not abrogate their homeland citizenship (Vink et al. 2019); the existence of external voting rights and the ability to vote in home-country elections while living abroad (Allen, Wellman, and Nyblade 2019); and the existence of formal government institutions/ministries for diaspora engagement (Gamlen 2019). In Figure 5.3, we plot the evolution of these institutions for between 100 and 186 countries over the last 60 years. While there are differences

---

[5] See Appendix Figure A5.1 for (the lack of) country coverage.

TABLE 5.1 *State–diaspora relations, 2010*

		External voting rights	
		Yes	No
Dual citizenship	Yes	AFG, **ARG**, AUS, **AZE**, **BDI**, BEL, **BEN**, **BFA**, **BGR**, BHR, **BLR**, BOL, **BRA**, CAN, **CHE**, COG, **COL**, COM, CPV, CRI, CYP, DJI, DOM, **DZA**, ECU, FIN, FRA, FSM, GAB, GBR, **GEO**, **GHA**, **GRC**, HND, HRV, **IRN**, IRQ, ISL, **ITA**, KGZ, LBN, LUX, **LVA**, MDA, **MDV**, **MEX**, MHL, MKD, **MLI**, **MOZ**, NAM, NIC, NRU, NZL, OMN, PAN, **PER**, PHL, PLW, **POL**, **PRT**, **RUS**, **RWA**, SDN, **SGP**, STP, SVK, **SVN**, SWE, **SYR**, TCD, **TGO**, TJK, TKM, **TUN**, TUR, **UKR**, USA, UZB, VEN, **YEM**	AGO, ALB, ARM, ATG, BHS, BLZ, BRB, CHL, DMA, EGY, ERI, GMB, GRD, GTM, GUY, HUN, IRL, ISR, **JAM**, JOR, KHM, KIR, KNA, **LCA**, LIE, **MAR**, MNG, MUS, MYS, **NGA**, PRY, QAT, SAU, **SLE**, **SLV**, SOM, SWZ, SYC, TLS, TON, TUV, **UGA**, URY, VCT, VNM, WSM
	No	AUT, **BGD**, BIH, BWA, CAF, CIV, **CZE**, DEU, DNK, **ESP**, EST, GIN, GNB, IDN, **JPN**, **KAZ**, **KEN**, **KOR**, LTU, MMR, MRT, NER, NLD, NOR, PNG, SEN, **THA**, VUT, ZAF	ARE, BRN, BTN, **CHN**, CMR, CUB, **ETH**, FJI, GNQ, **HTI**, **IND**, KWT, LBR, LBY, **LKA**, LSO, MDG, MWI, **NPL**, **PAK**, PRK, SLB, SUR, TTO, **TZA**, ZMB, ZWE

Note: Dual citizenship from Vink et al. (2019); external voting rights from Allen, Wellman, and Nyblade (2019); countries with diaspora institutions in **bold** from Gamlen (2019).

in terms of the adoption of these institutions (see Table 5.1) and the speed at which they have proliferated, homelands are increasingly reaching out to their diasporas. They are, to paraphrase Bauböck (2003), treating emigrants as part of their "extended-nation."

This growing embrace of external populations and rapid increase in diaspora-focused institutions has stimulated a rapidly developing literature on "state-diaspora relations." This literature yields several colorful phrases to capture how the connection between states and external populations reshapes conventional understandings of world politics. Homelands are often referred to as "emigration states" (Gamlen 2019), "emigration nations" (Collyer 2013), and "nations of emigrants" (FitzGerald 2008). Regardless of the specific terminology, this language is designed to recognize that states have shifted from at best ignoring and at worst vilifying their expatriates, to viewing expatriates as a vital resource for homeland populations and politicians.

We further discuss the origins and rise of diaspora institutions below. In summary, extant literature primarily explains the rise and nature of state-diaspora relations in terms of *tapping, transnationalism, and governance*. In the tapping account, states attempt to harness the financial, intellectual, or otherwise material assets of their diaspora to improve conditions for the homeland. By contrast, transnationalism is an approach that focuses on migrants as a resource beyond traditional state borders that can influence and transform political and cultural life through their "social" remittances (Levitt 1998). Finally, Gamlen (2019) suggests that diaspora institutions are attempts on behalf of the state to govern cross-border migration. In this view, international and nongovernmental organizations promote these institutions to capture the benefits of the diaspora, as well as to reassert the role of the state in the governance of global human mobility.

Why might countries interested in maintaining connections with their diaspora offer dual citizenship rights? Broadly speaking, citizenship connects a set of exclusive rights and responsibilities that apply to individuals born within that country's territorial borders. Citizens often have the right to own property, are eligible for employment, can access public education and other social programs, and are vested with the right to vote. As discussed in Chapter 3, some host countries require that migrants abrogate – or give up – their home-country citizenship before naturalizing in the host country. By extending dual citizenship, homelands continue to provide citizenship rights even if their émigrés naturalize abroad. From the perspective of an immigrant, dual citizenship obviates the need to obtain a visa to return home and allows the expatriate an opportunity to own property and make other investments in her homeland.

From this perspective, it is easy to understand how and why dual citizenship could be deployed instrumentally to shape attitudes and behaviors and signal who is part of the "in-group" and who is disconnected. Shain (1999b) remarked that governments use this power to "promote and sustain the attachment of the people to the motherland" (pp. 662–63). Østergaard-Nielsen (2003) argues that the Turkish government attempted to engage its diaspora to upgrade the country's image and facilitate entry into the EU, while Goldring (1998) and Itzigsohn (2000) suggest that the extension of dual citizenship is designed to persuade expatriates to become more involved in their home countries – an involvement that, we argue, leads to a steady flow of remittances.

In addition to symbolically linking diasporas with their homelands, the extension of dual citizenship is often used to encourage expatriates to naturalize in their host countries. Jones-Correa (2001) and Mazzolari (2009) use micro-level data and find ample evidence – based on Latin American immigrants to the United States – to support this conjecture. Encouraging naturalization, while seemingly at odds with the idea that sending countries attempt to strengthen ties with their diasporas, is a strategic decision. Freeman and Ögelman (1998) argue that "sending countries are likely to be strategic and directed toward such goals as enhancing their control and influence over their nationals living abroad and, through them, increasing their influence over the foreign and domestic policies of receiving states" (p. 771).

External voting rights similarly provide symbolic attachment to the homeland. By providing expatriates with the opportunity to participate in, and potentially influence the outcome of, home-country elections, policy makers signal the importance of these external constituents. Unlike dual citizenship, external voting rights do not afford expatriates the ability to easily transit back to their homeland; voting often occurs from abroad by mail or at consulates and embassies. Wellman (2021) argues that the explanation for external voting rights – specifically in sub-Saharan African countries but likely more generally – is the prospect that enfranchised external populations will support the incumbent politician. External voting rights may therefore reflect an electoral calculation rather than a strictly economic one.

The rise of diaspora ministries reflects a different logic. Here, diaspora ministries refer to official "government offices dedicated to emigrants and their descendants abroad" (Gamlen 2019). Examples include India's Ministry of Overseas Indian Affairs and Ireland's Irish Abroad Unit. These institutions are charged with a broad portfolio, which includes preserving cultural identity among expatriates, advertising opportunities for remittances and funneling those remittances into different projects, and managing the export of migrant labor. These may be instrumental – encouraging remittances and return – or they may be more symbolic, designed to remind expatriates about their connections to the homeland (Gamlen 2019).

The question, then, is whether these institutions help sending countries leverage the resources of their expatriate populations. While both dual citizenship and external voting rights are deployed instrumentally, the rationale behind enfranchising external populations is political rather than economic. The creation of diaspora ministries is a mixed bag, with some specifically designed to leverage the economic successes of their diasporas, while others are effectively symbolic reminders to expatriates about the importance of their homeland. We hypothesize that dual citizenship and diaspora ministries should influence remittance flows, with dual citizenship being most consequential, while external voting rights should not have any substantive effect.

ANALYSIS: DIASPORA ENGAGEMENT AND REMITTANCES

We deploy macro- and micro-level data to analyze the relationship between diaspora institutions and remittance inflows. We present a time-series cross-sectional analysis of countries, and then zoom in on a representative survey of migrants residing in Spain to estimate the individual-level effect of diaspora institutions on the propensity to remit.

Macro-level Analysis

We first assess the substantive and statistical importance of diaspora institutions in attracting remittances at the country level. We construct an unbalanced panel data set of approximately 110 lower- and middle-income countries from 1970 to 2018. The dependent variable is remittances as a share of the receiving country's GDP, obtained from the World Bank's WDI.[6] We log the dependent variable, as it highly skewed.[7] Some countries (like Bosnia and Herzegovina, Tajikistan, Tonga, and Tuvalu) have remittance-to-GDP shares of over 40 percent, while a dozen others receive less than 1/100 of 1 percent of their GDP in remittances. Our independent variables of interest are the existence of dual citizenship rights (Vink et al. 2019), external voting rights (Allen, Wellman, and Nyblade 2019), and diaspora ministries (Gamlen 2019). Each of these is measured as an indicator variable, coded one if the institution exists and zero otherwise.

---

[6] We ensure that our findings are robust to logged remittances per capita, an alternative cross-national measure of aggregate remittances.

[7] Prior to logging the variable, its mean is 4.6 percent and standard deviation is 1.4 percent.

Following Chami et al. (2005), we control for logged GDP per capita in constant 2010 US dollars and its square to capture differences in the average level of wealth in the migrant's homeland. The squared term accounts for the possibility of selection on the part of migrants whereby migration flows – and differences in the rate of emigration – change as countries undergo economic development. Chami et al. (2005) also include change in the country's exchange rate vis-à-vis the US dollar, which proxies for the opportunity cost of saving or consuming funds in the host country relative to sending it home. Both variables are from the WDI.

Yang (2011) argues that migrant remittances are countercyclical, rising when home-country households experience a negative shock. We include a measure of the financial cost of natural disasters as a share of GDP from EM-DAT, a leading data source for such data. We also control for a country's level of democracy using the polyarchy measure from V-Dem, as well as for the country's level of corruption using the V-Dem regime corruption score.

Finally, we argue that a country's remittances rise as the economic capacity of its diaspora grows. We construct $EconomicCapacity_{od}$ to capture the extent to which country o's diaspora is in countries d that are relatively wealthier than the home country at time t:

$$EconomicCapacity_{ot} = \sum_{d=1}^{d} \frac{Migrants_{odt}}{Migrants_{ot}} (GDPPC_{dt} - GDPPC_{ot})$$

where $Migrants_{odt}$ represents the number of people from country o residing in country d at time t, $Migrants_{ot}$ represents the total number of people from country o residing outside its borders at time t, and $GDPPC_{dt}$ and $GDPPC_{ot}$ represent the GDP per capita of countries d and o, respectively, at time t.[8] This calculation yields the GDP differential between country o and all other countries d at time t, weighted by the relative number of migrants from country o living in country d at time t. We log this variable to adjust for skewness. Data on migrant stocks comes from the GBMD (Özden et al. 2011).

We estimate a series of models using OLS, lag all independent variables by one year to decrease the risk of simultaneity, and report standard errors clustered by country to account for heterogeneity in cross-country error variance.

---

[8] When the value of $GDPPC_{jt} - GDPPC_{it}$ is negative, we recode it to zero.

We present our main results in Table 5.2, which includes a set of models that jointly include measures of all three diaspora institutions. In Appendix Tables A5.1, A5.2, and 5.3, we include these measures separately for each institution as an alternative estimation strategy. In Column (1) of Table 5.2, we present estimates from a pooled regression. The coefficient on dual citizenship is positive and statistically significant, in line with our expectations. As the dependent variable is logged, we can interpret the coefficient as indicating that, all else equal, countries with dual citizenship receive, on average, 49 percent more remittances as a share of their GDP than countries that do not provide dual citizenship to their expatriates.

To illustrate the magnitude of this effect, in Figure 5.4 we engage in a set of counterfactual analyses, estimating the effect of dual citizenship on remittances for a set of emerging economies. For this simulation, we hold all variables at their period means and predict the average rate of remittances if the country had dual citizenship during the estimation period. If India, a country that has not embraced dual citizenship, had this policy in place for the entire estimation period, our model predicts that remittances would have increased, on average, by $2 billion a year. For Mexico, a country that adopted dual citizenship in 1998, having dual citizenship increased remittances by almost $3 billion. In the pooled regression, diaspora ministries are also associated with greater remittance inflows, though the estimated effect is smaller. Meanwhile, the presence of external voting rights is not meaningfully related to remittance inflows.

Columns (2) through (4) of Table 5.2 leverage different fixed effects strategies: country fixed effects, year fixed effects, and country and year fixed effects, respectively. We include these to account for any country- or time-invariant factors that may influence remittance flows. Across the board, the effect of dual citizenship continues to be positive and statistically significant, though the estimates are attenuated. In the specification that includes country fixed effects, the effect of dual citizenship decreases to approximately 28 percent. Only dual citizenship is robustly associated with increased remittances across each of these alternative specifications. While there is again some evidence that diaspora ministries can increase remittances, this finding does not persist with the inclusion of country effects.

Regardless of specification, external voting rights are not associated with increased remittances. This suggests that voting rights cannot be deployed as part of a strategy to harness the economic power or strength of diaspora populations. Rather, as discussed above, policy makers likely use external voting as a mechanism to generate electoral support (Wellman

TABLE 5.2 *Diaspora institutions and remittances*

	Dependent variable: $\log(Remittances/GDP)_{ot}$			
	(1)	(2)	(3)	(4)
$DualCitizenship_{ot-1}$	0.498***	0.280***	0.461***	0.216**
	(0.103)	(0.0978)	(0.107)	(0.0888)
$VotingRights_{ot-1}$	−0.0479	−0.0481	−0.120	−0.159**
	(0.0996)	(0.0696)	(0.107)	(0.0756)
$DiasporaMinistry_{ot-1}$	0.357***	0.0577	0.281**	−0.0448
	(0.101)	(0.0671)	(0.112)	(0.0689)
$EconomicCapacity_{ot-1}$	0.185***	0.544***	0.160***	0.376***
	(0.0596)	(0.114)	(0.0598)	(0.113)
$GDPPC_{ot-1}$	2.080***	0.166	2.226***	0.554
	(0.628)	(0.692)	(0.618)	(0.642)
$GDPPC^2_{ot-1}$	−0.155***	−0.0151	−0.164***	−0.0597
	(0.0392)	(0.0432)	(0.0388)	(0.0422)
$ExRateChange_{ot-1}$	−0.0620	0.0500	−0.0487	0.0457
	(0.104)	(0.0703)	(0.0920)	(0.0613)
$NaturalDisaster_{ot-1}$	1.290***	0.324**	1.349***	0.352*
	(0.312)	(0.155)	(0.296)	(0.180)
$Polyarchy_{ot-1}$	0.379	0.0376	0.331	−0.180
	(0.289)	(0.204)	(0.305)	(0.193)
$Corruption_{ot-1}$	−0.289	−0.394*	−0.308	−0.548**
	(0.284)	(0.231)	(0.293)	(0.214)
Constant	−7.674***	−4.418	−7.886***	−2.745
	(2.244)	(2.671)	(2.193)	(2.450)
Observations	3,561	3,560	3,561	3,560
Country FEs	No	Yes	No	Yes
Year FEs	No	No	Yes	Yes

Note: * $p < 0.10$, ** $p < 0.05$, *** $p < 0.01$. All models estimated with OLS. Robust standard errors clustered by country in parentheses.

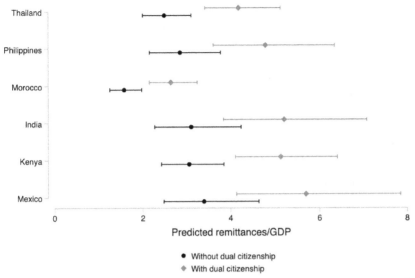

FIGURE 5.4 Predicted effect of dual citizenship on remittances as a percentage of GDP. Circles represent predicted remittances as a percentage of GDP and associated 95% confidence intervals when the country does not have dual citizenship; diamonds represent analogous predictions when the country does have dual citizenship. Predictions based on model in Column (1) of Appendix Table A5.1.

2021). Interestingly, in Column (4), the coefficient on external voting rights is negative and statistically significant, suggesting that the marginal contribution of external voting in countries with diaspora institutions and dual citizenships is to reduce, rather than increase, remittances. This effect is driven by collinearity between external voting rights and diaspora ministries, along with the full set of fixed effects. If we drop the diaspora ministries variable from the specification in Column (4), we find that external voting has no statistically significant effect on remittances.

Micro-level Analysis

The results thus far support the hypothesis that dual citizenship – more so than external voting rights or diaspora ministries – provides a motive for émigrés to remain connected to their homeland. This connection leads to higher remittances. We next turn to the individual level: Does dual citizenship increase the marginal propensity of a migrant to remit?

To answer this, we use the National Immigrant Survey of Spain (NIS).[9] Deployed in 2007, the NIS surveyed over 15,000 foreign-born persons who had been living in Spain for at least one year. What is unique about the NIS is the existence of the *Padron Municipal* – the municipal registrar – which is used to identify migrants. Migrants are incentivized to register with the local *Padron* because there is no need to have legal status when signing up for the *Padron,* and upon signing up, all registrants have access to medical care for themselves and their families, as well as the right to education for their children. This decreases the likelihood of undercounting migrants, a challenge that confronts almost every other survey of immigrants (Reher and Requena 2009).

The NIS includes two key questions: "Do you send money overseas?" and "How much did you send home last month?" The response to the first question is dichotomous, while the second is reported in constant US dollars. Interviewees are also asked a range of social, economic, and demographic questions, which we use as control variables. Unfortunately, the NIS does not ask respondents if they have acquired Spanish citizenship, so we are not able to directly test whether home-country dual citizenship counteracts naturalization.[10]

In Table 5.3, we estimate a set of mixed effects probit and tobit models, which allow us to incorporate unmeasured origin-country characteristics as level two random effects.[11] We also control for several individual-level characteristics: was the individual in contact with friends/family in the home country recently, was the individual employed last week, the individual's level of education, gender, year of birth, and whether they are retired/pensioner. We also include an indicator variable to control for migrants from countries in the Schengen Area, with the assumption being that free movement may decrease the transactions costs associated with relocating to Spain and may facilitate return.

In Column (1), we use a probit model to estimate the marginal propensity of an individual to remit. The baseline probability of remitting by individuals in this sample is 38%. The coefficient on dual citizenship in Column (1) is positive and statistically significant: All else equal,

---

[9] Data are available at www.ine.es/uc/1iua8d77

[10] It is likely that the NIS excluded this question due to fear that it would reduce response rates.

[11] We use mixed effects models as the NIS is only given at a single point in time. The use of country fixed effects would completely absorb the effect of dual citizenship.

the provision of home-country dual citizenship is associated with a 15-percentage point increase in the marginal propensity to remit.

Additionally, dual citizenship may facilitate larger flows of remittances because it encourages migrants to naturalize in their host country without sacrificing home-country ties. Existing evidence is consistent with this conjecture. Jones-Correa (2001) argues that dual citizenship encourages immigrant integration, naturalization, and incorporation in the host country because migrants would no longer have to sacrifice "symbolic or active" participation in the home country. Vink et al. (2013) find that home-country dual citizenship dramatically increases the naturalization rates of immigrants across a number of European countries. In many – if not most – advanced economies, entry into certain sectors of the labor market is restricted to that country's citizens. There is a multitude of reasons for this, ranging from partisan and labor union politics to the increasingly common use of occupational licensing requirements (Peterson, Pandya, and Leblang 2014). Focusing on changes in dual citizenship policies in Latin American countries, Jones-Correa (2001) and Mazzolari (2009) find that the provision of dual citizenship by the homeland led to increased naturalization rates among their expatriates residing in the United States, and this, in turn, led to higher employment rates and earnings.[12]

In Columns (2) through (4) of Table 5.3, we address this by examining the size of migrant remittances. On average, migrants in the NIS sample report send home $1,884 annually. This amount increases by approximately $372 to countries that provide their expatriates with dual citizenship rights. In Column (3), the coefficient on the Schengen Area indicator is positive and statistically significant: Migrants from the Schengen Area, all else equal, remit over $1,100 more than migrants from non-Schengen countries.

Why does dual citizenship increase the size of remittances? From the perspective of self-interest, immigrants will be more likely to remit, or remit more, if they intend to return home and consume or invest the resources they have remitted. Since dual citizenship may make the prospect of return – either permanent or circular – easier and more likely, it may increase remittances used for the maintenance of existing assets or for future consumption. In a study of migrants living in Germany, Zimmermann, Constant, and Gataullina (2009) find that immigrants who held a German passport – available only to German citizens (or dual

---

[12] Mazzolari (2009) finds that immigrants from countries granting dual citizenship were 3.6 percent more likely to find full time employment relative to immigrants from other Latin American countries.

TABLE 5.3 *Micro-level evidence on dual citizenship and remittance behavior*

Dependent variable:	$SendMoney_i$	$AmountSent_i$		
	(1)	(2)	(3)	(4)
$DualCitizenship_{ot-1}$	0.44*	372.57*	552.00**	507.08*
	(0.26)	(193.99)	(250.40)	(275.10)
$InTouchHomeland_i$	1.46**	262.69	292.31	355.28
	(0.12)	(391.78)	(414.68)	(387.98)
$Employed_i$	0.64**	408.00**	428.75**	342.17**
	(0.06)	(99.33)	(100.82)	(120.57)
$Education_i$	−0.10**	101.35**	96.95**	67.17
	(0.03)	(48.17)	(46.77)	(56.23)
$Male_i$	0.01	250.42**	239.40**	268.25**
	(0.04)	(106.02)	(106.46)	(119.33)
$BirthYear_i$	−0.00	−0.18	−0.20	0.29**
	(0.00)	(0.37)	(0.38)	(0.14)
$Retired_i$	−1.03**	1115.39	967.62	712.90
	(0.09)	(713.07)	(619.14)	(484.29)
$Schengen_o$			1145.45*	1283.45*
			(642.92)	(779.49)
$PlanReturn_i$				698.27**
				(322.02)
Constant	−1.76**	713.56	513.09	−367.95
	(0.41)	(911.72)	(963.52)	(661.95)
Observations	11,016	3,416	3,416	2,990

* $p < 0.10$, ** $p < 0.05$. Column (1) estimated using multilevel probit. Columns (2), (3), and (4) estimated using multilevel generalized least squared (GLS). Robust standard errors clustered by migrant origin country in parentheses.

citizens) – were more likely to engage in circular return as compared to those who did not hold a German passport.

In Column (4) of Table 5.3, we include an indicator variable from the NIS survey which is coded one if the migrant reports an "intention to return home" at some point in the future and zero otherwise. Our estimates indicate that three percent of those surveyed expressed an intention to return. Including this variable marginally reduces the coefficient on dual citizenship. The intention to return has a positive and statistically significant effect, with those expressing such an intention sending, on average, almost $700 more home as compared to those who do not express such an intention. This is consistent with the theory that self-interest, in part, motivates individuals to remit. That said, even after accounting for self-interest, dual citizenship is robustly associated with increased remittances.

Overall, both macro- and micro-level evidence support the idea that dual citizenship enables sending countries to harness the financial resources of their expatriate population. A potential complication, however, is that naturalization may be at odds with a country's attempt to use dual citizenship as a mechanism of symbolic attachment, as dual citizens may become attached to two homes. It is difficult to analyze this directly at the individual level due to a lack of consistent survey questions. But the case of Mexico – one of the largest sources of immigrants into developed countries – may be illustrative. In analyzing Mexico's transnational policies, DeSipio (2006) notes that dual citizenship as deployed by Mexico prevents what he calls the "development of undivided loyalty to the host country." Délano (2010) agrees, arguing that transnational connections prevent immigrants from acquiring a sense of loyalty to the host country.

Gutiérrez (1999) provides a rationale: Mexico's attempts to connect to expatriates in the United States (via voting rights and dual citizenship) are part of a general strategy to foster a diasporic identity, which helps foster a "wide-range of government objectives that include guaranteeing the flow of remittances to Mexico, defending Mexicans' rights in the United States, and possibly influencing the development of a lobbying group" (p. 551). He concludes by arguing that even if dual citizenship weakens ties between those who naturalize in the United States, the strategy helps to engage second- and third-generation citizens of Mexican descent to still consider themselves Mexican. More generally, Bloemraad (2004) argues that dual citizenship provides a mechanism to strengthen ties with the home country. By allowing for naturalization without consequence, she argues that home-country dual citizenship decreases the cost of cultural and political integration, which, in turn, increases the migrant's ability to maintain transnational ties.

The importance of transnational ties – especially for countries in the Global South that are competing for human and financial capital – cannot be overstated. Remittance flows are stable and are increasing, allowing households around the world access to capital to finance consumption and helping communities rise out of poverty. It would seem then, that dual citizenship would be ubiquitous: All countries should adopt it. Yet that is not what we observe. Some countries cut ties with their expatriates, preventing them from owning property and decreasing their attachments to the homeland. Why is this the case? In the next section, we develop an argument rooted in principal-agent theory to explain cross-national and -temporal variation in the adoption of diaspora engagement strategies.

EXPLAINING THE EMERGENCE OF DIASPORA INSTITUTIONS

Our argument and findings emphasize that diaspora institutions, especially the provision of dual citizenship, confer significant benefits on migrant-sending countries. States that build diaspora institutions experience increased remittance inflows. Yet these observations generate an immediate puzzle: If diaspora institutions are an economic boon to sending countries, why don't *all* countries build them? How can we explain a country's decision to build, or not to build, diaspora institutions?

Figure 5.3 and Table 5.1 illustrate the significant variation in the adoption of diaspora institutions, and no clear patterns immediately emerge. Countries with autocratic governments like Afghanistan and Saudi Arabia vary regarding dual citizenship and external voting rights. Democracies are likewise heterogeneous: Austria provides external voting rights but not dual citizenship, while Ireland provides dual citizenship but not external voting rights. Mexico and Morocco both have diaspora ministries but differ in their allowance of external voting rights. And across these comparisons, there are vast differences in the size of the diaspora.

Surprisingly few accounts help us explain cross-national and -temporal variation in the creation of diaspora institutions. Perspectives that focus on *tapping* might suggest that countries with larger, wealthier, and more educated diasporas benefit most from diaspora institutions and would be more likely to construct them. Yet this does not explain why poorer countries might also benefit – perhaps even more in relative terms – from having these institutions in place. *Embracing* and *governing* logics also grant little insight into variation in the creation of diaspora institutions across space and time.

We argue that one reason existing frameworks are unable to explain the rise of diaspora institutions is that they do little to explore the agency of diaspora members themselves. Tapping approaches, for instance, largely characterize migrants as a passive resource on which states can readily draw. Governing approaches similarly abstract away from diaspora members and focus on epistemic communities of elites. Yet *all* migrants are political and economic actors in their own right – individuals who have their own preferences and independent decision-making capabilities. Explaining the origins of diaspora institutions requires not only grappling with the incentives of states to form these institutions but also the incentives of migrants to engage with these institutions in ways beneficial to themselves and their homelands.

We propose a political economy theory of the decision to create diaspora institutions rooted in principal-agent theory. Broadly, we conceive of diaspora institutions as a solution to a principal-agent problem that migrant-sending countries face. Our argument generates testable hypotheses as to which countries are most likely to create diaspora institutions. We show how the incentives of diaspora members, as well as their level of political power abroad, interact with the sending country's interests to explain the spatial and temporal distribution of diaspora institutions.

Principal-agent (P-A) theory represents situations in which one actor acts on behalf of another to implement an agenda (Lupia and Mccubbins 2000). The principal must delegate some control over implementing its agenda to an agent charged with realizing the principal's preferences. This delegation occurs because the agent has valuable resources – typically information, skill, or time – for policy implementation that the principal does not have (Kiewiet and McCubbins 1991). Delegation is rational because the agent has some specific advantage important to implementing the principal's agenda.

If the interests of the principal and agent perfectly align, this relationship exists without incident – agents perfectly implement the agenda of the principal. When their interests do not align, a P-A problem emerges – agents, in pursuit of their own self-interest, act in ways that do not serve the interest of the principal (Aghion and Tirole 1997). The result of this misalignment is *agency loss* that can come in the form of *omission* (the agent fails to take an action that would benefit the principal) or *commission* (the agent takes some action contrary to the interests of the principal). Agency loss is magnified substantially when agents have a high degree of autonomy (Strøm 2000).

How can principals limit agency loss? P-A theory suggests that the creation of institutions aligns the incentives of principals and agents to help overcome the P-A problem. *Contract design* is an attempt by the principal to establish incentive compatibility between principals and agents. *Screening and selection* refer to mechanisms that attempt to prevent actors with substantial incentive incompatibility from becoming agents. *Monitoring requirements* force agents to share otherwise-hidden information about agenda implementation with the principal. Finally, *institutional checks* ensure that agents are held accountable by the veto of a third party. Building such institutions reduces agency loss substantially, but principals must weigh the amount of expected agency loss against the costs of constructing such institutions.

We argue that migrant-sending countries and their diasporas are in an informal principal-agent relationship. Migrant-sending countries are the principal, and migrants are agents. States in the international system want to ensure their own security, as well as increase their wealth and power.[13] Diaspora members can have substantial influence on the realization of the sending state's agenda as a function of their position in the international system. They can take (or not take) actions that influence the material interests of the home state. For instance, migrants can lobby migrant-receiving governments to increase foreign aid to their homeland (Bermeo and Leblang 2015). They may also lobby those states to act (or not act) on behalf of their home country in inter- or intra-state conflicts (Shain and Barth 2003).

Besides lobbying host states in pursuit of their home country's interests, the diaspora engages in a range of activities that stimulate economic development at home, as we highlight in the preceding chapters. Migrants can remit, invest, foster new trade links, attract new sources of capital, and return home with new wealth and skills. These actions serve the development interests of migrant-sending countries. In this sense, we see migrants as informal agents of their origin state, with substantial abilities to help the state advance its own interests.

However, migrants have their own interests, as well as substantial autonomy, since they fall outside the sovereign boundaries of their homeland. The potential divergence of interests, as well as the relatively high level of autonomy the diaspora enjoys, can generate substantial agency loss. In terms of *omission*, migrants may choose to take none of the actions we discuss above that further the interests of the state. Perhaps even worse for the state, diasporas engage in *commission*-related agency loss – that is, they take actions that are in direct conflict with the material interests of the sending state. For instance, migrants may financially support insurgencies or rebel groups in their home states, or they may lobby their host country government to support regime change or military intervention (Shain 2002).

---

[13] Politicians' electoral self-interest may be apparent if we focus on electoral institutions like external voting rights (e.g., Wellman 2021), but may not be relevant for dual citizenship or other types of institutions.

Given the potential for agency loss, sending states can turn to the institutional toolbox to reconcile this problem. Yet many of these tools, including *screening and selection* mechanisms, *monitoring* requirements, and *institutional checks*, are infeasible given the substantial spatial and legal autonomy that migrants enjoy. For all intents and purposes, states cannot selectively choose who emigrates and cannot monitor migrants living far from their own borders. One remaining option, however, is viable: contract design. We conceive of diaspora institutions, and particularly dual citizenship, as a form of contract design that induces stronger incentive compatibility between migrant-sending states and members of the diaspora. Diaspora institutions alter the incentive structure of migrants. These institutions help shape preferences and persuade migrants that it is in their material interest to take actions that benefit the principal – the home state. They can also foster identity-based links for migrants that might encourage favorable lobbying, remitting, return migrating, investing, and the fostering of new trade links.

Yet building diaspora institutions is costly, requiring the use of scarce financial and political resources on the part of the sending state. Many migrant-sending countries have limited state capacity to build new institutions and implement programs that alter the incentive structure of migrants. There are also significant opportunity costs: That capacity may be more effectively deployed toward other domestic or international priorities. Additionally, citizens who do not migrate may *oppose* emigration and disapprove of political projects designed to embrace expatriates (Kustov 2020). In short, building diaspora institutions is a political project and therefore requires expending political and fiscal capital. States must decide whether the potential benefits of diaspora institutions (limiting agency loss) outweigh the costs of using scarce resources and state capacity to cater to migrants.

We argue that in conditions where potential agency loss is the highest, we are likely to observe rapid building of diaspora institutions. It will be in these cases that a cost-benefit analysis will favor the use of scarce resources to build these institutions. We argue that the amount of agency loss is determined by the relative position of the diaspora in the international system, as well as the political power that members of the diaspora hold in host states. If a sending state's diaspora is primarily located in influential states (say, in the United States or Western Europe), the cost of not engaging migrants with diaspora institutions grows. This is especially the case when migrants hold political power in these powerful host countries – that is, via the host's integration policies, migrants are allowed to participate in the political process.

In short, when a sending state's diaspora is located primarily in economically and politically powerful host states, and those host states grant them political power, the potential for agency loss increases. Migrants can take acts of omission and commission that are costly for their home states. Such dynamics would make engaging the diaspora increasingly more vital to the interests of sending states, causing them to allocate political and financial resources toward the creation of diaspora institutions. By contrast, if a sending state's migrants are primarily located in less powerful states and are not granted the right to participate in the political process, the potential for agency loss falls, and states are likely to eschew the creation of diaspora institutions.

Our argument generates empirically testable propositions with regard to the position of diasporas in the international system, their level of political power, and the propensity of sending states to develop diaspora institutions. We first focus on a diaspora's relative level of *economic capacity*. We hypothesize that an increase in the share of a sending state's diaspora that is located in relatively wealthier countries is associated with an increased propensity to build diaspora institutions. We also analyze a diaspora's relative level of *lobbying capacity*: An increase in the ability of a sending state's diaspora to effectively lobby more powerful countries in the international system is associated with an increased propensity to build diaspora institutions.

Empirical Analysis

We test our hypotheses using data on the adoption of diaspora institutions by all countries between 1980–2017. We leverage information on the spatial distribution of migrants, as well as the political power that migrants hold, to measure the economic and political capacity of each country's diaspora. Using a survival modeling strategy, we identify which factors are associated with faster adoption of diaspora institutions, most notably dual citizenship provision for emigrants. We focus on explaining the emergence of dual citizenship rights. Secondarily, we analyze the creation of external voting rights and diaspora ministries, in line with our analyses above. We observe in what year each country adopts dual citizenship, as well as external voting rights and diaspora ministries. There are no instances of reversion once a country adopts these institutions.

We construct a series of independent variables that measure the relative economic and lobbying capacity of each country's diaspora. We already introduced $EconomicCapacity_{ot}$, which is designed to capture the extent to which country o's diaspora is located in countries d that are relatively wealthier than its home country at time t. This is our primary measure of the diaspora's economic capacity. In a similar fashion, we construct several variables designed to capture the lobbying capacity of a country's diaspora. We first create $VotingRights_{ot}$:

$$VotingRights_{ot} = \sum_{d=1}^{d} \frac{Migrants_{odt}}{Migrants_{ot}} * MigrantVotingRights_{dt}$$

where $MigrantVotingRights_{dt}$ is an indicator for whether country d extends voting rights to migrants at time t. This calculation reduces to the share of country o's diaspora that holds voting rights abroad at time t and is designed to capture the diaspora's ability to act politically on behalf of its homeland.

We create three variables that capture the relative strategic location of a country's diaspora in the international system. The first is $AidDonor_{ot}$:

$$AidDonor_{ot} = \sum_{d=1}^{d} \frac{Migrants_{odt}}{Migrants_{ot}} * AidDonor_{dot} * MigrantVotingRights_{dt}$$

where $AidDonor_{dit}$ is an indicator for whether country d is an aid donor to country o at time t. This calculation reduces to the share of country o's diaspora that lives in aid donors that grant migrants voting rights. We use the OECD's CRS to identify aid donor relationships. The next is $SecurityCouncil_{ot}$:

$$SecurityCouncil_{ot} = \sum_{d=1}^{d} \frac{Migrants_{odt}}{Migrants_{ot}} * SecurityCouncil_{dt} * MigrantVotingRights_{dt}$$

where $SecurityCouncil_{dt}$ is an indicator for whether country d is a voting member of the United Nations Security Council at time t. This calculation reduces to the share of country o's diaspora that resides in voting Security Council members that grant migrants voting rights. Security Council membership status is drawn from Dreher, Sturm, and Vreeland (2008). Finally, we create $Ally_{ot}$:

$$Ally_{ot} = \sum_{d=1}^{d} \frac{Migrants_{odt}}{Migrants_{it}} * Ally_{odt} * MigrantVotingRights_{dt}$$

where $Ally_{odt}$ is an indicator for whether countries o and d are in a formal alliance at time t. This calculation reduces to the share of country o's diaspora that is located in allied countries that grant migrants voting rights. We identify alliances using the ATOP dataset (Leeds et al. 2002).

We include a range of political and economic control variables in our models. Consistent with our remittance models, we include GDP per capita, polyarchy, migrant stocks, and natural disaster damage. We include an indicator for whether country *o* allows dual citizenship for immigrants living within its borders at time *t*. To capture the potential diffusion of diaspora institutions across borders, we include the count of countries bordering country *o* that allow dual citizenship at time *t* (Vink et al. 2019). Finally, we include the logged number of international students that country *o* has living abroad at time *t* to capture human capital tapping dynamics.

We employ Cox proportional hazards survival modeling to analyze which factors contribute to the faster adoption of diaspora institutions. We lag all independent variables by one year and cluster standard errors by country. We report hazard ratios rather than coefficients in all tables that follow to better illustrate which factors lead to slower or quicker adoption of dual citizenship and other diaspora institutions.

Results

Table 5.4 presents the main results, where time until the adoption of dual citizenship is the dependent variable. We include each of our measures of economic and lobbying capacity independently in Columns (1) through (5). Broadly, the results suggest that a diaspora's capacity to engage in international economic exchange and to influence foreign governments is strongly associated with the faster adoption of dual citizenship. When included separately in Column (1), the hazard ratio associated with *EconomicCapacity*$_{it}$ is greater than 1 and is statistically significant, indicating that countries with diasporas located in relatively wealthier states adopt dual citizenship more quickly. However, economic capacity is not statistically significant at conventional levels when included jointly with variables related to lobbying capacity.

Across the board, our measures of diaspora lobbying capacity are associated with faster adoption of dual citizenship provisions. When migrants can participate in the political process abroad, their home countries adopt dual citizenship more quickly. The same is true when relatively more members of the diaspora have voting rights in strategically important countries, such as aid donors, Security Council members, and allied countries. In sum, the results align with our expectations: Home countries that stand to lose the most from not building diaspora institutions are the countries that adopt dual citizenship most quickly.

TABLE 5.4 *The adoption of dual citizenship*

	Dependent variable: time until adoption of dual citizenship				
	(1)	(2)	(3)	(4)	(5)
EconomicCapacity$_{ot-1}$	1.680** (0.397)	1.193 (0.318)	1.065 (0.285)	1.127 (0.256)	1.223 (0.288)
VotingRights$_{ot-1}$		1.017* (0.00937)			
AidDonor$_{ot-1}$			1.019** (0.00924)		
SecurityCouncil$_{ot-1}$				1.025*** (0.00786)	
Ally$_{ot-1}$					1.026*** (0.00751)
GDPPC$_{ot-1}$	0.744* (0.125)	0.702** (0.120)	0.711* (0.132)	0.725* (0.120)	0.718* (0.122)
Democracy$_{ot-1}$	2.772 (2.429)	2.580 (2.247)	2.993 (2.635)	2.587 (2.303)	1.405 (1.375)

(continued)

TABLE 5.4 (*continued*)

	Dependent variable: time until adoption of dual citizenship				
	(1)	(2)	(3)	(4)	(5)
$DualCitizenship$ $Immigrants_{ot-1}$	4.797*** (1.874)	5.115*** (2.050)	5.402*** (2.303)	4.910*** (1.989)	4.903*** (1.904)
$NaturalDisaster_{ot-1}$	3.732 (3.336)	4.116 (3.919)	9.291* (11.50)	5.559* (5.127)	6.278* (5.934)
$BorderDC_{ot-1}$	2.237** (0.714)	2.140** (0.658)	1.901* (0.626)	1.945** (0.578)	1.880** (0.555)
$MigrantStock_{ot-1}$	0.155 (0.308)	0.0958 (0.203)	0.0804 (0.177)	0.0339 (0.0824)	0.0360 (0.0831)
$CollegeStudents_{ot-1}$	0.831** (0.0613)	0.871* (0.0719)	0.855 (0.0819)	0.857* (0.0699)	0.846* (0.0727)
Observations	3,875	3,875	2,926	3,875	3,875

Note: * $p < 0.10$, ** $p < 0.05$, *** $p < 0.01$. All models estimated using Cox proportional hazards regression. Hazard ratios reported. Robust standard errors clustered by country in parentheses.

Beyond our independent variables of interest, our control variables offer some interesting insights. Relatively lower income countries are quicker to adopt dual citizenship, as well as countries that themselves offer immigrants within their borders the right to maintain dual citizenship. Countries that experience greater damage from natural disasters also adopt dual citizenship relatively more quickly, potentially signaling a strategic move by countries facing crises to harness the resources of their diaspora. Finally, spatial diffusion appears to play an important role – when countries are bordered by relatively more countries that offer dual citizenship to their emigrants, they are more likely to adopt dual citizenship (Vink et al. 2019). Interestingly, the raw size of a country's diaspora appears to matter little in the decision to adopt dual citizenship provisions.

We replicate this set of models using time until the adoption of our two other diaspora institutions: external voting rights and the establishment of a diaspora ministry. Those results are presented in Appendix Tables A5.4 and A5.5.[14] In contrast to dual citizenship, our independent variables of interest do not consistently and robustly explain the adoption of these alternative diaspora institutions. Instead, factors like spatial diffusion and democracy tend to matter more in these cases. These results are consistent with the idea that the creation of these other diaspora institutions is based less on economical and more on social or political motivations.

CONCLUSION

Remittances are an important – and for some countries, households, and individuals, essential – financial resource, enabling consumption and investment in health, education, and welfare. For policy makers, the harnessing of external capital, be it financial or human, provides opportunities to enhance their electoral prospects as it increases economic activity, decreases inequality, and increases support for incumbents. The desire to increase remittances, however, does not always trump other strategic considerations as policy makers develop institutional ties to their expatriate populations. Politicians must balance other domestic and international priorities against their need and desire to improve their geopolitical standing vis-à-vis countries that host their diaspora.

While this chapter has emphasized the importance of receiving remittances for sending countries, enabling the flow of remittances may be of

---

[14] The diffusion variable is omitted in Appendix Table A5.5 because there is not sufficient variation in the count of bordering countries with diaspora ministries.

strategic importance for migrant host countries. As discussed in Chapter 2, migration from low- and middle-income countries is often the result of a family/household decision – a decision that is part of the household's effort to diversify economic risk and shield itself from negative economic shocks. Through that lens, remittances are essential. For destination countries, especially those that are concerned with regulating the flow of migrants across their borders, facilitating the flow of remittances may help influence the flow of migrants. That is the question we address in the next chapter.

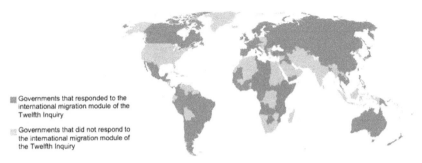

APPENDIX FIGURE A5.1 Responses to UN Population Policies Survey.
Source: United Nations "World Population Policies" (2019).

APPENDIX TABLE A5.1 *Dual citizenship provision and remittances*

	Dependent variable: $\log(Remittances/GDP)_{ot}$			
	(1)	(2)	(3)	(4)
$DualCitizenship_{ot-1}$	0.536***	0.311***	0.458***	0.211**
	(0.1000)	(0.0985)	(0.106)	(0.0957)
$EconomicCapacity_{ot-1}$	0.208***	0.560***	0.173***	0.386***
	(0.0615)	(0.100)	(0.0616)	(0.105)
$GDPPC_{ot-1}$	1.740***	0.381	1.959***	0.692
	(0.610)	(0.696)	(0.616)	(0.687)
$GDPPC^2_{ot-1}$	−0.134***	−0.0300	−0.148***	−0.0688
	(0.0383)	(0.0444)	(0.0388)	(0.0454)
$ExRateChange_{ot-1}$	−0.0675	0.0485	−0.0511	0.0467
	(0.103)	(0.0699)	(0.0903)	(0.0627)
$NaturalDisaster_{ot-1}$	1.054***	0.198	1.147***	0.222
	(0.351)	(0.197)	(0.319)	(0.212)
$Polyarchy_{ot-1}$	0.499*	0.0557	0.326	−0.204
	(0.278)	(0.195)	(0.305)	(0.191)
$Corruption_{ot-1}$	−0.274	−0.450**	−0.377	−0.586***
	(0.282)	(0.223)	(0.293)	(0.208)

(continued)

APPENDIX TABLE A5.1 *(continued)*

Constant	-6.539^{***}	-5.311^{**}	-6.871^{***}	-3.419
	(2.203)	(2.667)	(2.208)	(2.590)
Observations	3,956	3,955	3,956	3,955
Country FEs	No	Yes	No	Yes
Year FEs	No	No	Yes	Yes

Note: * $p < 0.10$, ** $p < 0.05$, *** $p < 0.01$. All models estimated with OLS. Robust standard errors clustered by country in parentheses.

APPENDIX TABLE A5.2 *External voting rights and remittances*

	Dependent variable: $\log(Remittances/GDP)_{ot}$			
	(1)	(2)	(3)	(4)
$VotingRights_{ot-1}$	0.140	0.0163	-0.0406	-0.119
	(0.105)	(0.0695)	(0.114)	(0.0748)
$EconomicCapacity_{ot-1}$	0.224^{***}	0.572^{***}	0.167^{**}	0.384^{***}
	(0.0710)	(0.104)	(0.0690)	(0.103)
$GDPPC_{ot-1}$	2.007^{***}	0.380	2.356^{***}	0.689
	(0.672)	(0.670)	(0.651)	(0.635)
$GDPPC^2_{ot-1}$	-0.146^{***}	-0.0252	-0.169^{***}	-0.0683
	(0.0421)	(0.0419)	(0.0411)	(0.0420)
$ExRateChange_{ot-1}$	-0.0836	0.0348	-0.0613	0.0305
	(0.102)	(0.0734)	(0.0824)	(0.0639)
$NaturalDisaster_{ot-1}$	1.183^{***}	0.342^{**}	1.326^{***}	0.363^*
	(0.407)	(0.164)	(0.348)	(0.187)
$Polyarchy_{ot-1}$	0.369	0.136	0.219	-0.0981
	(0.290)	(0.205)	(0.305)	(0.197)
$Corruption_{ot-1}$	-0.239	-0.391^*	-0.309	-0.490^{**}
	(0.305)	(0.216)	(0.312)	(0.208)
Constant	-7.693^{***}	-5.623^{**}	-8.283^{***}	-3.329
	(2.395)	(2.521)	(2.306)	(2.329)
Observations	3,623	3,622	3,623	3,622
Country FEs	No	Yes	No	Yes
Year FEs	No	No	Yes	Yes

Note: * $p < 0.10$, ** $p < 0.05$, *** $p < 0.01$. All models estimated with OLS. Robust standard errors clustered by country in parentheses.

APPENDIX TABLE A5.3 *Diaspora ministries and remittances*

	Dependent variable: $\log(Remittances/GDP)_{ot}$			
	(1)	(2)	(3)	(4)
$DiasporaMinistry_{ot-1}$	0.427***	0.125*	0.287**	0.00316
	(0.100)	(0.0737)	(0.118)	(0.0789)
$EconomicCapacity_{ot-1}$	0.191***	0.551***	0.160**	0.382***
	(0.0682)	(0.0967)	(0.0674)	(0.0931)
$GDPPC_{ot-1}$	1.982***	0.529	2.191***	0.861
	(0.626)	(0.650)	(0.625)	(0.640)
$GDPPC^2_{ot-1}$	−0.144***	−0.0389	−0.158***	−0.0793*
	(0.0388)	(0.0417)	(0.0391)	(0.0429)
$ExRateChange_{ot-1}$	−0.0713	0.0297	−0.0533	0.0305
	(0.0984)	(0.0745)	(0.0857)	(0.0649)
$NaturalDisaster_{ot-1}$	1.053***	0.203	1.153***	0.233
	(0.332)	(0.216)	(0.314)	(0.222)
$Polyarchy_{ot-1}$	0.305	0.123	0.138	−0.141
	(0.290)	(0.189)	(0.314)	(0.187)
$Corruption_{ot-1}$	−0.287	−0.435*	−0.400	−0.594***
	(0.295)	(0.220)	(0.304)	(0.210)
Constant	−7.382***	−5.744**	−7.659***	−3.970*
	(2.255)	(2.515)	(2.232)	(2.394)
Observations	4,060	4,059	4,060	4,059
Country FEs	No	Yes	No	Yes
Year FEs	No	No	Yes	Yes

Note: * $p < 0.10$, ** $p < 0.05$, *** $p < 0.01$. All models estimated with OLS. Robust standard errors clustered by country in parentheses.

APPENDIX TABLE A5.4 *The adoption of external voting rights*

	(1)	(2)	(3)	(4)	(5)
	Dependent variable: time until adoption of external voting rights				
$EconomicCapacity_{ot-1}$	0.855 (0.0933)	0.912 (0.127)	0.802 (0.113)	0.845 (0.104)	0.803* (0.0948)
$VotingRights_{ot-1}$		0.995 (0.00567)			
$AidDonor_{ot-1}$			1.001 (0.00566)		
$SecurityCouncil_{ot-1}$				1.001 (0.00523)	
$Ally_{ot-1}$					1.007* (0.00433)
$GDPPC_{ot-1}$	0.985 (0.0955)	1.009 (0.101)	0.990 (0.101)	0.981 (0.0973)	0.971 (0.0955)
$Democracy_{ot-1}$	1.351 (0.638)	1.437 (0.684)	1.478 (0.735)	1.335 (0.634)	1.076 (0.530)
$NaturalDisaster_{ot-1}$	0.0000115 (0.0000117)	0.0000239 (0.000229)	0.0000232 (0.000241)	0.0000963 (0.0000986)	0.00000712 (0.0000748)

$BorderEV_{ot-1}$	1.487**	1.477*	1.497**	1.489**	1.505**
	(0.299)	(0.297)	(0.302)	(0.299)	(0.300)
$MigrantStock_{ot-1}$	0.140	0.150	0.118	0.135	0.112
	(0.210)	(0.228)	(0.186)	(0.206)	(0.172)
$CollegeStudents_{ot-1}$	0.999	0.986	0.978	1.000	1.006
	(0.0677)	(0.0669)	(0.0678)	(0.0680)	(0.0704)
Observations	4,069	3,249	2,283	3,249	3,249

Note: * $p < 0.10$, ** $p < 0.05$, *** $p < 0.01$. All models estimated using Cox proportional hazards regression. Hazard ratios reported. Robust standard errors clustered by country in parentheses.

APPENDIX TABLE A5.5 *The creation of diaspora ministries*

	Dependent variable: time until creation of diaspora ministry				
	(1)	(2)	(3)	(4)	(5)
$EconomicCapacity_{ot-1}$	0.830**	0.867	0.828	0.779***	0.784***
	(0.0737)	(0.103)	(0.0961)	(0.0712)	(0.0722)
$VotingRights_{ot-1}$		0.997			
		(0.00732)			
$AidDonor_{ot-1}$			0.998		
			(0.00770)		
$SecurityCouncil_{ot-1}$				1.008	
				(0.00638)	
$Ally_{ot-1}$					1.008
					(0.00639)
$GDPPC_{ot-1}$	0.646***	0.656***	0.649***	0.619***	0.618***
	(0.0683)	(0.0776)	(0.0760)	(0.0705)	(0.0700)
$Democracy_{ot-1}$	6.753***	7.019***	7.936***	7.070***	6.102***
	(3.678)	(3.889)	(4.573)	(3.976)	(3.617)
$NaturalDisaster_{ot-1}$	1.54e-10	3.04e-11	3.65e-10	5.61e-13	1.02e-12
	(2.72e-09)	(6.02e-10)	(6.84e-09)	(1.28e-11)	(2.27e-11)

	(1)	(2)	(3)	(4)	(5)
MigrantStock$_{ot-1}$	4.307	3.226	3.274	3.332	3.180
	(5.107)	(3.855)	(3.957)	(3.846)	(3.642)
CollegeStudents$_{ot-1}$	1.655***	1.633***	1.630***	1.694***	1.692***
	(0.170)	(0.171)	(0.176)	(0.180)	(0.182)
Observations	4,143	3,335	2,400	3,335	3,335

Note: * $p < 0.10$, ** $p < 0.05$, *** $p < 0.01$. All models estimated using Cox proportional hazards regression. Hazard ratios reported. Robust standard errors clustered by country in parentheses.

167

6

Destination Statecraft

Labor Market Policy and the Regulation of Migration

Thus far, we have examined the factors and forces associated with international migration, and we have shown how migrants channel global investment and remittance flows to their homelands. These financial flows – whether they accrue to corporate entities or immigrant households – help drive domestic investment and consumption, support employment, and generate tax revenue. In Chapter 5, we discussed the conditions under which governments of sending countries encourage the political, economic, and social participation of expatriate populations, as expatriates are an essential source of external financing. We found that support for diaspora engagement is not universal; not all countries expend the political and economic resources that foster inclusion of external populations.

What about destination countries? Are attitudes and policies similarly mixed? From an economic perspective, it is remarkably inefficient to implement barriers to the free movement of people. Economists have found that restrictions on immigration – because they generate distortions from optimal exchange – are tantamount to leaving "trillion-dollar bills" on the sidewalk (Clemens 2011; Clemens and Pritchett 2019). This, in a nutshell, is one of the fundamental puzzles of political economy: In the face of expected economic gain, why do politicians in advanced democracies see controlling immigration – particularly from developing countries – as a key policy goal? Restrictionist policy makers argue that migration increases labor market competition and burdens the welfare state. By fueling social conflict, some politicians stoke these grievances, fueling nativist political movements (Mayda 2006; Dancygier 2010; Norris and Inglehart 2019).[1]

Seeking electoral advantage, politicians promote a variety of policies to limit immigration. While the use of border walls and third-party agreements with other countries has increased markedly, politicians also use tools of *economic statecraft* in an effort to exercise immigration control beyond the border's edge (FitzGerald 2020; Schon and Leblang 2021). Policy makers engage in economic statecraft when they deploy foreign economic policy to influence the behavior of foreign actors towards a specific end (Baldwin 2020). In the case of immigration, politicians often propose using foreign aid and free trade agreements to reduce immigration. While foreign aid and trade agreements often generate little public support, politicians wrap these policies in the promise that they will spur economic development in the Global South, which in turn will tamp down the "root causes" of migration we identify in Chapter 2, such as economic deprivation and absence of public goods provision (Asencio et al. 1990; Bermeo and Leblang 2015; Peters 2015a).

Examples of this logic abound. The EU charges its development assistance agencies with addressing the "root causes" of immigration, while the United States considered decreasing immigration a central goal of the North American and Central American Free Trade Agreements (NAFTA and CAFTA) (Knoll and Sheriff 2017). Some of the first executive orders issued by the Biden administration similarly focused on increasing development aid to El Salvador, Guatemala, and Honduras to address the "root causes" of migration (White House 2021). While policy makers remain enthusiastic about using development assistance and economic cooperation to stem emigration, the academic community is more skeptical. In fact, recent contributions by migration scholars suggest that aid and trade not only do not *decrease* the demand for exit, but they may even *increase* migration in the short run (Clemens and Postel 2018).

We argue for a broader notion of economic statecraft within the context of immigration policy. While extant research foregrounds aid and trade, policy makers seldom discuss the role for increasing *remittances* to reduce immigration pressures. Figure 1.3 shows that remittances are stable and have consistently grown over the last decade; remittances

---

[1] Whether these concerns are rooted in material reality or in psychological dispositions like ethnocentrism is strongly disputed by a wealth of scholarly research (see Hainmueller and Hopkins 2014). Yet to politicians who want to stay in office, this debate is mostly irrelevant, as anti-immigrant sentiment is a political reality regardless of its origins.

dwarf foreign aid flows to low- and middle-income countries (World Bank Group 2016). However, unlike aid or trade flows, it is critical to emphasize that remittances accrue directly to households – friends and family members who remain at home. This means that remittances can directly and immediately improve the well-being of home-country households far beyond that promised by aid or trade. In this chapter, we explore whether remittances can reduce subsequent immigration pressure from home countries.

Ultimately, the answer to this question depends on how remittances affect the decision calculus of potential immigrants. Some scholars argue that remittances signal to others that immigration "pays off," demonstrating immigration's material benefits to the émigré (Aslany et al. 2021). Household members who aspire to emigrate may also use remittances to finance migration. From this perspective, granting migrants labor market access to foster remittances has the potential to *increase* – not decrease – immigration.

We foreground a competing hypothesis. As noted in the previous chapter, remittances are a critical source of income for households, allowing them to finance consumption and increasing their ability to secure daily needs without migrating (Adams and Page 2005). Households use remittances to insure against risks emanating from economic crises or natural disasters, blunting the financial blow of such events (Yang 2011). And households often use remittances to invest in immobile assets and privately access traditionally public goods like health and education (Adams and Cuecuecha 2010). Through these channels, remittances may decrease the need and desire for subsequent household members to leave, reducing aggregate immigration pressures.

It is challenging to directly test this hypothesis. Existing cross-sectional survey data – even the most comprehensive – focuses on *unrealized* or potential migration: individuals who have not yet migrated. Survey data – unless it is based on household panels – allows us to identify factors associated with *intention* but are not suited to parse which mechanism is more important to a household's actual decision to go abroad. Consequently, we harness macro-level data on *realized or observed* immigration. Using dyadic panel data for a global sample of countries, we show that increased bilateral remittance flows are strongly associated with *decreased* bilateral migration. Importantly, in this chapter, we examine the effect of remittances alongside foreign aid and international trade flows and find that only remittances are robustly associated with decreased immigration. We also find that remittances decrease demand for *unauthorized* immigration using annual data on migrant apprehensions in the United States.

We then turn to identifying some tools that high-income destinations can use to increase remittances to origin countries, focusing on augmenting labor market access for migrants. Guest worker programs – which provide temporary non-immigrant visas to foreign-born workers – have been used across industrialized democracies since World War I (Peters 2019). These programs expand access to host-country labor markets, which increases the earnings of current migrants and augments their capacity to remit. In both the United States and European contexts, we find that temporary worker visa programs are strongly associated with increased remittances to migrant origin countries. We explore a separate but substantively similar policy in the United States – Temporary Protected Status (TPS) – and find similar results (see also Helms and Leblang, 2022).

Finally, we probe our proposed mechanism using individual-level data from the GWP, which we introduced in Chapter 2. We find that individuals who receive remittances are more satisfied with their access to public goods and report higher levels of economic and intersubjective well-being, which, we argue and find in Chapter 2, are associated with reduced emigration intentions.

This chapter proceeds as follows. First, we review extant scholarship on the use of economic statecraft to control immigration. This provides the foundation for our argument that remittances decrease migration. Next, we evaluate the relationship between remittances and migration using a global sample of data. We then examine the effectiveness of a range of guest-worker policies at stimulating remittance flows. Before concluding, we validate the micro-level mechanism of our argument using data from the GWP.

CONTROLLING IMMIGRATION

Politicians worry about the electoral consequences of growing foreign-born populations. Increases in immigration are often associated with events that threaten the political survival of leaders (Moriconi, Peri, and Turati 2018). Many voters believe that immigrants depress wages, impose new burdens on public services, and generate increased social conflict (Hainmueller and Hopkins 2014). Nativist movements capitalize on these sentiments by advocating for policies that reduce the current foreign-born population and subsequent immigrant inflows. Nativist parties give voters who are concerned about immigration a credible way to electorally punish leaders they view as contributing to the current level of immigration. As a result, incumbent politicians attempt to limit immigration out of electoral self-interest.[2]

Controlling immigration requires an array of policy tools. Scholars traditionally focus on policies that restrict the ability of immigrants to enter the country or limit the rights of entering immigrants (Czaika and de Haas 2011). These include the construction of physical barriers like walls and fences, investment of budgetary resources into immigration enforcement agencies, and quotas or bans that limit the number of migrants who can enter from a specific country of origin. Anti-immigration political manifestos often also include the restriction of political and economic rights for foreign-born persons after they have immigrated (Ruhs 2013).

Du jour thinking about limiting migration gives pride of place to the construction of border walls, checkpoints, and other physical barriers (Gülzau and Mau 2021). Motivated by the desire to limit the movement of foreigners – who are often characterized as "illegals" or "potential terrorists," these border fortifications are more for political show than for actual effect. Linebarger and Braithwaite (2020) show that border walls do little to enhance security broadly, while Nanes and Bachus (2021) show that walls delay, but do not deter, terrorist attacks. Regarding actual migration, Schon and Leblang (2021) show that border walls can *increase* cross-border migration, as these barriers result in a shift from labor migration to asylum claims.

These standard policy tools stop at the border's edge. Politicians who want to proactively limit immigration are well-served to reach for tools that reduce the *demand for exit* from origin countries. These tools fall within the realm of economic statecraft: They attempt to change the incentives of a foreign economic actor (in this case, potential emigrants) to achieve a policy goal (reducing immigration) using economic instruments (Baldwin 2020). The rationale underlying this approach is straightforward: If destination countries can improve the lives of potential emigrants in their countries of origin, or at least prevent them from becoming materially worse, they may be able to reduce subsequent demand for exit, leading to smaller immigration flows. This is the motivation behind efforts to address the "root causes" of immigration, such as poverty, conflict, and youth unemployment (European Union Trust Fund for Africa 2016). As a result, many governments channel foreign aid

---

[2] The literature on the political consequences of immigration is voluminous. See Kunovich (2004), Mayda (2006), Dancygier (2010), and Zamora-Kapoor and Verea (2014) for a variety of different approaches and perspectives.

toward countries of origin in the hopes of reducing subsequent immigration (Bermeo and Leblang 2015).

Similarly, using the logic of neoclassical models, increasing trade flows should decrease emigration (Peters 2015a; Totten 2017). This was the explicit motivation behind Presidents Clinton and Bush's support for NAFTA and CAFTA, which were cast as market-oriented policies to reduce immigration from Mexico and Central America.[3] Beyond aid and trade, recent research suggests that migrant destinations leverage their power, both bilaterally and via multilateral institutions, to prevent subsequent immigration by granting generous sovereign bailouts to large migrant origin countries (Angin, Shehaj, and Shin 2021; Tobin, Leblang, and Schneider 2021).

The logic behind the use of aid and trade, along with other policy tools, relies on an assumption that these policies meaningfully alter the well-being of households in recipient nations. It is not immediately clear that this assumption is grounded in empirical reality. Compared to the magnitude of underdevelopment in migrant-sending countries, foreign aid flows are extremely small. This means that aid – at least at current levels – is likely not up to the challenge of limiting immigration (Clemens and Postel 2018). Additionally, the gains from aid and international trade are unevenly distributed and unlikely to quickly accrue to those considering emigration (Clemens et al. 2012; Qian 2015; Artuc, Porto, and Rijkers 2019). Some scholars even argue that initial increases in development stimulate *more* immigration by decreasing the individual's financial constraint, which would otherwise prevent emigration (Clemens and Postel 2018; Dao et al. 2018).[4] As a result, there is understandable skepticism that the tools of economic statecraft meaningfully control immigration.

CAN REMITTANCES CONTROL IMMIGRATION?

Yet aid and trade do not exhaust the cross-border economic flows that influence a potential emigrant's quality of life. Remittances, as described in Chapter 5, are sought by both policy makers and households in home countries. Few policy makers propose increasing remittances to reduce

[3] For example, President Clinton in his remarks at the NAFTA signing ceremony claimed that "there will be less illegal immigration because more Mexicans will be able to support their children by staying home" (White House 1993).

[4] This logic is similar to the mobility transition., a cross-national finding that emigration first increases with marginal increases in economic development to a critical point, and then decreases thereafter (Dao et al. 2018). It also has resonance with what some scholars call the "emigration life cycle" (Clemens 2020).

immigration, yet there are reasons to expect that they could pack a more powerful punch than other economic flows. While foreign aid is too small in magnitude to address the "root causes" of migration, remittances now represent the largest economic flow to many low- and middle-income countries. And unlike international trade flows, the benefits of which trickle down to a country's population only with a significant lag, remittances accrue immediately and directly to households in migrant-sending countries. Migrants may then use these resources to improve their material well-being, investing in goods and services that measurably reduce their desire to exit. Can increasing remittances to migrant origins reduce subsequent immigration pressures?

The answer to this question hinges on how remittances shape the decision-making of people who have not yet migrated but may do so in the future, and the picture is not immediately clear. Competing theoretical perspectives suggest that remittances may either *increase* or *decrease* immigration, and evaluating these competing hypotheses is difficult with survey data.

There are at least two arguments that suggest remittances *increase* immigration. First, remittances may serve as a signal of economic success that current immigrants enjoy in their host country. Those considering immigration may see remittances as a signal that immigration will similarly "pay off" for them and choose to migrate in response (Aslany et al. 2021). Second, remittances are a source of capital that households might use to alleviate existing credit constraints and send additional members abroad (Dao et al. 2018).[5] Both logics suggest efforts to increase remittances could increase, rather than decrease, subsequent emigration from the recipient's homeland.

On the other hand, remittances can plausibly *decrease* immigration. As we highlight in the preceding chapter, households primarily use remittances to increase and smooth consumption at home (Adams and Page 2005; Combes and Ebeke 2011). Remittances allow households to accumulate savings and overcome local credit deficiencies, and these capital flows play a crucial role in helping households diversify economic risk, reducing economic volatility (Stark 1984). More broadly, remittances are often used to improve access to, and the quality of, local public goods enjoyed by migrant hometowns through non-state provision (Lee, Walter-Drop, and Wiesel 2014). In Mexico, for instance, households and hometowns use remittances to improve the availability and quality of public goods enjoyed by households, including clean water and sanitation

---

[5] While not directly about remittances, Angelucci (2015) similarly suggests that the alleviation of credit constraints increases emigration.

(Adida and Girod 2011; Duquette-Rury 2014) and physical security (Pérez-Armendáriz and Duquette-Rury 2021).

This phenomenon is broader than Mexico: Cross-national evidence indicates that remittances lead to improved well-being outcomes that are consistent with greater access to traditionally public goods and services (Lee, Walter-Drop, and Wiesel 2014). A growing body of scholarship demonstrates that remittances allow households to shield themselves from the consequences of weak local governance (Doyle 2015) and help protect households from negative income shocks like economic crises and natural disasters (Singer 2010). Our results in Chapter 2 suggest that access to public goods such as clean water, education, and healthcare matter more than financial resources in a potential emigrant's calculus (see also Dustmann and Okatenko 2014).

Cross-sectional survey data of individuals considering emigration, however, is not well-suited to parsing theoretical consequences of remittances. Some analyses of individual-level emigration intentions include measures of remittance receipt,[6] often finding that receiving remittances is associated with increased emigration *aspirations*. However, this work fails to consider how remittances increase well-being at home, which may also *decrease* emigration aspirations.

Remittances and Authorized Migration

Given these challenges and the absence of household panel surveys that include questions related to remittances and realized migration, we focus on the relationship between macro-level remittances and realized immigration flows using dyadic panel data. To investigate the relationship between migrant stocks and remittances, we adopt the gravity model framework utilized in Chapters 3 and 4. Data on bilateral remittances come from the World Bank's bilateral remittance matrices, while data on bilateral migrant stocks come from the UN. Combining these datasets results in a dyadic panel dataset of bilateral migration and remittances from 2010 to 2019, with a total of almost 38,000 country pairs. Because global data on migrant stocks is available only every two or three years, we have a panel with uneven time periods of those lengths.[7] We create our dependent variable –

---

[6] See Aslany et al.'s (2021) systematic review of remittances as a potential driver of emigration aspirations.

[7] Bilateral migration and lagged remittance data are jointly available for years 2010, 2013, 2015, 2017, and 2019. Lagging the bilateral remittance data limits us to four time points per dyad: 2013, 2015, 2017, and 2019.

the logged bilateral emigration rate from country o to country d at time t, using the following procedure. We first calculate migration *flows* using data on migration *stocks* by differencing migration stocks from country o in country d at time t and time t-1, replacing negative values with zeros. We then divide migration flows by the population of origin country o at time t to calculate the bilateral migration rate, and then take the natural log.

Bilateral migrant stocks and remittances are also logged, and all independent variables are lagged by one period to decrease the chance of simultaneity. In line with similar analyses (e.g., Beine and Parsons 2015) and our models in Chapter 3, we use PPML estimation.[8] We include a set of origin*year and destination*year fixed effects to capture time-varying origin- and destination-specific factors that may influence bilateral remittances and emigration rates. This means that we identify the effect of remittances using only information that varies over time within dyads. We report robust standard errors clustered by dyad.

We summarize our main results in Figure 6.1, which presents a marginal effects plot from two fully specified models of bilateral migration with different samples: a global sample of dyads, and a subsample that represents migration from the Global South to the Global North.[9] These models include measures of bilateral foreign aid and trade flows. In both cases, an increase in bilateral remittances is associated with a *lower* subsequent bilateral emigration rate, all else equal. These results are consistent with our hypothesis that remittances allow households in the Global South to better manage economic risk and access public goods, decreasing the need or desire to emigrate. While remittances may signal the benefits of migration or alleviate credit constraints, our results suggest that these effects are more than offset by alternate mechanisms that reduce immigration pressures.[10]

Figure 6.2 illustrates the predicted bilateral emigration rate across the range of logged bilateral remittances, using Column (1) of Appendix Table A6.1. The figure shows that bilateral emigration rates fall

---

[8] We discuss in further detail why we use PPML in Chapter 3.

[9] We present underlying model estimates in Appendix Table A6.1. As with our analyses in other chapters, we use OECD membership to classify countries as belonging to the Global North and Global South.

[10] In results not reported, we explore the possibility of a non-linear relationship between remittances and migration by including a square term. The estimated coefficient on this square term is positive and statistically significant at $p < .01$; however, in magnitude it is roughly 1/20 the size of the linear term, and the negative linear effect of remittances dominates across virtually the entire range of remittances. These results are available upon request.

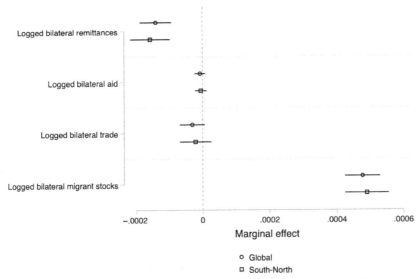

FIGURE 6.1 Bilateral remittances and bilateral migration. Marginal effects of primary variables of interest with 95 percent confidence intervals. Estimates from Models (3) and (4) of Appendix Table A6.1.

precipitously as bilateral remittances increase. A one-standard-deviation increase in remittances above the mean is associated with a roughly 25 percent decline in the bilateral emigration rate, all else equal. These results suggest that bilateral remittances have both substantive and statistical significance for reducing emigration rates.

What about other tools of economic statecraft: foreign aid and trade flows? While it is difficult to compare coefficient estimates across models due to different underlying samples, we note that bilateral remittances continue to have a negative and statistically significant relationship with bilateral emigration rates even after controlling for bilateral aid and trade. The estimated coefficients on bilateral aid and trade are also negative, but they do not reach conventional levels of statistical significance, either in the global sample or within the South–North corridor. This finding is consistent with existing work finding that aid flows are too small to meaningfully reduce migration flows, and that trade flows do not meaningfully shape the decision calculus of potential migrants (Clemens and Postel 2018).[11]

---

[11] While our baseline models are quite conservative, we estimate alternative models to evaluate the robustness of the baseline findings. In Appendix Table A6.2, we add dyad (country pair) fixed effects. The inclusion of dyad fixed effects excludes from the

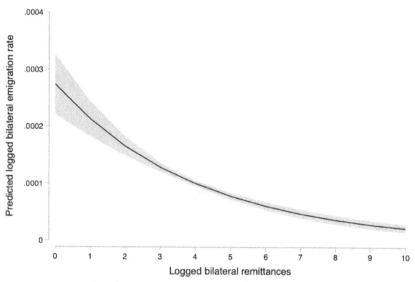

FIGURE 6.2 Predicted bilateral emigration rate across range of logged bilateral remittances. Predictions based on Model (1) of Appendix Table A6.1.

Remittances and Unauthorized Migration

To this point, we have shown that increased bilateral remittances are associated with decreased bilateral migration, both in a global sample and for the South–North corridor. However, these results rely on data that measures solely *authorized* immigration – migrants who have entered a destination country through sanctioned channels. Politicians interested in controlling immigration often focus on *unauthorized* migration – migrants who enter through non-sanctioned channels. Do remittances have the potential to decrease the demand for unauthorized immigration?

The primary challenge to evaluating whether remittances reduce unauthorized immigration is measurement. Assuming that immigration

estimation country pairs that experience zero migration over the entire time period; Beine and Parsons (2015) note that this may induce selection bias. Yet dyad fixed effects eliminate any dyad-specific confounding factors that are time-invariant. We continue to find that increased remittances are associated with decreased emigration rates. For the South–North corridor, the estimated coefficient continues to be negative, but is not statistically significant at conventional levels; this is likely due to the relatively small sample size and inclusion of many fixed effects. In Appendix Table A6.3, we measure logged remittances in first differences. Our baseline relationship continues to hold using this alternative measurement strategy.

authorities want to prevent unauthorized entry,[12] and that unauthorized immigrants wish to remain undetected, observing unauthorized immigration is difficult, if not impossible. To overcome this challenge, we zoom in on unauthorized immigration to the United States, the world's largest immigrant destination. We proxy for the demand for unauthorized entry by measuring the number of people who are apprehended while attempting to enter the United States without inspection (i.e., migrant apprehensions). We obtain data on the number of individuals apprehended by Customs and Border Patrol (CBP) annually between 1998–2015, disaggregated by country of origin, and use this to measure unauthorized entry into the United States.

While imperfect, assuming "that the *apprehension rate* is constant, changes in apprehensions are a direct indicator of changes in illegal inflows" (Office of Immigration Statistics 2017). We cannot directly test whether the apprehension rate is constant, but we can control for factors, such as the number of Border Patrol agents employed yearly, that may influence the apprehension rate.[13] We use data on apprehensions to calculate an analogous apprehension rate, dividing the number of individuals who were apprehended from country i at time t by the population of country i, and taking the natural log.

We, unfortunately, lack comparable annual data on bilateral remittances from the United States to countries of origin across all years in our sample. As a result, we instead use logged total remittances received by country i at time t as a proportion of GDP as our primary measure; this measure comes from the WDI. While this variable captures remittances received from destinations other than the United States, we note that the United States is the largest source of remittances in the world (McAuliffe and Khadria 2020).

We include a battery of control variables[14] to capture the push and pull factors driving unauthorized migration to the United States, including

---

[12] A crack-down on unauthorized migrants would hinder the labor supply and push up wages in sectors such as agriculture, construction, and hospitality. That would decrease wages for business owners in some politically sensitive and geographically concentrated areas. See, for example, Root (2016) for a discussion of the sensitivity of immigration enforcement in Texas.

[13] Our preferred enforcement measure is line-watch hours, however, the Department of Homeland Security stopped reporting this information after 2009. The correlation between line-watch hours and number of officers is 0.987.

[14] See Stark (1984); Clark, Hatton, and Williamson (2007); and Fitzgerald, Leblang, and Teets (2014), which contain reviews and empirical tests of these variables.

relative wages (home-country GDP/US GDP per capita), relative economic inequality (home-country Gini Index/US Gini index), and the size of existing migrant networks.[15] We also include two variables to capture factors that potentially "push" migrants to exit their country: the ratio of the number of deaths from natural disasters in the country of origin to total population and the existence of an ongoing civil war. We include the log of origin-country population to control for the pool of potential migrants. All independent variables are lagged by one year, except for migrant stocks, since current social networks are most relevant for current flows of migration. Additionally, because stocks measure accumulated flows, including them contemporaneously de facto captures lagged values of migration flows.

We also add a number of variables suggested in earlier studies of unauthorized migration. We first include the logged number of Border Patrol agents to capture relative levels of enforcement. We proxy for changes in labor demand using changes in the United States unemployment rate. To account for shortages of visas for authorized entry, we include the total number of visas (all categories) issued by the United States in the prior year. Finally, we include a measure of the backlog to receive an asylum hearing. Backlogs in asylum courts may signal to potential migrants either that they will not be granted a hearing in a timely fashion, or that immigration officials are purposefully delaying hearings with the intent of deterring asylum seekers. We proxy for asylum backlogs using the logged average number of days it takes for an asylum case to be heard, disaggregated by country of origin (Hanson and Spilimbergo 1999; Bohn and Pugatch 2015).

We again estimate this model using PPML, including origin country fixed effects and clustering standard errors by origin country. We present the main results in Figure 6.3; underlying model estimates are available in Appendix Table A6.4. We present the results for both a global sample, and a subsample limited to countries in the Western Hemisphere, from which most unauthorized migration to the United States originates. The results are in line with our hypothesis. All else equal, increased remittances are associated with a decline in the apprehension rate, whether we

---

[15] It is important to note that the stock of the foreign-born population can also have a policy interpretation within the context of legal migration to the US. As the vast majority of immigrant visas are issued for the purpose of family reunification, the foreign-born population can be interpreted as a proxy for the number of families who are attempting to reunify with family members from abroad.

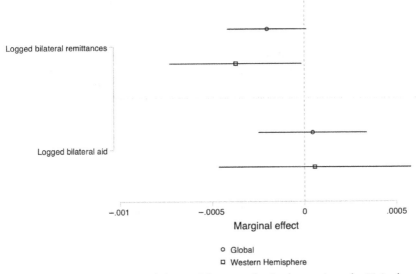

FIGURE 6.3 Remittances and demand for unauthorized entry into the United States. Marginal effects of primary variables of interest with 95 percent confidence intervals. Estimates from Models (3) and (4) of Appendix Table A6.4.

analyze all non-OECD countries or just those in the Western Hemisphere. Notably, remittances have a negative and statistically significant relationship with apprehensions even when accounting for bilateral foreign aid flows; aid itself has no statistically significant effect, either for the global sample or within the Western Hemisphere. We take this as evidence that remittances can meaningfully reduce the demand for both authorized *and unauthorized* migration.

USING ECONOMIC STATECRAFT TO INCREASE REMITTANCES

Our results suggest that increased remittances – unlike foreign aid or international trade – are robustly associated with a reduction in migration flows. These empirical results are consistent with our hypothesis that remittances help would-be migrants increase and smooth consumption, shield themselves from economic shocks, and privately access essential goods such that migration becomes undesirable or unnecessary. This implies that if policy makers could intervene to increase remittances, they could meaningfully reduce the demand for entry from origin countries, while also increasing the well-being of those who remain at home. How can policy makers foster greater remittance flows?

We hypothesize that by expanding current migrants' access to the domestic labor market via guest worker programs, migrant destinations can increase remittances to origins and decrease subsequent immigration pressures. The Bracero program – a program in place from 1942 to 1964 designed to bring Mexican labor into the United States – is perhaps the best-known guest worker program, but countries across Europe also used temporary migrant worker programs after World War II as a strategy to help rebuild their economies (Boucher and Gest 2018; Peters 2019). While these temporary visa programs have expanded – they now provide access for international students, working holidaymakers (a combination of tourism and work permits), or family reunification – the large majority of temporary visas issued by OECD countries are guest workers' visas, which allow foreign visitors (not permanent immigrants) to enter destination countries for a designated period of time to engage in temporary work.[16]

These programs continue to play an important role in the policy arsenal of developed countries. Figure 6.4 shows that in 2017, OECD countries issued almost five million temporary non-immigrant visas, which is almost equivalent to the number of permanent immigrant visas issued (OECD 2020). On a per capita basis, Australia, Canada, and New Zealand lead the way in temporary visa provision, with the United States issuing the largest absolute number of these permits. While much research focuses on how countries use these policies to achieve domestic economic goals (e.g., Messina 2007), we suggest that they have positive externalities for politicians who want to curb immigration. As a result, they can be powerful tools of migration statecraft – states can use guest worker programs to influence the calculus of potential migrants by fostering greater remittance flows.

Can policy makers leverage labor market policy as a tool of immigration statecraft? Unfortunately, data to directly evaluate whether migrants who are granted labor market access remit more does not exist. However, existing evidence shows that status-enhancing policies for immigrants provide economic benefits. Rivera-Batiz (1999) and Kossoudji and Cobb-Clark (2002) find that a shift to permanent legal status in the United States increases the wages of an immigrant by 6–13 percent on

---

[16] Discussions of the role and importance of guest worker programs can be found in Boucher and Gest (2018). Surak (2015) and Zolberg (2000) provide critiques of guest worker programs, arguing that they are exploitative and a modern form of imperialism.

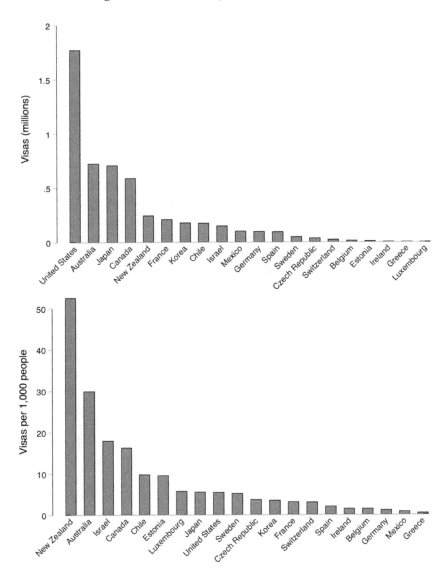

FIGURE 6.4 Use of temporary visas across OECD countries, 2017. Top panel:
total number of visas issued. Bottom panel: number of visas issued per
1,000 people.
Source: OECD (2020).

average.[17] Devillanova, Fasani, and Frattini (2018) and Kaushal (2006) find, in the Italian and American context, respectively, that when undocumented immigrants are eligible for amnesty, they are significantly more likely to find employment than those who are ineligible.

Labor market access, in turn, provides migrants with the potential to send more remittances. This potential is borne out: Using surveys of migrants residing in the United States, France, Germany, Italy, Spain, and Australia, Bollard, McKenzie, and Morten (2009) and Bollard et al. (2011) find that even after controlling for a wide array of demographic, economic, and social characteristics, higher wages are associated with an increase in both the frequency and amount of remittances sent home.

We evaluate this claim using data on guest worker programs in the United States, and as an extension, in Europe. While the OECD collects information on visa issuances, these data do not distinguish between higher- and lower-skilled temporary worker visas, and they do not allow us to identify visas that allow temporary workers to be accompanied by family members. As a result, available OECD data are insufficient to isolate the labor market access-enhancing component of temporary migration programs. Consequently, we focus on US guest worker programs, not just because they are the largest of their kind, but because they also allow us to differentiate among visa classes. Our focus is on the US H2-B visa program, which provides access to the US labor market for a maximum of one year and is capped at 65,000 visas yearly. The H2-B visa program is a non-immigrant visa program, designed exclusively for temporary work, and does not permit its recipients to bring accompanying family members.

We expect that greater participation in the H2-B visa program will result in origin countries receiving more remittances. As a placebo test, we examine the H1-B visa program, which is also currently capped at 65,000 a year and allows labor market access for higher-skilled migrants. The H1-B program is a useful placebo because it provides a visa for three years and is renewable for another three years; it focuses on highly educated migrants who earn higher wages than H2-B visa holders, which may increase the ability of these visa holders to bring

---

[17] Amuedo-Dorantes and Bansak (2014) and Pan (2012) reach differing conclusions regarding the effect of legal permanent resident status on employment for women in particular, with Amuendo-Dorantes and Bansak finding that women are more likely to exit the workforce once they obtain status, while Pan finds the opposite effect.

family members with them. Importantly, family members of H2-B visa holders are eligible for entry into the United States under the H-4 visa category. As a result, while we would expect greater H2-B participation to increase remittances, we would not expect the same for greater H1-B participation.

Visa Policy and Remittances

We first examine the relationship between US temporary visa policy and remittance inflows to a global sample of non-OECD countries between 1990–2015. Our dependent variable is logged remittances received by country i at time t as a share of that country's GDP.[18] We construct our measure of H2-B visa participation as the logged percentage of people from country i who hold an H2-B visa at time t.[19] Because the US Department of State records and reports visa statistics on a fiscal rather than an annual year basis, we utilize a two-year moving average of this variable. We construct an analogous measure of H1-B visa participation for a placebo test.

We include the same set of control variables that we include in our model of remittances in Chapter 5. We estimate this model using OLS and include origin country fixed effects, and we lag all variables by one year. Robust standard errors are clustered by origin country. Table 6.1 displays our findings. In Column (1), we find that as the percentage of country i's population holding an H2-B visa increases, that country's receipt of remittances increases, all else equal. A one-standard-deviation increase in the percentage of country i's population holding an H2-B visa is associated with a roughly 4 percent increase in logged remittances as a percentage of GDP, on average. This suggests that temporary visa policies can meaningfully increase remittance flows to migrant countries of origin.

As a placebo test, we replace H2-B visas with H1-B visas in Column (2). Because H1-B visas are both longer-term and renewable, and accrue to higher-skilled and higher-income individuals who can bring family members with them, we expect this variable to be insignificant. The results suggest that H1-B visas, indeed, are not meaningfully associated with remittance receipt for origin countries. We include H1-B and H2-B

---

[18] Again, annual data on bilateral remittance flows from the United States to other countries is unavailable for the period on which we focus.

[19] In other words, we divide the number of H2-B visa holders from country i at time t by the population of country i and multiply by 100. We then take the log.

TABLE 6.1 *Labor market access policy and remittances*

	Dependent variable: $\log\left(Remittances/GDP_{it}\right)$			
	(1)	(2)	(3)	(4)
$\log\left(H2BRate_{it-1}\right)$	3.209***		3.250***	
	(0.956)		(1.052)	
$\log\left(H1BRate_{it-1}\right)$		2.486	−0.544	
		(5.480)	(5.234)	
TPS_{it-1}				0.460**
				(0.188)
$\log\left(MigrantStock_{it-1}\right)$	0.240***	0.242***	0.241***	0.237***
	(0.060)	(0.061)	(0.060)	(0.059)
Constant	−1.158*	−1.170*	−1.162*	−1.122*
	(0.600)	(0.607)	(0.605)	(0.593)
Observations	2,854	2,854	2,854	2,854
Controls	Yes	Yes	Yes	Yes
Origin FEs	Yes	Yes	Yes	Yes

Note: ***$p < .01$ **$p < .05$ *$p < .1$. Models estimated using OLS. All models include country fixed effects and control variables: change in origin country exchange rate, GDP ratio, natural disaster death rate, civil war, change in US unemployment rate, and logged migrant stocks. Robust standard errors clustered by origin country in parentheses.

visa participation jointly in Column (3); while H2-B visas continue to be positively associated with remittance receipt, H1-B visas continue to have no detectable effect.

To extend our results, we evaluate the impact of one additional US policy that has implications for migrant labor market access: TPS. The US Immigration Act of 1990 established TPS, which provides temporary legal status to foreign nationals from countries experiencing a natural disaster, political and economic instability, or violent conflict, but who do not legally qualify as refugees. TPS offers two crucial benefits to foreign nationals that make it a useful case to test our argument: 1) a temporary stay in deportation proceedings and 2) legal access to the labor market. Crucially, TPS is only extended to foreign nationals *who are already in the United States* at the time of the precipitating crisis. TPS is initially granted for two years and can be renewed indefinitely, but can also be terminated at the discretion of the executive branch. As with temporary visas, we expect countries with foreign nationals covered by TPS to receive more remittances than countries whose migrants were not granted TPS (see Helms and Leblang, forthcoming).[20] In Column (4) of Table 6.1, we replace temporary visa participation with an indicator variable coded as one if country i's current migrants are covered by TPS at time $t - 1$ and zero otherwise. Like H2-B visa participation, TPS is associated with a statistically significant increase in remittance receipt.

To explore whether these results travel to other contexts, we estimate analogous models of remittances using data on temporary visa programs for 28 destination countries that belong to the EU. Data on temporary visa issuances for these countries is available via Eurostat for 2010–2017. Unfortunately, these data only differentiate between classes of visas for a small subset of countries and years. As a result, we analyze aggregated temporary visas regardless of type. These results are available in Appendix Table A6.5. They broadly confirm that temporary visas in European countries also increase remittances to migrant origin countries.

MICRO-LEVEL MECHANISMS

At the macro-level, our results broadly support the hypothesis that labor market access policies that augment remittances are effective tools of migration statecraft. Increases in remittances are associated with a decrease in subsequent immigration. These observables, we argue, are driven by the effect that remittances have on individual and household satisfaction in the homeland. As noted above, remittances are different from aid and trade flows because they accrue immediately and directly to households (Escribà-Folch, Meseguer, and Wright 2015), smoothing consumption, substituting for absent public goods, and, more broadly, positively influencing individuals' perceptions of economic conditions in their homelands (Ahmed 2017).

We investigate whether the receipt of remittances has effects consistent with this literature at the micro-level using survey data from the GWP. We discuss the GWP in detail in Chapter 2 and refer readers to that discussion for details. Our hypothesis is that receipt of remittances increases an individual's reported level of satisfaction with a variety of amenities, and in the aggregate, their standard of living, their income, and their outlook on life. The GWP includes a question asking whether the individual has received money or goods from someone living in another country

---

[20] Orrenius and Zavodny (2015) find that Salvadoran immigrants with TPS are more likely to find employment as compared to Salvadorans in the US without authorization and that, on average, the jobs they find pay higher wages.

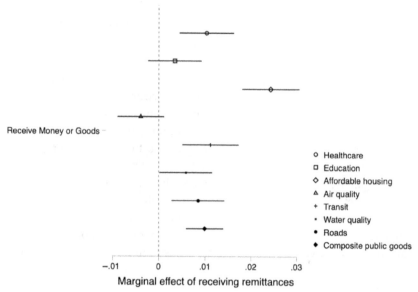

Receive Money or Goods

○ Healthcare
□ Education
◇ Affordable housing
△ Air quality
+ Transit
· Water quality
• Roads
♦ Composite public goods

−.01   0   .01   .02   .03
Marginal effect of receiving remittances

FIGURE 6.5 Remittance receipt and satisfaction with public goods. Marginal effect of receiving remittances on public goods with 95 percent confidence intervals. Underlying model estimates from Appendix Table A6.6.

in the past year. To this independent variable of interest, we add a battery of control variables, including level of education, gender, age, income quintile, employment status, and household size. All models are estimated using OLS and include a set of country*year fixed effects to account for time-varying country-specific factors that may influence the dependent variables. We include survey weights and report standard errors clustered by country-year. These models are consistent with those in Chapter 2.

We present the results with respect to satisfaction with public goods in Figure 6.5.[21] This figure presents the effect of receiving remittances across eight different public goods outcomes. The results indicate that, all else equal, receiving remittances increases the likelihood that an individual reports being satisfied with healthcare, housing, transit, water quality, and roads. There is no statistically significant effect of remittances on reported satisfaction with education or air quality. In the final model, we combine responses to each of these areas of public goods into a single, continuous scale using PCA, as we did in Chapter 2, and again find a

[21] Underlying model estimates are available in Appendix Table A6.6.

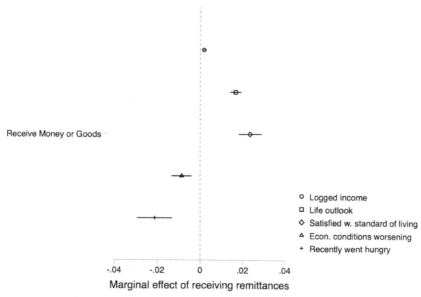

FIGURE 6.6 Remittance receipt and well-being. Marginal effects of receiving remittances on range of well-being outcomes with 95% confidence intervals. Underlying model estimates from Appendix Table A6.7.

positive relationship between receipt of remittances and satisfaction with local public goods and amenities.

Figure 6.6 shows the effect of receiving remittances on a range of outcomes related to material well-being.[22] We use five variables reported by the GWP; all are rescaled to fall in the 0–1 interval for ease of comparison: 1) reported income, 2) reported current well-being on a scale of 0 (worst) to 10 (best), 3) satisfaction with personal standard of living, 4) personal perceptions of national economic conditions, and 5) self-report of whether they or their family have gone hungry in the past 12 months. We find – consistent with the literature discussed earlier – that receiving remittances is associated with better material conditions, even after controlling for a broad range of socioeconomic and demographic confounders. Remittance recipients, on average, report higher income, higher overall well-being, increased satisfaction with their current standard of living, decreased probability of perceiving national economic conditions as getting worse, and decreased probability of reporting having gone hungry in the past year.

---

[22] Underlying model estimates are available in Appendix Table A6.7.

These results are consistent with the logic that remittances allow households in the Global South to avoid the negative consequences of poor governance and limited access to public goods, and they lend meaningful support to the micro-level mechanism that we suggest links remittances and decreased subsequent immigration. When households receive remittances, they report being happier with the quality of and access to a wide variety of public amenities. They also report better overall well-being and are better able to manage economic risk.

CONCLUSION

Policy makers in migrant destinations have experimented with a variety of economic statecraft tools to decrease immigration, and so far, have little to show for their efforts. We suggest – and provide evidence – that remittances increase recipients' satisfaction with local amenities which, we argue, manifests in lower subsequent emigration. This, by itself, is an important extension of existing work on the political consequences of remittances (e.g., Ahmed 2012; Doyle 2015). Using bilateral migration data for a global sample of dyads and panel data for unauthorized immigration to the United States, we show that remittances are associated with decreased migration. And we demonstrate that the United States – and other migrant origin countries – can increase remittances by using temporary guest worker programs and disaster-related protections that provide immigrants with labor market access.

We contribute to a growing literature on how advanced democracies respond to migration. Unlike most of this literature, which focuses on building of walls (Hassner and Wittenberg 2015), the use of foreign aid and trade (Carbaugh 2007; Bermeo and Leblang 2015), or the deployment of military force (Weiner and Münz 1997), our arguments and evidence suggest that an effective way to manage demand for entry is to allow migrants temporary labor market access. Our emphasis on host-country labor market policies and their effect on subsequent migration also puts us in dialogue with emergent literature on what Hollifield (2004) called the "migration state" and what a new wave of scholars terms "migration diplomacy" (Adamson and Tsourapas 2019). Finally, we add to a burgeoning literature on the social, economic, and political consequences of remittances (e.g., Katz and Stark 1986; Massey et al. 1993; Singer 2010; Doyle 2015; Escribà-Folch, Wright, and Meseguer 2022).

From a theoretical perspective, these results suggest that labor market policies should be included in the arsenal of tools related to economic statecraft – they belong to a set of policies that politicians can use to control immigration (Adamson and Tsourapas 2019). Allowing some migrants an opportunity to work in the destination country's labor market induces higher migrant wages which, in turn, results in larger remittance flows. Our argument highlights the fact that, unlike aid or trade, remittances accrue quickly and directly to potential emigrants. This means that remittances can be more expediently deployed to enhance the recipient's satisfaction with local amenities than more aggregated and slower-moving flows like aid or trade. As advanced democracies increasingly seek to leverage conventional tools of economic statecraft to limit immigration, we suggest they turn to policies that increase remittances to developing countries. By contrast, policies that discourage or reduce these flows, such as a remittance tax or outright prohibition, may have the unintended consequence of increasing immigration.

APPENDIX TABLE A6.1 *Bilateral remittances and bilateral migration*

	Dependent variable: $\log(EmigrationRate_{odt})$			
	Global	South–North	Global	South–North
	(1)	(2)	(3)	(4)
$\log(Remittances_{odt-1})$	−0.252***	−0.308***	−0.397***	−0.441***
	(0.025)	(0.059)	(0.067)	(0.085)
$\log(Aid_{odt-1})$			−0.021	−0.014
			(0.023)	(0.025)
$\log(Trade_{odt-1})$			−0.088	−0.060
			(0.055)	(0.068)
$\log(MigrantStock_{odt-1})$	1.209***	1.233***	1.350***	1.376***
	(0.025)	(0.063)	(0.069)	(0.086)
Constant	−17.613***	−16.919***	−17.130***	−17.613***
	(0.466)	(1.060)	(1.482)	(1.724)
Observations	92,904	16,046	11,327	9,808
Gravity controls	Yes	Yes	Yes	Yes
Origin*year FEs	Yes	Yes	Yes	Yes
Destination*year FEs	Yes	Yes	Yes	Yes

Note: ***$p < 0.01$, **$p < 0.05$, *$p < 0.1$. Models estimated using PPML. All models include origin*year and destination*year fixed effects and a standard set of gravity controls: logged distance, contiguity, previously same country, common official language, and historical colonial relationship. Robust standard errors clustered by country pair in parentheses.

APPENDIX TABLE A6.2 *Bilateral remittances and bilateral migration: dyad fixed effects*

	Dependent variable: $\log(EmigrationRate_{odt})$			
	Global	South–North	Global	South–North
	(1)	(2)	(3)	(4)
$\log(Remittances_{odt-1})$	–0.177**	–0.084	–0.771***	–0.316
	(0.071)	(0.161)	(0.166)	(0.295)
$\log(Aid_{odt-1})$			–0.008	–0.016
			(0.030)	(0.031)
$\log(Trade_{odt-1})$			0.143	0.489**
			(0.224)	(0.247)
$\log(MigrantStock_{odt-1})$	5.238***	7.513***	6.349***	7.914***
	(0.430)	(0.579)	(0.703)	(0.931)
Constant	–60.104***	–82.769***	–73.290***	–92.334***
	(4.700)	(6.023)	(7.823)	(10.093)
Observations	45,131	14,309	9,661	8,690
Origin*year FEs	Yes	Yes	Yes	Yes
Destination*year FEs	Yes	Yes	Yes	Yes
Dyad FEs	Yes	Yes	Yes	Yes

Note: ***$p < 0.01$, **$p < 0.05$, *$p < 0.1$. Models estimated using PPML. All models include origin*year, destination*year, and dyad fixed effects. Robust standard errors clustered by country pair in parentheses.

APPENDIX TABLE A6.3 *Bilateral remittances and bilateral migration:*
first differences

	Dependent variable: $\log(EmigrationRate_{odt})$			
	Global	South–North	Global	South–North
	(1)	(2)	(3)	(4)
$\log(Remittances_{odt-1})$	−0.098**	−0.147	−0.263**	−0.809***
	(0.049)	(0.157)	(0.116)	(0.244)
$\log(Aid_{odt-1})$			−0.007	−0.006
			(0.022)	(0.021)
$\log(Trade_{odt-1})$			0.058	0.089
			(0.128)	(0.138)
$\log(MigrantStock_{odt-1})$	1.022***	0.976***	1.014***	1.014***
	(0.017)	(0.032)	(0.034)	(0.039)
Constant	−16.211***	−15.313***	−16.528***	−16.536***
	(0.446)	(0.945)	(0.881)	(0.937)
Observations	45,646	10,847	6,817	6,163
Gravity controls	Yes	Yes	Yes	Yes
Origin*year FEs	Yes	Yes	Yes	Yes
Destination*year FEs	Yes	Yes	Yes	Yes

Note: ***$p < 0.01$, **$p < 0.05$, *$p < 0.1$. Models estimated using PPML. Measures of remittances, aid, and trade are all in first differences. All models include origin*year and destination*year fixed effects and a standard set of gravity controls: logged distance, contiguity, previously same country, common official language, and historical colonial relationship. Robust standard errors clustered by country pair in parentheses.

APPENDIX TABLE A6.4 *Remittances and the demand for unauthorized entry to the United States*

	Dependent variable: $\log(ApprehensionRate_{it})$			
	Global (1)	Western Hemisphere (2)	Global (3)	Western Hemisphere (4)
$\log(Remittances/GDP_{it-1})$	−0.377* (0.194)	−0.406** (0.193)	−0.338* (0.183)	−0.386** (0.189)
$\log(Aid/GDP_{it-1})$			0.074 (0.251)	0.058 (0.277)
$\log(MigrantStock_{it-1})$	5.142*** (1.039)	5.473*** (1.048)	5.318*** (1.091)	5.641*** (1.105)
Constant	−14.247 (49.201)	−11.738 (50.881)	−14.154 (48.800)	−12.171 (49.446)
Observations	714	374	586	361
Controls	Yes	Yes	Yes	Yes
Origin country FEs	Yes	Yes	Yes	Yes

Note: *** $p < 0.01$, ** $p < 0.05$, * $p < 0.1$. Models estimated using PPML. All models include country fixed effects and control variables: GDP ratio, Gini ratio, logged origin country population, natural disaster death rate, civil war, logged average days for asylum hearing, logged Border Patrol staff, logged total visas, change in US unemployment rate, origin country homicide rate, and logged migrant stocks. Robust standard errors clustered by origin country in parentheses.

		Dependent variable: $\log(Remittances/GDP_{it})$			
	(1)	(2)	(3)	(4)	(5)
$\log(AllVisas_{odt-1})$	0.016***				
	(0.00)				
$\log(SeasonalVisas_{odt-1})$		0.014			
		(0.01)			
$\log(SkillVisas_{odt-1})$			−0.007		
			(0.00)		
$\log(EdVisas_{odt-1})$				0.001	
				(0.00)	
$\log(FamilyVisas_{odt-1})$					0.018***
					(0.00)
$\log(MigrantStock_{odt-1})$	0.019***	0.125***	0.055***	0.025***	0.013***
	(0.00)	(0.03)	(0.01)	(0.00)	(0.00)
Constant	0.333*	8.674***	3.180***	0.436**	0.498**
	(0.19)	(3.16)	(0.92)	(0.20)	(0.21)
Observations	17,187	611	3,695	16,473	16,667
Controls	Yes	Yes	Yes	Yes	Yes
Origin*year FEs	Yes	Yes	Yes	Yes	Yes
Destination*year FEs	Yes	Yes	Yes	Yes	Yes

Note: *** $p < 0.01$, ** $p < 0.05$, * $p < 0.1$. Models estimated using OLS. All models include origin*year and destination*year fixed effects. Controls: GDP per capita ratio, change in exchange rate ratio, logged migrant stocks, logged distance, contiguity, previously same country, common official language, and historical colonial relationship. Robust standard errors clustered by country pair in parentheses.

APPENDIX TABLE A6.6: *Remittance receipt and satisfaction with public goods*

Dependent variable:	Healthcare (1)	Education (2)	Affordable housing (3)	Air quality (4)	Transit (5)	Water quality (6)	Roads (7)	Local amen. (PCA) (8)
Receive remit.	0.010*** (0.003)	0.003 (0.003)	0.024*** (0.003)	-0.004 (0.003)	0.011*** (0.003)	0.006** (0.003)	0.008*** (0.003)	0.010*** (0.002)
Secondary ed.	-0.021*** (0.003)	-0.029*** (0.003)	-0.021*** (0.003)	-0.041*** (0.002)	-0.010*** (0.003)	-0.019*** (0.002)	-0.015*** (0.003)	-0.021*** (0.002)
Tertiary ed.	-0.060*** (0.004)	-0.095*** (0.004)	-0.057*** (0.004)	-0.093*** (0.003)	-0.057*** (0.004)	-0.058*** (0.003)	-0.045*** (0.004)	-0.066*** (0.003)
Female	0.017*** (0.002)	0.023*** (0.002)	0.003* (0.002)	-0.014*** (0.001)	0.020*** (0.001)	-0.001 (0.001)	0.033*** (0.002)	0.013*** (0.001)
Age	-0.000*** (0.000)	0.000*** (0.000)	-0.000* (0.000)	0.000*** (0.000)	0.000*** (0.000)	-0.000 (0.000)	0.001*** (0.000)	0.000*** (0.000)
2nd incomequint.	0.019*** (0.002)	0.014*** (0.002)	0.026*** (0.003)	-0.001 (0.002)	0.019*** (0.002)	0.014*** (0.002)	0.014*** (0.002)	0.016*** (0.002)

(continued)

APPENDIX TABLE A6.6: (continued)

3rd income quint.	0.027***	0.018***	0.039***	-0.011***	0.033***	0.019***	0.030***	0.023***
	(0.003)	(0.003)	(0.003)	(0.002)	(0.003)	(0.003)	(0.003)	(0.002)
4th income quint.	0.047***	0.027***	0.055***	-0.021***	0.049***	0.025***	0.042***	0.034***
	(0.003)	(0.003)	(0.003)	(0.003)	(0.003)	(0.003)	(0.003)	(0.002)
5th income quint.	0.068***	0.033***	0.073***	-0.035***	0.061***	0.038***	0.055***	0.045***
	(0.004)	(0.004)	(0.004)	(0.004)	(0.004)	(0.003)	(0.004)	(0.003)
Unemployed	-0.024***	-0.023***	-0.045***	-0.030***	-0.012***	-0.019***	-0.008***	-0.023***
	(0.003)	(0.003)	(0.003)	(0.003)	(0.003)	(0.003)	(0.003)	(0.002)
Household size	-0.001***	-0.001***	0.002***	-0.001***	-0.001**	-0.001**	-0.002***	-0.001***
	(0.000)	(0.000)	(0.000)	(0.000)	(0.000)	(0.000)	(0.000)	(0.000)
Constant	0.521***	0.635***	0.464***	0.793***	0.535***	0.649***	0.454***	0.575***
	(0.005)	(0.005)	(0.005)	(0.004)	(0.005)	(0.004)	(0.005)	(0.004)
Observations	978,616	984,850	950,276	997,746	978,085	1,002,175	992,703	829,677
Country*year FEs	Yes	Yes	Yes	Yes	Yes	Yes	Yes	Yes

Note: * $p < 0.10$, ** $p < 0.05$, *** $p < 0.01$ All models estimated using OLS and country*year combination fixed effects. Robust standard errors clustered by country*year combination in parentheses.

APPENDIX TABLE A6.7 *Remittance receipt and well-being*

Dependent variable:	log(income)	Well-being (0–10)	Satisfied w/ standard of living	Econ. conditions worsening	Gone hungry in last year
	(1)	(2)	(3)	(4)	(5)
Receive remit.	0.036***	0.168***	0.024***	-0.009***	-0.021***
	(0.008)	(0.013)	(0.003)	(0.002)	(0.004)
Secondary ed.	0.057***	0.314***	0.007**	0.016***	-0.044***
	(0.006)	(0.010)	(0.003)	(0.002)	(0.004)
Tertiary ed.	0.042***	0.603***	0.024***	0.027***	-0.056***
	(0.010)	(0.014)	(0.004)	(0.003)	(0.005)
Female	-0.001	0.135***	0.014***	0.003*	-0.003
	(0.003)	(0.009)	(0.002)	(0.001)	(0.002)
Age	-0.003***	-0.013***	-0.002***	0.001***	0.0002***
	(0.000)	(0.000)	(0.000)	(0.000)	(0.000)
2nd income quint.	1.606***	0.336***	0.053***	-0.016***	-0.059***
	(0.039)	(0.013)	(0.003)	(0.002)	(0.004)

(continued)

APPENDIX TABLE A6.7 *(continued)*

3rd income quint.	2.125***	0.588***	0.100***	-0.026***	-0.092***
	(0.046)	(0.016)	(0.003)	(0.002)	(0.006)
4th income quint.	2.576***	0.840***	0.150***	-0.035***	-0.116***
	(0.050)	(0.019)	(0.004)	(0.003)	(0.008)
5th income quint.	3.306***	1.223***	0.227***	-0.045***	-0.135***
	(0.055)	(0.022)	(0.005)	(0.003)	(0.010)
Unemployed	-0.064***	-0.420***	-0.106***	0.039***	0.058***
	(0.008)	(0.016)	(0.003)	(0.003)	(0.006)
Household size	0.188***	0.058***	0.009***	-0.002***	-0.007***
	(0.004)	(0.002)	(0.000)	(0.000)	(0.001)
Constant	5.761***	4.396***	0.495***	0.257***	0.230***
	(0.047)	(0.030)	(0.006)	(0.004)	(0.010)
Observations	1,084,734	1,068,550	1,047,533	1,084,734	239,700
Country*year FEs	Yes	Yes	Yes	Yes	Yes

Note: * $p < 0.10$, ** $p < 0.05$, *** $p < 0.01$. All models estimated using OLS and country*year combination fixed effects. Robust standard errors clustered by country*year combination in parentheses.

7

Conclusion

Migration and the Future of Globalization

International migration is a defining phenomenon of our time. While humans have moved across long distances for millennia, migration has taken on renewed political importance in the current era. Even before COVID-19 put an abrupt end to cross-border migration in 2020, restrictions on border entry and citizenship have increased as policymakers increasingly see immigration as a space where they can score easy political points. COVID-19 has disrupted supply chains, altered migration routes, and scuttled (some) efforts toward increased multilateralism. Domestically, advanced democracies are seeing structural adjustments in their labor markets, as citizens fundamentally rethink the role of work in their daily lives. Labor shortages and increased wages should, at least in theory, give rise to coalitions supporting the liberalization of immigration. Yet the politics of immigration have become so polarized that this may be the new "third rail" of democratic politics.

The arguments advanced in the prior chapters do not directly address social, cultural, or nativist concerns over migration. Nor do we advance normative recommendations regarding the level or rate of immigration. Our purpose in this book is to examine the nature of global migration and the effect of migration on globalization. Financial globalization we take to be a net good; access to global capital markets decreases borrowing costs to firms and governments and finances activities that increase economic growth. And remittances – financial flows which now exceed flows of FDI – accrue directly to families who use this income for consumption and investment. Beyond the relationship between migration and globalization, we have explored and synthesized arguments about why people emigrate, what influences the selection of destinations, and how migrants economically re-engage with their homeland. We have examined how and why migrant-sending and -receiving countries leverage policy tools to achieve immigration-related economic goals.

While we have covered vast amounts of theoretical and empirical ground in this volume, we want to emphasize three overarching contributions. First and fundamentally, politics is an essential component of any framework attempting to understand the decision to migrate and the processes informing a migrant's destination. Potential migrants respond to domestic conditions – their perceptions of effective governance, provision of public goods, and prospects for political inclusion – both in their homelands and in their range of potential destinations.

In a sense, this is hardly surprising. Political decisions directly affect human well-being, which, in turn, influences migration decisions. More surprising is that little political economy research on migration focuses on political conditions at origin, or a destination country's internal political environment. This is in contrast to scholars in conflict studies who examine when civil war and regime transitions generate "forced" migration (e.g., Adhikari 2012; Braithwaite, Salehyan, and Savun 2019) and to research in migration studies that emphasizes the role of natural disasters and climate change in influencing an individual's aspiration to emigrate (e.g., Carling 2002; Aslany et al. 2021). Yet little attention is paid to how more regular, "day-to-day" political dynamics influence emigration decision-making. Our analysis in Chapter 2 represents an important step in this direction, demonstrating that potential emigrants' everyday perceptions of the political environment in which they live significantly shape whether they see emigration as attractive. Similarly, Chapter 3 shows that everyday modes of political inclusion intimately shape how emigrants select among potential destinations. Politics matters, not just for understanding large-scale conflict and displacement events, but also for understanding more regularized international labor migration. Political factors influence the environment where migrants choose to live and their ability to enter into civic and labor relationships with their host country. Institutional considerations matter, as do the potential migrant's perception of the hostility of the political environment, governance quality, control of corruption, and the rule of law.

Second, our work emphasizes that migration is an essential component of globalization. Immigration itself represents the globalization of labor markets; it is the transfer of skilled and unskilled labor across national borders. As we discuss in Chapters 4 and 5, migrants are also essential agents of *financial* globalization, facilitating the movement of portfolio and foreign direct investment. Because migrants have location-specific information – along with knowledge of home-country culture, language, and markets – they grease the wheels of international financial markets. Above and beyond a migrant's influence on a firm's investment behavior, migrants themselves transfer enormous financial sums across national borders in the form of remittances. These remittances have direct benefits to recipient households and generate political spillovers to recipient countries. As a whole, migrants as entrepreneurs, as conduits of information, and as remitters, help bind home and host markets and countries together in ways above and beyond what should be expected from a set of competitive, autonomous nation-states.

Third, both home and host countries use political tools to shape their connections with migrant populations. Migrant homelands are not passive agents in the global political economy. We show in Chapter 5 that fundamental decisions about who is part of a political community – who is a citizen – are influenced by home-country preferences regarding their expatriate population. The extension of citizenship rights by the homeland helps harness financial and human capital, essential for economic development and poverty reduction. But the provision of political rights to expatriates is a decision made by sovereign states; decisions that are, as we discuss in Chapter 5, often driven by political and economic calculation. Finally, in Chapter 6, we make a novel policy proposal: Migrant-receiving countries can decrease the flow of permanent migrants by opening up their labor markets. Expanding temporary labor market access to current migrants and increasing remittance flows dampens subsequent demand for migrant entry, an important finding in an era when policymakers tend to rely on less effective tools like foreign aid and free trade agreements.

MIGRATION, CLIMATE CHANGE, PANDEMICS, AND POPULISM

As we complete this manuscript during the early months of 2022, much has changed in the global political economy, while a great deal remains the same. Climate change continues to drive individuals and households to seek better lives in countries of the Global North, as it induces greater food insecurity and increases the frequency of natural disasters that generate human displacement. The current COVID-19 pandemic provides a simple rationale used by destination countries to close their borders to those seeking entry. The Biden administration has found it difficult, if not impossible, to end border restrictions erected during Donald Trump's presidency.

Restrictive entry policies in destination countries will continue to generate conflict so long as there is an enduring desire on the part of individuals to improve the quality of their own lives and those of their families. The most recent rounds of the GWP (2018–20) indicate that 25 percent of those surveyed intend to move abroad, with 63 percent of those people indicating a preferred destination in the Global North. As discussed in Chapter 2, there is a wide gap between intended and observed migration. But with the Intergovernmental Panel on Climate Change reporting in August 2021 that human-induced climate change continues to affect weather, generating "heatwaves, heavy precipitation, droughts, and tropical cyclones" (Masson-Delmotte et al. 2021, p. 1), the demand for exit will likely only increase. One critical question, of course, is whether climate change will increase migration within the Global South, or if it will drive more citizens from the Global South to pursue destinations in the Global North.

COVID-19 has led countries in the Global North to close their borders and implement unprecedented mobility restrictions that may be difficult to reverse. This casts a shadow of uncertainty on business travel and tourism, as well as on permanent and temporary migration. It is too early to tell whether migration in a post-COVID world will resemble patterns of mobility observed in 2019, or if it will be more like 1929 when destination countries, worried about unemployment and the spread of communism, largely kept their borders and labor markets closed to foreigners. The pandemic has unleashed a wave of scientific populism (Mede and Schäfer 2020) and energized those who seek to use a "fear of foreignness" as a justification to exclude migrants (Olivas Osuna and Rama 2021). It seems likely, but not certain, that these forces will help mobilize radical right-wing factions, generating political pressure to maintain border restrictions even after concerns over COVID-19 abate.

The COVID-19 pandemic does, however, shine light on the importance of migration and migrant networks for home countries. While too early for a full assessment, early indications are that migrant remittances are remarkably stable. Even with border closings limiting circular migration and business closures reducing economic opportunity, migrants continued to send extraordinary financial sums back to their homelands. Indications at the end of 2020 are that remittance flows continue to rise both in raw terms and as a share of the receiving country's GDP, while other economic flows saw dramatic declines.

What does the future hold for remittances? In Chapter 5, we show that migrant homelands can harness the financial capital of their diasporas by leveraging citizenship policy – providing expatriates with home-country citizenship after they naturalize abroad. Given that host-country entry and labor market policies are uncertain in a post-COVID world, it is in the homeland's economic interest to liberalize dual citizenship policies and work to remain connected to their diaspora. While renewed restrictions on entry may limit *new* migrant flows, homelands can work to deepen *existing* relationships with their expatriate communities to facilitate a continued transfer of financial and human capital and maintain international connections.

The provision of dual citizenship has important knock-on effects on global economic ties. In Appendix Table A7.1, we replicate the models of portfolio and foreign direct investment developed in Chapter 4 and include Vink et al.'s (2019) measure of dual citizenship provision.[1] The effect of dual citizenship is substantial: For portfolio investment, countries offering dual citizenship receive, on average, 62% more portfolio investment and 46% more FDI. With the disruption of supply chains and volatility of international trade, these results suggest that extending dual citizenship may be a strategic move for countries that see global economic integration as an engine of economic development for the migrant's homeland.

Migration also has important implications for host countries. As the United States and Western Europe emerge from pandemic-induced recessions, employers face an undersupply of labor in key industries, which hampers economic recovery. The result has been rapidly increasing labor costs, widespread labor shortages within some industries, and broader fears of inflationary pressures. Foreign labor has proved a crucial ingredient for economic growth in advanced economies, filling gaps in the workforce and contributing significantly to economic growth (Papademetriou and Sumption 2013). We suggest that lifting current restrictions on migration and human mobility may be crucial to a fuller economic recovery. Taking a longer-run look, wealthy democracies continue to face rapidly aging populations, raising concerns about labor supply and the ability to maintain current levels of social spending. Increasing immigration is likely to be essential to maintaining a globally competitive workforce (W. R. Kerr 2018).

A wealth of empirical research also documents that immigrants are more willing than natives to take on the risks of entrepreneurship. Immigrants are much more likely to use their skills to start businesses

---

[1] Because we include a variable measuring conditions in the investment recipient country, we exclude destination*year fixed effects and instead control for the recipient country's level of democracy and corruption.

that create new job opportunities for native workers (Azoulay et al. 2020). Often cited is the fact that immigrant entrepreneurs are largely responsible for the growth of leading technology firms in the US and Europe (S. P. Kerr and Kerr 2017). Migrants are engines of technological innovation, creating intellectual property at much higher rates than natives (Hunt and Gauthier-Loiselle 2010). Immigrants achieve all of this – filling labor force gaps, starting new businesses, and creating new jobs – with minimal labor market impacts for native workers. The most advanced empirical research finds that immigrants do not meaningfully displace natives, either in the form of reduced wages or employment (Card 1990; S. P. Kerr and Kerr 2011; Clemens and Hunt 2019; Peri and Yasenov 2019). The consensus is that on net, immigration is an economic boon to migrant-receiving countries, not a harm.

The arguments and evidence we present in Chapter 4 focus on the importance of migrant-specific information for capital allocation and economic gains for migrant *homelands*. With destination countries seeking to recover from the COVID-related recessions, the question whether migrants foster investment *into their host societies* is equally relevant.[2] As described in this book, migrants provide co-ethnics with information about opportunities, markets, products, and labor quality that exist in host countries. Migrants are likely to possess unique and actionable knowledge about business opportunities and market structures; they also likely have the expertise necessary to navigate administrative and legal regulations in their host country (Morales 2021). As low- and middle-income countries become larger *sources* of investment capital, migrant networks could play a particularly important role in allocating these capital flows (Perea and Stephenson 2017).

Does investment follow migrants into their host countries in a more systematic fashion? We extend our analysis in Chapter 4 here, analyzing

---

[2] Anecdotes of migrant-led investment in destination countries abound. For example, Intesa Sanpaolo, one of the largest banks in Italy today, opened offices in New York in the early 1900s, applying for a banking license to take deposits. The head of the Intesa Sanpaolo archives explained their rationale as follows: "The most important factor at the outset [of the twentieth century] was the focus on Italian migrants and the emergence of numerous Italian colonies in the United States" (Costa 2017). Italian banks at the turn of the twentieth century followed their migrants to the United States because the government of Italy wanted to ensure a steady flow of remittances back to the homeland (Zeitz and Leblang 2021). In the case of Italian banks, and financial institutions in general, the logic is that firms follow migrants because migrants are a potential customer base.

FDI flows into OECD countries as a function of international migration.[3] Greenfield FDI, projects that are new investments, provide a different way to examine the importance of migrant networks. Using data from the *Financial Times* fDi Markets dataset, we have information on foreign investment projects from media sources, internal sources, reports from industry and investment promotion agencies, market research, and publication companies (fDi Markets 2021).[4] Importantly, fDi Markets provides the investment origin country o and investment destination country d for each project. We use these project-level data to create a dyadic panel dataset of greenfield FDI and bilateral migration flows. We focus on the *count* of new projects from country o to country d at time t as our primary dependent variable, but we also leverage additional data on estimated *job creation*.

As with our earlier analyses, we utilize PPML estimation with origin*-year and destination*year fixed effects to analyze bilateral greenfield FDI flows. Our results are presented in Appendix Table A7.2. Column (1) shows that increased migrant *flows* from country o to country d are associated with increased greenfield FDI flows along that same corridor. Each 20 percent increase in logged bilateral migrant flows is associated with an additional foreign investment project each year, on average. While we do not have data on the net economic impact of these investments, we separately model the estimated number of new jobs associated with bilateral greenfield FDI in Column (2). Our results again suggest that migrant flows stimulate increases in employment opportunity in migrant destination countries. In short, these results demonstrate that migrants not only facilitate investment back to their home countries; they also facilitate investment *into their host countries*. This is another critical economic benefit of international migration.

Given this empirical reality, how should policymakers in destination countries approach immigration? One clear implication is that countries would economically benefit from increasing immigration flows. Our results in Chapter 3 suggest that one efficient means to do this is by creating a more welcoming political environment for migrants. When countries provide a more permissive configuration of citizenship rights – and resist the rise of radical right, anti-immigrant parties – they are better able to attract migrants from around the world. These factors also have

---

[3] We focus on OECD destinations because they are the only countries for which we have annual bilateral migration flow data.
[4] See Owen (2019) for further discussion of the fdi Markets data.

an independent effect on foreign investment flows. Anecdotally, anti-immigrant legislation in the United States, specifically the passage of SB 1070 in Arizona, signaled that state's hostility to foreigners, which spilled over to foreign investment inflows (Andrews, Leblang, and Pandya 2018). Additionally, restrictions imposed on foreign countries as part of Donald Trump's travel ban led to an increase in offshoring, resulting in economic harm to localities (Glennon 2020). The lesson is clear: Crafting an attractive political environment for potential immigrants makes countries more economically competitive, while restricting immigrant rights creates new economic harms.

We test this proposition directly in Columns (3) and (4) of Appendix Table A7.2, adding our measures of investment destination country *d*'s citizenship policies and support for radical right parties. The political environment for immigrants has a direct, independent relationship with both the count of new bilateral FDI projects and the estimated number of new jobs created. A three-point increase in the political environment index is associated with two additional foreign investment projects each year, and roughly 75 new jobs; these opportunities, especially if they flow to areas that are depressed or experiencing economic transition, are an unambiguous benefit for the receiving community. By contrast, increasing support for the radical right parties depresses investment. By creating a political environment that is open to the political integration of migrants, countries can attract foreign investment and create new jobs. As countries continue to confront the economic fallout of COVID-19, it is essential to remember that restricting migration also restricts globalization, with deleterious economic consequences.

SUMMING UP AND LOOKING AHEAD: DIRECTIONS FOR FUTURE RESEARCH

There is a strong backlash to international migration and globalization in advanced democracies. Whatever its causes, our results suggest that there will be meaningful, negative economic consequences of this backlash. Communities in the United States and Europe will miss out on new economic opportunities and may experience more acute labor shortages. Capital flows to emerging economies may stall in response. The growth in remittances is likely to slow if migration restrictionists have their way, leading to increasing poverty and inequality and also reducing house-holds' ability to cope with economic crisis, climate change, and food insecurity. We do not make a normative case for or against international migration in this book – something accomplished by others elsewhere.[5] However, our findings do contribute to a growing scholarly consensus that immigration confers significant benefits on the world economy – benefits that flow to both migrant-receiving and -sending countries (Clemens 2011).

Our efforts in this volume are to integrate theories and evidence regarding migration into the broader study of globalization. As globalization is a human construct, situating migration at the center makes sense. Moving research forward requires an appreciation that studies of migration, unlike those focusing on trade and capital flows, are limited by the availability of comprehensive and comparable data. International organizations such as the IMF and the WTO track global economic flows in a systematic fashion. Most data on migration stocks and flows are collected by destination countries, where there are differences in terms of the definition of who is a migrant and how the migrant's country of origin – country of birth, country of citizenship, or country of residence – is measured. Host countries also differ regarding the measurement of a migrant's level of education or skill level. Interestingly, and a subject well outside of this volume's focus, host countries rarely, if ever, measure exit or return migration.

The absence of an international organization governing migration does not mean that focusing on bilateral or multilateral agreements is a worthless endeavor. The WTO's General Agreement in Trade in Services includes Mode 4, a provision that attempts to capture the movement of persons who are party to service trade. The European Community's charter embraces free movement, and the Schengen Area is one where individuals can cross national borders without need of a passport or other official documentation. With the exception of an early paper by Orefice (2015), there is little scholarly work examining the relationship between trade agreements and temporary or permanent mobility. It is likely that these agreements stimulate both migration and, concomitantly, the movement of investment capital as well.

Additional efforts focusing on the determinants of irregular, undocumented, or mixed migration are also essential from a policy-making and humanitarian perspective. Both the United States and the EU are on the receiving end as millions of men, women, children, and families cross borders in hopes of obtaining a better life. Some, perhaps most, are fleeing

---

[5] Recent empirical studies that make normative claims in favor of migration include Legrain (2020) and Nowrasteh and Powell (2020). Collier (2013) and Borjas (2016) take the opposite position.

persecution, war, and conflict and are thus subject, in theory at least, to protection under the 1951 United Nations Refugee Convention. Others, however, are fleeing natural disasters – such as those fleeing Hurricanes Eta and Iota, which hit Central America's Northern Triangle in November of 2020 – or slow onset climate change that has ravaged agriculture across the African continent for the last three decades.

The tools utilized in this volume and the frameworks provided may help us better understand the factors that generate climate migration. While climate change is an existential challenge, some communities are able to leverage technology to help with adaptation, resulting in stable food supplies, while others experience levels of food insecurity such that technological fixes are impossible. Migration, especially under conditions of climate change, is adaptation, providing households with mechanisms to help support their families. Whether remittances help communities build resilience, or help recipient households become food secure from season to season, is an increasingly urgent question with human and policy consequences.

Likewise, a deeper examination of temporary migration programs that help transfer human and financial capital to home countries may be a mechanism that serves homelands, while pacifying nativist and radical right-wing factions in destination countries. These groups may be more accommodating of policies that provide entry for temporary labor and that have the promise of building the economies of countries of origin such that it decreases the demand for entry. This, of course, depends on the ability of political entrepreneurs to craft policies and political messages that tie economic progress to the promise of migration.

A focus on the role of adaptation to climate change is intimately related to another blind spot in existing research: the dynamics of migration *within* the Global South. This belies the fact that the *plurality* of international migration occurs between countries in the Global South (World Bank Group 2016). While there is certainly some literature on this phenomenon (Hujo and Piper 2007; Ratha and Shaw 2007; and Gindling 2009), political economy scholars have yet to sufficiently tackle this project.[6] Our efforts to track both the flow of migrants across South–South corridors and the knock-on effect of financial flows within this same corridor is just the tip of the iceberg; much more work in this area would be a welcome addition to the vast majority of existing literature that focuses on advanced

---

[6] See Gaikwad, Hanson, and Toth (2021) for a notable and innovative exception.

economies as the only primary destinations. Do the same push and pull factors that motivate people to migrate to the Global North apply equally to destinations in the Global South, especially those who are induced to migrate as a form of adaptation to climate change? Do we need to construct new theories of international migration with less emphasis on factors such as wage differentials and political tolerance, or are these sufficient to understand this facet of the phenomenon? If we fail to answer these questions, we may miss explaining a significant proportion of migration with its own consequences and policy implications.

PUBLIC OPPOSITION TO IMMIGRATION

Despite the clear implication that international migration is a net economic good, the political reality is that mass publics in advanced democracies often oppose immigration. This is especially the case in the current era. While public opinion on immigration has not become more restrictionist per se (see Kustov, Laaker, and Reller 2021), the politicization of existing immigration attitudes has led to a surging anti-immigrant political movement in the United States and Western Europe. In the United States, this manifested in the election of Donald Trump, and in Europe, the successful Brexit referendum and the rise of radical right parties (Jensen, Quinn, and Weymouth 2017; Colantone and Stanig 2019). In each case, concerns about the economic and social impact of immigration were at the forefront of debate.

Why do voters oppose immigration on the grounds that it generates economic and social harms, despite a broad consensus that the *opposite* is true? Answering this question is outside the scope of our volume, but we highlight recent research on the broader impacts of economic globalization. Our research concludes that if countries want to harness the economic benefits of globalization, embracing immigration is essential. Support for globalization, however, is hardly unambiguous. While globalization brings benefits, it also has distributional consequences and increases exposure to exogenous economic shocks, generating winners and losers. Politicians, especially those representing perspectives distant from the median voter, exploit this distributional conflict by laying the blame for society's woes at the feet of globalization. Politicians signal support for protectionist policies to gain electoral advantage (Feigenbaum and Hall 2015), especially in districts exposed to international trade shocks (e.g., Autor et al. 2020; Baccini and Weymouth 2021). But politicians not only appeal to voters' material interests. They also cultivate support by stoking cultural conflict, harping on the ways in which foreign ideas, cultures, norms, and, ultimately, people, compete with home-country traditions and values (Margalit 2012, 2019; Inglehart and Norris 2017).

It is clear how migration enters this equation. Unemployment (Golder 2003) and recession-induced economic anxiety (Goldstein and Peters 2014) generate increased opposition to immigration, especially in areas where foreign-born populations live in key constituencies (Dancygier 2010). Economic harms – or prospective fears of future harms – may trigger anxieties related to status loss and lead to more immigration opposition (Jetten, Mols, and Postmes 2015; Mols and Jetten 2016; Smeekes et al. 2018; Jetten, Mols, and Steffens 2021; Parker 2021) and greater support for far-right parties (Betz 1994; Margalit 2019; Rhodes-Purdy, Navarre, and Utych 2021), especially among (white) men (Baccini and Weymouth 2021). This suggests that the distributional effects of globalization likely drive both opposition to immigration and support for far-right, anti-globalization parties. In other words, it is likely not the distributional effects of migration itself – again, the weight of evidence indicates that migrants create economic benefits for natives – but rather broader opposition to globalization and the public's concerns about the distributional consequences of global economic integration. Immigration serves as a useful scapegoat for politicians and other political entrepreneurs, who mobilize supporters by characterizing globalization as embodying cultural and economic forces beyond their control (Inglehart and Norris 2017; Colantone and Stanig 2019).

The political reality, therefore, is that many citizens of migrant destinations desire to limit or control immigration, and reelection-seeking politicians will pursue policies that restrict human mobility. How do our argument and findings speak to this fact? In Chapter 2, we stress another empirical reality: Most people would *rather not migrate* unless they felt it was necessary. When potential emigrants are satisfied with the political environment in which they live, they are far less likely to pursue emigration. Quality delivery of public goods, transparent and accountable political institutions, and a sense of physical safety all foster *voluntary immobility* – in other words, they make non-migration preferable to migration.

A clear policy implication follows: if politicians in migrant-receiving countries can foster improved governance in migrant-sending countries, they may be able to reduce immigration pressures. How might they achieve this? We made clear in Chapter 6 that the general use of development assistance – foreign aid – is unlikely to meaningfully reduce immigration. However, aid that is specifically targeted at improving public goods, making political institutions more accountable, and providing physical safety may be more effective. Indeed, some recent results suggest that *targeted* aid that improves social services can reduce migration flows (Lanati and Thiele 2018). In short, politicians interested in reducing immigration pressures must recognize that most people would rather *not* emigrate – especially if they could enjoy a more amenable political environment without having to do so.

Even in the face of weak governance, the desire to remain at home is strong – if potential migrants have sufficient *private* resources to acquire basic needs and invest in education, health, and safety. Our results in Chapter 6 show that when migrant-sending countries receive greater private capital in the form of remittances, emigration decreases significantly. This is consistent with the notion that remittances foster voluntary immobility. Politicians who want to control immigration can leverage this relationship: By stimulating greater remittance flows, they can meaningfully dampen immigration pressures. Destination countries, then, can leverage a range of policies to stimulate remittances, including regulating the fees charged by money transfer services, providing mechanisms to help migrants access banking (e.g., Zeitz and Leblang 2021), and, as we suggest in Chapter 6, broadening labor market access for temporary migrants, especially those from crisis-stricken countries.

In short, given that politicians face an electorate that wants to restrict immigration, we draw out policy proposals that achieve this goal. We emphasize policies that improve material conditions in migrant-sending countries such that potential emigrants no longer aspire to leave. We contend that such policies – which get at the heart of a migrant's decision calculus – are more likely to achieve the goal of controlling immigration than deterrence-focused policies, such as border fortifications and immigration enforcement. This suggests shifting the paradigm away from measures that focus on deterrence and toward programs that contribute to more transparent governance, the expansion of public goods, and the provision of basic human needs.

APPENDIX TABLE A7.1   *Dual citizenship and international investment*

Dependent variable:	$\log(PortfolioInvestment_{odt})$	$\log(FDI_{odt})$
	(1)	(2)
$DualCitizenship_{dt-1}$	0.488**	0.381**
	(0.122)	(0.139)
$\log(MigrantStock)_{odt-1}$	0.180**	0.285**
	(0.0281)	(0.0305)
$\log(Distance_{od})$	0.808**	−0.826**
	(0.110)	(0.121)
$Contiguous_{od}$	0.909**	1.282**
	(0.424)	(0.434)
$CommonLanguage_{od}$	0.910**	0.909**
	(0.230)	(0.247)
$GrowthCorr_{odt-1}$	0.206**	0.259**
	(0.0411)	(0.0530)
$CommonPeg_{odt-1}$	0.584**	0.468**
	(0.148)	(0.172)
$TaxTreaty_{odt-1}$	2.774**	3.250**
	(0.177)	(0.222)
$PTAs_{odt-1}$	−0.248**	−0.137**
	(0.0477)	(0.0511)
$Democracy_{dt-1}$	4.540**	1.329**
	(0.283)	(0.350)
$Corruption_{dt-1}$	−2.483**	−0.578*
	(0.255)	(0.299)
$\log(Trade_{odt-1})$	1.227**	0.933**
	(0.0306)	(0.0332)
Constant	−24.70**	−4.569**
	(1.147)	(1.293)
Observations	62,737	34,779
Origin*year FEs	Yes	Yes
Destination FEs	Yes	Yes

Note: * $p < 0.10$, ** $p < 0.05$. Models estimated with OLS. All models include origin * year fixed effects. All time-varying variables lagged by one year. Robust standard errors clustered by both origin and destination countries in parentheses.

APPENDIX TABLE A7.2 *Political environment in migrant destinations and greenfield FDI*

	Dependent variable: $FDIProjects_{odt}$			
	(1)	(2)	(3)	(4)
$\log(MigrantFlows_{odt-1})$	0.263**	0.232**	0.638**	0.693**
	(0.034)	(0.056)	(0.045)	(0.056)
$RightsIndex_{dt-1}$			0.189**	0.187**
			(0.027)	(0.041)
$RadicalRightChange_{dt-1}$			−0.021**	−0.043**
			(0.008)	(0.010)
$\log(Distance_{od})$	−0.216**	−0.285**	−0.074	0.140
	(0.040)	(0.054)	(0.084)	(0.098)
$Contiguous_{od}$	0.094	−0.046	0.021	0.139
	(0.112)	(0.181)	(0.181)	(0.281)
$CommonLanguage_{od}$	0.325**	0.089	0.013	0.028
	(0.080)	(0.114)	(0.175)	(0.209)
$GrowthCorr_{odt-1}$	−0.011	0.002	0.005	0.008
	(0.019)	(0.029)	(0.053)	(0.065)
$CommonPeg_{odt-1}$	−0.289**	−0.183**	−0.383*	−0.020
	(0.062)	(0.085)	(0.197)	(0.233)
$TaxTreaty_{odt-1}$	0.494**	1.022**	−0.127	0.020
	(0.120)	(0.197)	(0.250)	(0.277)
$PTAs_{odt-1}$	0.034**	0.058**	−0.006	−0.006
	(0.015)	(0.022)	(0.036)	(0.043)
Constant	2.309**	7.398**	−2.277**	−0.499
	(0.462)	(0.720)	(0.953)	(1.151)
Observations	29,899	29,686	19,639	19,501
Origin*year FEs	Yes	Yes	Yes	Yes

Note: * $p < 0.10$, ** $p < 0.05$. All models estimated using PPML. All time-varying variables lagged by one year. Robust standard errors clustered by both origin and destination countries in parentheses.

References

Abdih, Yasser, Ralph Chami, Jihad Dagher, and Peter Montiel. 2012. "Remittances and Institutions: Are Remittances a Curse?" *World Development* 40 (4): 657–66. https://doi.org/10.1016/j.worlddev.2011.09.014.

Acosta, Pablo, Cesar Calderón, Pablo Fajnzylber, and Humberto Lopez. 2008. "What Is the Impact of International Remittances on Poverty and Inequality in Latin America?" *World Development* 36 (1): 89–114. https://doi.org/10.1016/j.worlddev.2007.02.016.

Adams, Richard H., and Alfredo Cuecuecha. 2010. "Remittances, Household Expenditure and Investment in Guatemala." *World Development* 38 (11): 1626–41. https://doi.org/10.1016/j.worlddev.2010.03.003.

——— 2013. "The Impact of Remittances on Investment and Poverty in Ghana." *World Development* 50 (October): 24–40. https://doi.org/10.1016/j.worlddev.2013.04.009.

Adams, Richard H., and John Page. 2005. "Do International Migration and Remittances Reduce Poverty in Developing Countries?" *World Development* 33 (10): 1645–69. https://doi.org/10.1016/j.worlddev.2005.05.004.

Adamson, Fiona B., and Gerasimos Tsourapas. 2019. "Migration Diplomacy in World Politics." *International Studies Perspectives* 20 (2): 113–28. https://doi.org/10.1093/isp/ekyo15.

Adhikari, Prakash. 2012. "The Plight of the Forgotten Ones: Civil War and Forced Migration." *International Studies Quarterly* 56 (3): 590–606. https://doi.org/10.1111/j.1468-2478.2011.00712.x.

Adida, Claire L., and Desha M. Girod. 2011. "Do Migrants Improve Their Hometowns? Remittances and Access to Public Services in Mexico, 1995–2000." *Comparative Political Studies* 44 (1): 3–27. https://doi.org/10.1177/0010414010381073.

Agerberg, Mattias. 2019. "The Curse of Knowledge? Education, Corruption, and Politics." *Political Behavior* 41 (2): 369–99. https://doi.org/10.1007/s11109-018-9455-7.

Aggarwal, Reena, Asli Demirgüç-Kunt, and Maria Soledad Martínez Pería. 2011. "Do Remittances Promote Financial Development?" *Journal of Development Economics* 96 (2): 255–64. https://doi.org/10.1016/j.jdeveco.2010.10.005.

Aghion, Philippe, and Jean Tirole. 1997. "Formal and Real Authority in Organizations." *Journal of Political Economy* 105 (1): 1–29. https://doi.org/10.1086/262063.

Ahmed, Faisal Z. 2012. "The Perils of Unearned Foreign Income: Aid, Remittances, and Government Survival." *American Political Science Review* 106 (1): 146–65. https://doi.org/10.1017/S0003055411000475.

———. 2017. "Remittances and Incumbency: Theory and Evidence." *Economics & Politics* 29 (1): 22–47. https://doi.org/10.1111/ecpo.12086.

Alarian, Hannah M., and Michael Neureiter. 2021. "Values or Origin? Mandatory Immigrant Integration and Immigration Attitudes in Europe." *Journal of Ethnic and Migration Studies* 47 (5): 1006–27. https://doi.org/10.1080/1369183X.2019.1668756.

Alfaro, Laura, Sebnem Kalemli-Ozcan, and Vadym Volosovych. 2008. "Why Doesn't Capital Flow from Rich to Poor Countries? An Empirical Investigation." *Review of Economics and Statistics* 90 (2): 347–68. https://doi.org/10.1162/rest.90.2.347.

Allen, Nathan, Elizabeth Iams Wellman, and Benjamin Nyblade. 2019. "Extraterritorial Rights and Restrictions Dataset." https://www.evrrdataset.com/.

Amuedo-Dorantes, Catalina, and Cynthia Bansak. 2014. "Employment Verification Mandates and the Labor Market Outcomes of Likely Unauthorized and Native Workers." *Contemporary Economic Policy* 32 (3): 671–80. https://doi.org/10.1111/coep.12043.

Andrews, Sarah, David Leblang, and Sonal S. Pandya. 2018. "Ethnocentrism Reduces Foreign Direct Investment." *Journal of Politics* 80 (2): 697–700. https://doi.org/10.1086/694916.

Angelucci, Manuela. 2015. "Migration and Financial Constraints: Evidence from Mexico." *Review of Economics and Statistics* 97 (1): 224–28. https://doi.org/10.1162/REST_a_00487.

Angin, Merih, Albana Shehaj, and Adrian Shin. 2021. "IMF: International Migration Fund." Working paper.

Artuc, Erhan, Guido Porto, and Bob Rijkers. 2019. "Trading off the Income Gains and the Inequality Costs of Trade Policy." *Journal of International Economics* 120 (September): 1–45. https://doi.org/10.1016/j.jinteco.2019.05.001.

Asencio, Diego C. 1990. "Unauthorized Migration: An Economic Development Response." *Report of the Commission for the Study of International Migration and Cooperative Economic Development.* Washington, DC: Government Printing Office.

Aslany, Maryam, Jørgen Carling, Mathilde Bålsrud Mjelva, and Tone Sommerfelt. 2021. "Systematic Review of Determinants of Migration Aspirations." *QuantMig deliverable* 2.2. Southampton, UK: University of Southampton. https://www.prio.org/Publications/Publication/?x=12613.

Autor, David, David Dorn, Gordon Hanson, and Kaveh Majlesi. 2020. "Importing Political Polarization? The Electoral Consequences of Rising Trade Exposure." *American Economic Review* 110 (10): 3139–83. https://doi.org/10.1257/aer.20170011.

Awases, Magda, Akpa R. Gbary, Jennifer Nyoni, and Rufaro Chatora. 2004. *Migration of Health Professionals in Six Countries: A Synthesis Report.* Report. World Health Organization. www.afro.who.int/publications/migration-health-professionals-six-countries-synthesis-report.

Azizi, SeyedSoroosh. 2021. "The Impacts of Workers' Remittances on Poverty and Inequality in Developing Countries." *Empirical Economics* 60 (2): 969–91.

Azoulay, Pierre, Benjamin Jones, J. Daniel Kim, and Javier Miranda. 2020. "Immigration and Entrepreneurship in the United States." Working paper 27778. National Bureau of Economic Research. www.nber.org/papers/w27778.

Baccini, Leonardo, and Stephen Weymouth. 2021. "Gone For Good: Deindustrialization, White Voter Backlash, and US Presidential Voting." *American Political Science Review* 115 (2): 550–67. https://doi.org/10.1017/S0003055421000022.

Bailey, Thomas, and Roger Waldinger. 1991. "Primary, Secondary, and Enclave Labor Markets: A Training Systems Approach." *American Sociological Review* 56 (4): 432–45. https://doi.org/10.2307/2096266.

Baldwin, David A. 2020. *Economic Statecraft.* New edition. Princeton, NJ: Princeton University Press. https://press.princeton.edu/books/paperback/9780691204420/economic-statecraft.

Bancroft, George. 1849. "Letter to Lord Palmerson, January 26, 1849," Reprinted in Sen. *Ex. Docs.* 38, 36th Congress, 1st Session. 160(1860).

Bandelj, Nina. 2002. "Embedded Economies: Social Relations as Determinants of Foreign Direct Investment in Central and Eastern Europe." *Social Forces* 81 (2): 411–44. https://doi.org/10.1353/sof.2003.0001.

———. 2007. *From Communists to Foreign Capitalists: The Social Foundations of Foreign Direct Investment in Postsocialist Europe.* Princeton, NJ: Princeton University Press. https://press.princeton.edu/books/hardcover/9780691129129/from-communists-to-foreign-capitalists.

Bauböck, Rainer. 2003. "Towards a Political Theory of Migrant Transnationalism." *International Migration Review* 37 (3): 700–23. https://doi.org/10.1111/j.1747-7379.2003.tb00155.x.

Beine, Michel, and Christopher Parsons. 2015. "Climatic Factors as Determinants of International Migration." *Scandinavian Journal of Economics* 117 (2): 723–67. https://doi.org/10.1111/sjoe.12098.

Beine, Michel, Pauline Bourgeon, and Jean-Charles Bricongne. 2019. "Aggregate Fluctuations and International Migration." *Scandinavian Journal of Economics* 121 (1): 117–52. https://doi.org/10.1111/sjoe.12258.

Beine, Michel, Simone Bertoli, and Jesús Fernández-Huertas Moraga. 2016. "A Practitioners' Guide to Gravity Models of International Migration." *The World Economy* 39 (4): 496–512. https://doi.org/10.1111/twec.12265.

Bermeo, Sarah Blodgett, and David Leblang. 2015. "Migration and Foreign Aid." *International Organization* 69 (3): 627–57. https://doi.org/10.1017/S0020818315000119.

Bertocchi, Graziella, and Chiara Strozzi. 2008. "International Migration and the Role of Institutions." *Public Choice* 137 (1): 81–102. https://doi.org/10.1007/s11127-008-9314-x.

Bertoli, Simone, and Jesús Fernández-Huertas Moraga. 2013. "Multilateral Resistance to Migration." *Journal of Development Economics, Migration and Development,* 102 (May): 79–100. https://doi.org/10.1016/j.jdeveco.2012.12.001.

Betts, Alexander. 2009. "Institutional Proliferation and the Global Refugee Regime." *Perspectives on Politics* 7 (1): 53–58. https://doi.org/10.1017/S1537592709090082.

Betz, Hans-Georg. 1994. *Radical Right-Wing Populism in Western Europe.* London: Macmillan. https://doi.org/10.1007/978-1-349-23547-6.

Bloemraad, Irene. 2000. "Citizenship and Immigration: A Current Review." *Journal of International Migration and Integration* 1 (1): 9–37. https://doi.org/10.1007/s12134-000-1006-4.

———. 2004. "Who Claims Dual Citizenship? The Limits of Postnationalism, the Possibilities of Transnationalism, and the Persistence of Traditional Citizenship." *International Migration Review* 38 (2): 389–426. https://doi.org/10.1111/j.1747-7379.2004.tb00203.x.

Blonigen, Bruce A., and Miao Wang. 2004. "Inappropriate Pooling of Wealthy and Poor Countries in Empirical FDI Studies." Working paper 10378. National Bureau of Economic Research. https://www.nber.org/papers/w10378.

Böcker, Anita G.M. 1994. "Chain Migration over Legally Closed Borders: Settled Immigrants as Bridgeheads and Gatekeepers." *Netherlands' Journal of Social Sciences* 2: 87–106.

Bohn, Sarah, and Todd Pugatch. 2015. "U.S. Border Enforcement and Mexican Immigrant Location Choice." *Demography* 52 (5): 1543–70. https://doi.org/10.1007/s13524-015-0416-z.

Bollard, Albert, David McKenzie, and Melanie Morten. 2009. "The Remitting Patterns of African Migrants in the OECD." *Discussion paper 0921. CReAM Discussion Paper Series. Centre for Research and Analysis of Migration (CReAM),* Department of Economics, University College London. http://www.cream-migration.org/publ_uploads/CDP_21_09.pdf.

Bollard, Albert, David McKenzie, Melanie Morten, and Hillel Rapoport. 2011. "Remittances and the Brain Drain Revisited: The Microdata Show That More Educated Migrants Remit More." *World Bank Economic Review* 25 (1): 132–56. https://doi.org/10.1093/wber/lhr013.

Borjas, George J. 1989. "Economic Theory and International Migration." *International Migration Review* 23 (3): 457–85. https://doi.org/10.2307/2546424.

———. 2000. "Introduction." In *Issues in the Economics of Immigration,* edited by George J. Borjas, 1–14. Chicago: University of Chicago Press. https://www.nber.org/books-and-chapters/issues-economics-immigration/introduction-issues-economics-immigration.

2016. *We Wanted Workers: Unraveling the Immigration Narrative.* New York: WW Norton. https://wwnorton.com/books/We-Wanted-Workers/.

Boucher, Anna K., and Justin Gest. 2018. *Crossroads: Comparative Immigration Regimes in a World of Demographic Change.* Cambridge: Cambridge University Press. https://doi.org/10.1017/9781316416631.

Boyd, Monica. 1989. "Family and Personal Networks in International Migration: Recent Developments and New Agendas." *International Migration Review* 23 (3): 638–70. https://doi.org/10.1177/019791838902300313.

Braithwaite, Alex, Idean Salehyan, and Burcu Savun. 2019. "Refugees, Forced Migration, and Conflict: Introduction to the Special Issue." *Journal of Peace Research* 56 (1): 5–11. https://doi.org/10.1177/0022343318814128.

Brücker, Herbert, and Abdeslam Marfouk. 2013. *"Education, Gender and International Migration: Insights from a Panel-Dataset 1980–2010."* Mimeo. IAB. https://www.iab.de/en/daten/iab-brain-drain-data.aspx#How%20to%20cite.

Büthe, Tim, and Helen V. Milner. 2008. "The Politics of Foreign Direct Investment into Developing Countries: Increasing FDI through International Trade Agreements?" *American Journal of Political Science* 52 (4): 741–62. https://doi.org/10.1111/j.1540-5907.2008.00340.x.

Calderón Chelius, Leticia. 2003. *Voting at a Distance: Comparative Experiences of the Extension of Political Rights to Migrants.* Mexico City: Instituto Mora.

Cameron, A. Colin, Jonah B. Gelbach, and Douglas L. Miller. 2011. "Robust Inference With Multiway Clustering." *Journal of Business & Economic Statistics* 29 (2): 238–49. https://doi.org/10.1198/jbes.2010.07136.

Cameron, A. Colin, and Pravin K. Trivedi. 2005. *Microeconometrics: Methods and Applications.* Cambridge: Cambridge University Press. https://doi.org/10.1017/CBO9780511811241.

Carbaugh, Robert J. 2007. "Is International Trade a Substitute for Migration?" *Global Economy Journal* 7 (3). https://doi.org/10.2202/1524-5861.1297.

Card, David. 1990. "The Impact of the Mariel Boatlift on the Miami Labor Market." *ILR Review* 43 (2): 245–57. https://doi.org/10.1177/001979399004300205.

Carling, Jørgen. 2002. "Migration in the Age of Involuntary Immobility: Theoretical Reflections and Cape Verdean Experiences." *Journal of Ethnic and Migration Studies* 28 (1): 5–42. https://doi.org/10.1080/13691830120103912.

Carling, Jørgen, and Kerilyn Schewel. 2018. "Revisiting Aspiration and Ability in International Migration." *Journal of Ethnic and Migration Studies* 44 (6): 945–63. https://doi.org/10.1080/1369183X.2017.1384146.

Carrington, William, and Enrica Detragiache. 1998. *"How Big Is the Brain Drain?" Working paper 98/102.* Washington, DC: International Monetary Fund. https://www.imf.org/en/Publications/WP/Issues/2016/12/30/How-Big-is-the-Brain-Drain-2677.

Catrinescu, Natalia, Miguel Leon-Ledesma, Matloob Piracha, and Bryce Quillin. 2009. "Remittances, Institutions, and Economic Growth." *World Development* 37 (1): 81–92. https://doi.org/10.1016/j.worlddev.2008.02.004.

Cavalli-Sforza, Luigi Luca, Paolo Menozzi, and Alberto Piazza. 1994. *The History and Geography of Human Genes.* Princeton, NJ: Princeton University Press.

Chami, Ralph, Adolfo Barajas, Thomas F. Cosimano, Connel Fullenkamp, Michael T. Gapen, and Peter Montiel. 2008. *"Macroeconomic Consequences of Remittances." Occasional paper 259.* Washington, DC: International Monetary Fund. https://www.imf.org/external/pubs/ft/op/259/op259.pdf.

Chami, Ralph, Connel Fullenkamp, and Samir Jahjah. 2005. "Are Immigrant Remittance Flows a Source of Capital for Development?" *IMF Staff Papers* 52 (1): 55–81. https://doi.org/10.2307/30035948.

Chiozza, Giacomo, and H.E. Goemans. 2011. *Leaders and International Conflict.* Cambridge: Cambridge University Press.

Chiswick, Barry R., and Paul W. Miller. 1995. "The Endogeneity between Language and Earnings: International Analyses." *Journal of Labor Economics* 13 (2): 246–88. https://doi.org/10.1086/298374.

Choi, Inbom. 2003. "Korean Diaspora in the Making: Its Current Status and Impact on the Korean Economy." In *The Korean Diaspora in the World Economy: Special Report 15*, edited by C. Fred Bergsten and Inbom Choi, 9–29. Washington, DC: Peterson Institute for International Economics.

Clark, Ximena, Timothy J. Hatton, and Jeffrey G. Williamson. 2007. "Explaining U.S. Immigration, 1971–1998." *Review of Economics and Statistics* 89 (2): 359–73. https://doi.org/10.1162/rest.89.2.359.

Clemens, Michael A. 2011. "Economics and Emigration: Trillion-Dollar Bills on the Sidewalk?" *Journal of Economic Perspectives* 25 (3): 83–106. https://doi.org/10.1257/jep.25.3.83.

——— 2020. "The Emigration Life Cycle: How Development Shapes Emigration from Poor Countries." Discussion paper 13614. IZA. https://docs.iza.org/dp13614.pdf

Clemens, Michael A., and Hannah M. Postel. 2018. "Deterring Emigration with Foreign Aid: An Overview of Evidence from Low-Income Countries." *Population and Development Review* 44 (4): 667–93. https://doi.org/10.1111/padr.12184.

Clemens, Michael A., and Jennifer Hunt. 2019. "The Labor Market Effects of Refugee Waves: Reconciling Conflicting Results." *ILR Review* 72 (4): 818–57. https://doi.org/10.1177/0019793918824597.

Clemens, Michael A., and Lant Pritchett. 2019. "The New Economic Case for Migration Restrictions: An Assessment." *Journal of Development Economics* 138 (May): 153–64. https://doi.org/10.1016/j.jdeveco.2018.12.003.

Clemens, Michael, and Mariapia Mendola. 2020. "Migration from Developing Countries: Selection, Income Elasticity and Simpson's Paradox." Discussion paper 13612. IZA. http://ftp.iza.org/dp13612.pdf.

Clemens, Michael A., Steven Radelet, Rikhil R. Bhavnani, and Samuel Bazzi. 2012. "Counting Chickens When They Hatch: Timing and the Effects of Aid on Growth." *The Economic Journal* 122 (561): 590–617. https://doi.org/10.1111/j.1468-0297.2011.02482.x.

Cohen, Robin. 1997. *Global Diasporas: An Introduction.* London: Routledge. https://www.routledge.com/Global-Diasporas-An-Introduction/Cohen/p/book/9780415435512.

Cohen, Yinon, and Yitchak Haberfeld. 2001. "Self-Selection and Return Migration: Israeli-Born Jews Returning Home from the United States

During the 1980s." *Population Studies* 55 (1): 79–91. https://doi.org/10
.1080/00324720127675.

Colantone, Italo, and Piero Stanig. 2019. "The Surge of Economic Nationalism in
Western Europe." *Journal of Economic Perspectives* 33 (4): 128–51. https://
doi.org/10.1257/jep.33.4.128.

Collier, Paul. 2013. *Exodus: How Migration Is Changing Our World*. Oxford:
Oxford University Press. https://www.oxfordmartin.ox.ac.uk/publications/
exodus-how-migration-is-changing-our-world/.

Collyer, Michael. 2005. "When Do Social Networks Fail to Explain Migration?
Accounting for the Movement of Algerian Asylum-Seekers to the UK."
Journal of Ethnic and Migration Studies 31 (4): 699–718. https://doi.org/10
.1080/13691830500109852.

———, ed. 2013. *Emigration Nations: Policies and Ideologies of Emigrant
Engagement. Migration, Diasporas and Citizenship*. New York: Palgrave
Macmillan. https://doi.org/10.1057/9781137277107.

Combes, Jean-Louis, and Christian Ebeke. 2011. "Remittances and Household
Consumption Instability in Developing Countries." *World Development*,
Special Section (pp. 1204–70): Foreign Technology and Indigenous
Innovation in the Emerging Economies, 39 (7): 1076–89. https://doi.org/10
.1016/j.worlddev.2010.10.006.

Constant, Amelie, and Douglas S. Massey. 2002. "Return Migration by German
Guestworkers: Neoclassical versus New Economic Theories." *International
Migration* 40 (4): 5–38. https://doi.org/10.1111/1468-2435.00204.

Cooray, Arusha, and Friedrich Schneider. 2016. "Does Corruption Promote
Emigration? An Empirical Examination." *Journal of Population Economics*
29 (1): 293–310. https://doi.org/10.1007/s00148–015-0563-y.

Coppedge, Michael, John Gerring, Carl Henrik Knutsen, Staffan I. Lindberg, Jan
Teorell, David Altman, Michael Bernhard, et al. 2021. "V-Dem Codebook
V11." ID 3802627. Rochester, New York: V-Dem Institute. https://doi.org/
10.2139/ssrn.3802627.

Correia, Sergio. 2017. "A Feasible Estimator for Linear Models with Multi-Way
Fixed Effects." Working paper. http://scorreia.com/research/hdfe.pdf.

Correia, Sergio, Paulo Guimarães, and Tom Zylkin. 2020. "Fast Poisson
Estimation with High-Dimensional Fixed Effects." *Stata Journal* 20 (1):
95–115. https://doi.org/10.1177/1536867X20909691.

Costa, Barbara. 2017. "Mapping Italy's Banking History." Intesa Sanpaolo
World. 2017. https://www.world.intesasanpaolo.com/mapping-italys-
banking-history/.

Coval, Joshua D., and Tobias J. Moskowitz. 1999. "Home Bias at Home: Local
Equity Preference in Domestic Portfolios." *Journal of Finance* 54 (6):
2045–73. https://doi.org/10.1111/0022-1082.00181.

———. 2001. "The Geography of Investment: Informed Trading and Asset Prices."
Journal of Political Economy 109 (4): 811–41. https://doi.org/10.1086/322088.

Crawley, Heaven. 2010. *Chance or Choice? Understanding Why Asylum Seekers
Come to the UK*. London: British Refugee Council. https://pureportal
.coventry.ac.uk/en/publications/chance-or-choice-understanding-why-
asylum-seekers-come-to-the-uk.

Croke, Kevin, Guy Grossman, Horacio A. Larreguy, and John Marshall. 2016. "Deliberate Disengagement: How Education Can Decrease Political Participation in Electoral Authoritarian Regimes." *American Political Science Review* 110 (3): 579–600. https://doi.org/10.1017/S0003055416000253.

Czaika, Mathias, and Christopher R. Parsons. 2017. "The Gravity of High-Skilled Migration Policies." *Demography* 54 (2): 603–30. https://doi.org/10.1007/s13524-017-0559-1.

Czaika, Mathias, and Hein de Haas. 2011. "The Effectiveness of Immigration Policies." DEMIG Project paper 3. International Migration Institute. https://ora.ox.ac.uk/objects/uuid:7769e8a1-cd85-4d8e-ba2b-09420bd6cd83.

Dahl, Robert. 1971. *Polyarchy: Participation and Opposition.* New Haven, CT: Yale University Press. https://yalebooks.yale.edu/book/9780300015652/polyarchy.

Dancygier, Rafaela M. 2010. Immigration and Conflict in Europe. *Cambridge Studies in Comparative Politics.* Cambridge: Cambridge University Press. https://doi.org/10.1017/CBO9780511762734.

Dao, Thu Hien, Frédéric Docquier, Chris Parsons, and Giovanni Peri. 2018. "Migration and Development: Dissecting the Anatomy of the Mobility Transition." *Journal of Development Economics* 132 (May): 88–101. https://doi.org/10.1016/j.jdeveco.2017.12.003.

Délano, Alexandra. 2010. "Immigrant Integration vs. Transnational Ties? The Role of the Sending State." *Social Research* 77 (1): 237–68.

DeSipio, Louis. 2006. "Transnational Politics and Civic Engagement: Do Home-Country Political Ties Limit Latino Immigrant Pursuit of United States Civic Engagement and Citizenship?" In *Transforming Politics, Transforming America*, edited by Taeku Lee, S. Karthick Ramakrishnan, and Ricardo Ramírez, 106–26. Charlottesville, Virginia: University of Virginia Press.

Desmet, Klaus, Michel Le Breton, Ignacio Ortuno-Ortın, and Shlomo Weber. 2009. "Stability of Nations and Genetic Diversity." Working paper. https://www.eco.uc3m.es/personal/iortuno/stability27april2009.pdf.

Devillanova, Carlo, Francesco Fasani, and Tommaso Frattini. 2018. "Employment of Undocumented Immigrants and the Prospect of Legal Status: Evidence from an Amnesty Program." *ILR Review* 71 (4): 853–81. https://doi.org/10.1177/0019793917743246.

Diaz-Cayeros, Alberto, Beatriz Magaloni, and Barry R. Weingast. 2003. "Tragic Brilliance: Equilibrium Party Hegemony in Mexico." Unpublished manuscript. https://doi.org/10.2139/ssrn.1153510.

Dimant, Eugen, Tim Krieger, and Daniel Meierrieks. 2013. "The Effect of Corruption on Migration,1985–2000." *Applied Economics Letters*, June. https://www.tandfonline.com/doi/full/10.1080/13504851.2013.806776.

Dimant, Eugen, and Guglielmo Tosato. 2018. "Causes and Effects of Corruption: What Has Past Decade's Empirical Research Taught Us? A Survey." *Journal of Economic Surveys* 32 (2): 335–56. https://doi.org/10.1111/joes.12198.

Disdier, Anne-Célia, and Thierry Mayer. 2007. "Je t'aime, Moi Non plus: Bilateral Opinions and International Trade." *European Journal of*

Political Economy 23 (4): 1140–59. https://doi.org/10.1016/j.ejpoleco.2006
.09.021.

Docquier, Frédéric, Aysit Tansel, and Riccardo Turati. 2020. "Do Emigrants Self-Select Along Cultural Traits? Evidence from the MENA Countries." *International Migration Review* 54 (2): 388–422. https://doi.org/10.1177/0197918319849011.

Dodge, Rachel, Annette P. Daly, Jan Huyton, and Lalage D. Sanders. 2012. "The Challenge of Defining Wellbeing." *International Journal of Wellbeing* 2 (3). https://www.internationaljournalofwellbeing.org/index.php/ijow/article/view/89.

Dowding, Keith, and Peter John. 2008. "The Three Exit, Three Voice and Loyalty Framework: A Test with Survey Data on Local Services." *Political Studies* 56 (2): 288–311. https://doi.org/10.1111/j.1467-9248.2007.00688.x.

Dowding, Keith, Peter John, Thanos Mergoupis, and Mark Van Vugt. 2000. "Exit, Voice and Loyalty: Analytic and Empirical Developments." *European Journal of Political Research* 37 (4): 469–95. https://doi.org/10.1023/A:1007134730724.

Doyle, David. 2015. "Remittances and Social Spending." *American Political Science Review* 109 (4): 785–802. https://doi.org/10.1017/S0003055415000416.

Dreher, Axel, Jan-Egbert Sturm, and James Vreeland. 2009. "Development Aid and International Politics: Does membership on the UN Security Council influence World Bank decisions?" *Journal of Development Economics* 88: 1–18.

Duquette-Rury, Lauren. 2014. "Collective Remittances and Transnational Coproduction: The 3 × 1 Program for Migrants and Household Access to Public Goods in Mexico." *Studies in Comparative International Development* 49 (1): 112–39. https://doi.org/10.1007/s12116-014-9153-3.

Dustmann, Christian, and Anna Okatenko. 2014. "Out-Migration, Wealth Constraints, and the Quality of Local Amenities." *Journal of Development Economics, Land and Property Rights*, 110 (September): 52–63. https://doi.org/10.1016/j.jdeveco.2014.05.008.

Dustmann, Christian, and Francesco Fasani. 2016. "The Effect of Local Area Crime on Mental Health." *The Economic Journal* 126 (593): 978–1017. https://doi.org/10.1111/ecoj.12205.

Eichengreen, Barry, and Marc Flandreau. 1997. *Gold Standard In Theory & History*. 2nd ed. London: Routledge. https://www.routledge.com/Gold-Standard-In-Theory–History/Eichengreen-Flandreau/p/book/9780415150613.

Eichengreen, Barry, and David Leblang. 2008. "Democracy and Globalization." *Economics & Politics* 20 (3): 289–334. https://doi.org/10.1111/j.1468-0343.2007.00329.x.

Eichengreen, Barry, and Pipat Luengnaruemitchai. 2006. "Bond Markets as Conduits for Capital Flows: How Does Asia Compare?" Working paper 12408. National Bureau of Economic Research. https://www.nber.org/papers/w12408.

Elton, Edwin J., Martin J. Gruber, Stephen J. Brown, and William N. Goetzmann. 2003. *Modern Portfolio Theory and Investment Analysis*. Hoboken, NJ: Wiley.

Escobar, Cristina. 2017. "Migration and Franchise Expansion in Latin America." Comparative report 2017/1. Fiesole, Italy: Robert Schuman Centre for Advanced Studies, European University Institute.

Escribà-Folch, Abel, Covadonga Meseguer, and Joseph Wright. 2015. "Remittances and Democratization." *International Studies Quarterly* 59 (3): 571–86. https://doi.org/10.1111/isqu.12180.

———. 2018. "Remittances and Protest in Dictatorships." *American Journal of Political Science* 62 (4): 889–904. https://doi.org/10.1111/ajps.12382.

Escribà-Folch, Abel, Joseph Wright, and Covadonga Meseguer. 2022. *Migration and Democracy*. Princeton, NJ: Princeton University Press. https://press.princeton.edu/books/hardcover/9780691199382/migration-and-democracy.

European Union Trust Fund for Africa. 2016. "Annual Report."

Eurostat. 2020. "Eurostat – Migration and Asylum." 2020. https://ec.europa.eu/eurostat/web/migration-asylum.

Faist, Thomas. 2000. "Transnationalization in International Migration: Implications for the Study of Citizenship and Culture." *Ethnic and Racial Studies* 23 (2): 189–222. https://doi.org/10.1080/014198700329024.

fDi Markets. 2021. "fDi Markets: The In-Depth Crossborder Investment Monitor from the Financial Times." 2021. https://www.fdimarkets.com/.

Feigenbaum, James J., and Andrew B. Hall. 2015. "How Legislators Respond to Localized Economic Shocks: Evidence from Chinese Import Competition." *Journal of Politics* 77 (4): 1012–30. https://doi.org/10.1086/682151.

Felbermayr, Gabriel J., and Farid Toubal. 2012. "Revisiting the Trade-Migration Nexus: Evidence from New OECD Data." *World Development* 40 (5): 928–37. https://doi.org/10.1016/j.worlddev.2011.11.016.

Ferraz, Claudio, and Frederico Finan. 2011. "Electoral Accountability and Corruption: Evidence from the Audits of Local Governments." *American Economic Review* 101 (4): 1274–1311. https://doi.org/10.1257/aer.101.4.1274.

Fiorina, Morris P. 1978. "Economic Retrospective Voting in American National Elections: A Micro-Analysis." *American Journal of Political Science* 22 (2): 426–43. https://doi.org/10.2307/2110623.

FitzGerald, David. 2008. *A Nation of Emigrants: How Mexico Manages Its Migration*. Berkeley, California: University of California Press.

FitzGerald, David Scott. 2020. "Remote Control of Migration: Theorising Territoriality, Shared Coercion, and Deterrence." *Journal of Ethnic and Migration Studies* 46 (1): 4–22. https://doi.org/10.1080/1369183X.2020.1680115.

Fitzgerald, Jennifer. 2018. *Close to Home: Local Ties and Voting Radical Right in Europe*. Cambridge Studies in Public Opinion and Political Psychology. Cambridge: Cambridge University Press. https://doi.org/10.1017/9781108377218.

Fitzgerald, Jennifer, David Leblang, and Jessica C. Teets. 2014. "Defying the Law of Gravity: The Political Economy of International Migration." *World Politics* 66 (3): 406–45. https://doi.org/10.1017/S0043887114000112.

Fong, Eric, and Emi Ooka. 2002. "The Social Consequences of Participating in the Ethnic Economy." *International Migration Review* 36 (1): 125–46. https://doi.org/10.1111/j.1747-7379.2002.tb00074.x.

Fougère, Denis, and Mirna Safi. 2009. "Naturalization and Employment of Immigrants in France (1968-1999)." *International Journal of Manpower* 30 (1/2): 83–96. https://doi.org/10.1108/01437720910948410.

Freeman, Gary P. 1994. "Can Liberal States Control Unwanted Migration?" *The Annals of the American Academy of Political and Social Science* 534 (1): 17–30. https://doi.org/10.1177/0002716294534001002.

——— 1995. "Modes of Immigration Politics in Liberal Democratic States." *International Migration Review* 29 (4): 881–902. https://doi.org/10.1177/019791839502900401.

Freeman, Gary P., and Nedim Ögelman. 1998. "Homeland Citizenship Policies and the Status of Third Country Nationals in the European Union." *Journal of Ethnic and Migration Studies* 24 (4): 769–88. https://doi.org/10.1080/1369183X.1998.9976665.

Freinkman, Lev. 2002. *Role of the Diasporas in Transition Economies: Lessons from Armenia*. Washington, DC: World Bank.

French, Kenneth R., and James M. Poterba. 1991. "Investor Diversification and International Equity Markets." *American Economic Review* 81 (2): 222–26.

Frieden, Jeffry A. 1994. "Exchange Rate Politics: Contemporary Lessons from American History." *Review of International Political Economy* 1 (1): 81–103. https://doi.org/10.1080/09692299408434269.

——— 2012. "From the American Century to Globalization." In *The Short American Century: A Postmortem*, edited by Andrew J. Bacevich. Cambridge, Massachusetts: Harvard University Press. https://www.hup.harvard.edu/catalog.php?isbn=9780674725690&content=toc.

Fussell, Elizabeth. 2010. "The Cumulative Causation of International Migration in Latin America." *The Annals of the American Academy of Political and Social Science* 630 (1): 162–77. https://doi.org/10.1177/0002716210368108.

Gaikwad, Nikhar, Kolby Hanson, and Aliz Toth. 2021. *"Do International Employment Opportunities Impact Individuals' Political Preferences and Behavior?"* Unpublished manuscript. https://nikhargaikwad.com/resources/Gaikwad-Hanson-Toth-2021.pdf.

Gallup. 2021. "Gallup World Poll." 2021. https://www.gallup.com/analytics/318875/global-research.aspx.

Gamlen, Alan. 2008. "The Emigration State and the Modern Geopolitical Imagination." *Political Geography* 27 (8): 840–56. https://doi.org/10.1016/j.polgeo.2008.10.004.

——— 2019. *Human Geopolitics: States, Emigrants, and the Rise of Diaspora Institutions*. Oxford: Oxford University Press. https://doi.org/10.1093/oso/9780198833499.001.0001.

Gamlen, Alan, Michael E. Cummings, and Paul M. Vaaler. 2019. "Explaining the Rise of Diaspora Institutions." *Journal of Ethnic and Migration Studies* 45 (4): 492–516. https://doi.org/10.1080/1369183X.2017.1409163.

Gibson, John, and David McKenzie. 2011. "Eight Questions about Brain Drain." *Journal of Economic Perspectives* 25 (3): 107–28. https://doi.org/10.1257/jep .25.3.107.

———. 2012. "The Economic Consequences of 'Brain Drain' of the Best and Brightest: Microeconomic Evidence from Five Countries." *The Economic Journal* 122 (560): 339–75. https://doi.org/10.1111/j.1468-0297.2012.02498.x.

Gindling, Tim H. 2009. "South–South Migration: The Impact of Nicaraguan Immigrants on Earnings, Inequality and Poverty in Costa Rica." *World Development* 37 (1): 116–26. https://doi.org/10.1016/j.worlddev.2008.01 .013.

Giuliano, Paola, Antonio Spilimbergo, and Giovanni Tonon. 2006. "Genetic, Cultural and Geographical Distances." Discussion paper 2229. IZA. http:// ftp.iza.org/dp2229.pdf.

Giuliano, Paola, and Marta Ruiz-Arranz. 2009. "Remittances, Financial Development, and Growth." *Journal of Development Economics* 90 (1): 144–52. https://doi.org/10.1016/j.jdeveco.2008.10.005.

Glennon, Britta. 2020. "How Do Restrictions on High-Skilled Immigration Affect Offshoring? Evidence from the H-1B Program." Working paper 27538. National Bureau of Economic Research. https://www.nber.org/papers/ w27538.

Golder, Matt. 2003. "Explaining Variation in the Success Of Extreme Right Parties In Western Europe." *Comparative Political Studies* 36 (4): 432–66. https://doi.org/10.1177/0010414003251176.

Goldring, Luin. 1998. "The Power of Status in Transnational Social Fields." In *Transnationalism from Below*, edited by Michael Peter Smith and Luis Eduardo Guarnizo. New Brunswick, NJ: Transaction.

Goldstein, Judith L., and Margaret E. Peters. 2014. "Nativism or Economic Threat: Attitudes Toward Immigrants During the Great Recession." *International Interactions* 40 (3): 376–401. https://doi.org/10.1080/ 03050629.2014.899219.

Goodman, Sara Wallace. 2015. "Conceptualizing and Measuring Citizenship and Integration Policy: Past Lessons and New Approaches." *Comparative Political Studies* 48 (14): 1905–41. https://doi.org/10.1177/0010414015592648.

Goodman, Sara Wallace, and Thomas B. Pepinsky. 2021. "The Exclusionary Foundations of Embedded Liberalism." *International Organization* 75 (2): 411–39. https://doi.org/10.1017/S0020818320000478.

Gould, David M. 1994. "Immigrant Links to the Home Country: Empirical Implications for U.S. Bilateral Trade Flows." *Review of Economics and Statistics* 76 (2): 302–16. https://doi.org/10.2307/2109884.

Graham, Benjamin A.T. 2019. *Investing in the Homeland: Migration, Social Ties, and Foreign Firms*. Ann Arbor, Michigan: University of Michigan Press. https://doi.org/10.3998/mpub.10011255.

Granovetter, Mark S. 1973. "The Strength of Weak Ties." *American Journal of Sociology* 78 (6): 1360–80. https://doi.org/10.1086/225469.

Greif, Avner. 1989. "Reputation and Coalitions in Medieval Trade: Evidence on the Maghribi Traders." *Journal of Economic History* 49 (4): 857–82. https:// doi.org/10.1017/S0022050700009475.

1993. "Contract Enforceability and Economic Institutions in Early Trade: The Maghribi Traders' Coalition." *American Economic Review* 83 (3): 525–48.

Grinblatt, Mark, and Matti Keloharju. 2001. "How Distance, Language, and Culture Influence Stockholdings and Trades." *Journal of Finance* 56 (3): 1053–73. https://doi.org/10.1111/0022-1082.00355.

Grogger, Jeffrey, and Gordon H. Hanson. 2011. "Income Maximization and the Selection and Sorting of International Migrants." *Journal of Development Economics, Symposium on Globalization and Brain Drain*, 95 (1): 42–57. https://doi.org/10.1016/j.jdeveco.2010.06.003.

Grzymala-Busse, Anna, Didi Kuo, Francis Fukuyama, and Michael McFaul. 2020. "Global Populisms and Their Challenges." Stanford: Freeman Spogli Institute for International Studies. https://fsi.stanford.edu/global-populisms/global-populisms-and-their-challenges.

Guiso, Luigi, Paola Sapienza, and Luigi Zingales. 2009. "Cultural Biases in Economic Exchange?" *Quarterly Journal of Economics* 124 (3): 1095–131. https://doi.org/10.1162/qjec.2009.124.3.1095.

Gülzau, Fabian, and Steffen Mau. 2021. "Walls, Barriers, Checkpoints, Landmarks, and 'No-Man's-Land.' A Quantitative Typology of Border Control Infrastructure." *Historical Social Research* 46 (3): 23–48.

Gupta, Sanjeev, Catherine A. Pattillo, and Smita Wagh. 2009. "Effect of Remittances on Poverty and Financial Development in Sub-Saharan Africa." *World Development* 37 (1): 104–15. https://doi.org/10.1016/j.worlddev.2008.05.007.

Gutiérrez, Carlos González. 1999. "Fostering Identities: Mexico's Relations with Its Diaspora." *Journal of American History* 86 (2): 545–67. https://doi.org/10.2307/2567045.

Haas, Hein de, Simona Vezzoli, and Katharina Natter. 2014. "*DEMIG POLICY.*" Dataset. International Migration Institute. https://www.migrationinstitute.org/data/demig-data/demig-policy-1.

Habib, Mohsin, and Leon Zurawicki. 2002. "Corruption and Foreign Direct Investment." *Journal of International Business Studies* 33 (2): 291–307. https://doi.org/10.1057/palgrave.jibs.8491017.

Hagan, Jacqueline Maria. 1998. "Social Networks, Gender, and Immigrant Incorporation: Resources and Constraints." *American Sociological Review* 63 (1): 55–67. https://doi.org/10.2307/2657477.

Hainmueller, Jens, and Daniel J. Hopkins. 2014. "Public Attitudes Toward Immigration." *Annual Review of Political Science* 17 (1): 225–49. https://doi.org/10.1146/annurev-polisci-102512-194818.

Hainmueller, Jens, and Michael J. Hiscox. 2010. "Attitudes toward Highly Skilled and Low-Skilled Immigration: Evidence from a Survey Experiment." *American Political Science Review* 104 (1): 61–84. https://doi.org/10.1017/S0003055409990372.

Halleröd, Björn, Bo Rothstein, Adel Daoud, and Shailen Nandy. 2013. "Bad Governance and Poor Children: A Comparative Analysis of Government Efficiency and Severe Child Deprivation in 68 Low- and Middle-Income Countries." *World Development* 48 (August): 19–31. https://doi.org/10.1016/j.worlddev.2013.03.007.

Hansen, Randall. 2009. "The Poverty of Postnationalism: Citizenship, Immigration, and the New Europe." *Theory and Society* 38 (1): 1–24. https://doi.org/10.1007/s11186-008-9074-0.

Hanson, Gordon H., and Antonio Spilimbergo. 1999. "Illegal Immigration, Border Enforcement, and Relative Wages: Evidence from Apprehensions at the U.S.-Mexico Border." *American Economic Review* 89 (5): 1337–57. https://doi.org/10.1257/aer.89.5.1337.

Hassner, Ron E., and Jason Wittenberg. 2015. "Barriers to Entry: Who Builds Fortified Boundaries and Why?" *International Security* 40 (1): 157–90. https://doi.org/10.1162/ISEC_a_00206.

Hatton, Timothy J. 2020. "Asylum Migration to the Developed World: Persecution, Incentives, and Policy." *Journal of Economic Perspectives* 34 (1): 75–93. https://doi.org/10.1257/jep.34.1.75.

Hatton, Timothy J., and Jeffrey G. Williamson. 1998. *The Age of Mass Migration: Causes and Economic Impact*. 1st edition. Oxford: Oxford University Press.

——— 2003. "Demographic and Economic Pressure on Emigration out of Africa." *Scandinavian Journal of Economics* 105 (3): 465–86. https://doi.org/10.1111/1467-9442.t01-2-00008.

——— 2005. *Global Migration and the World Economy: Two Centuries of Policy and Performance*. Cambridge, Massachusetts: MIT Press. https://mitpress.mit.edu/books/global-migration-and-world-economy.

——— 2011. "Are Third World Emigration Forces Abating?" *World Development* 39 (1): 20–32. https://doi.org/10.1016/j.worlddev.2010.05.006.

Head, Keith, Thierry Mayer, and John Ries. 2010. "The Erosion of Colonial Trade Linkages After Independence." *Journal of International Economics* 81 (1): 1–14. https://doi.org/10.1016/j.jinteco.2010.01.002.

Helbling, Marc, and David Leblang. 2019. "Controlling Immigration? How Regulations Affect Migration Flows." *European Journal of Political Research* 58 (1): 248–69. https://doi.org/10.1111/1475-6765.12279.

Helbling, Marc, and Dorina Kalkum. 2018. "Migration Policy Trends in OECD Countries." *Journal of European Public Policy* 25 (12): 1779–97. https://doi.org/10.1080/13501763.2017.1361466.

Helbling, Marc, Liv Bjerre, Friederike Römer, and Malisa Zobel. 2017. "Measuring Immigration Policies: The IMPIC Database." *European Political Science* 16 (1): 79–98. https://doi.org/10.1057/eps.2016.4.

Helliwell, John F., and Haifang Huang. 2008. "How's Your Government? International Evidence Linking Good Government and Well-Being." *British Journal of Political Science* 38 (4): 595–619. https://doi.org/10.1017/S0007123408000306.

Helliwell, John F., Haifang Huang, Shawn Grover, and Shun Wang. 2018. "Empirical Linkages between Good Governance and National Well-Being." *Journal of Comparative Economics* 46 (4): 1332–46. https://doi.org/10.1016/j.jce.2018.01.004.

Helms, Benjamin, and David Leblang. 2019. "Global Migration: Causes and Consequences." *Oxford Research Encyclopedia of Politics, February*. https://doi.org/10.1093/acrefore/9780190228637.013.631.

2022. "Labor Market Policy as Immigration Control: The Case of Temporary Protected Status." *International Studies Quarterly* 6 (3): sqac042.

Henisz, Witold J. 2000. "The Institutional Environment for Multinational Investment." *Journal of Law, Economics, and Organization* 16 (2): 334–64. https://doi.org/10.1093/jleo/16.2.334.

Henry, Ruby. 2009. "Does Racism Affect a Migrant's Choice of Destination?" Discussion paper 4349. IZA. http://ftp.iza.org/dp4349.pdf.

Hily, Marie-Antoinette, and Michel Poinard. 1987. "Portuguese Associations in France." In *Immigrant Associations in Europe*, edited by John Rex, Danièle Joly, and Czarina Wilpert. Aldershot, UK: Gower Publishing.

Hirschman, Albert O. 1970. *Exit, Voice, and Loyalty: Responses to Decline in Firms, Organizations, and States.* Cambridge, Massachusetts: Harvard University Press. https://www.hup.harvard.edu/catalog.php?isbn=9780674276604.

Holland, Alisha C., and Margaret E. Peters. 2020. "Explaining Migration Timing: Political Information and Opportunities." *International Organization* 74 (3): 560–83. https://doi.org/10.1017/S002081832000017X.

Hollifield, James F. 1992. *Immigrants, Markets, and States: The Political Economy of Postwar Europe.* Cambridge, Massachusetts: Harvard University Press. https://www.hup.harvard.edu/catalog.php?isbn=9780674444232.

2004. "The Emerging Migration State." *International Migration Review* 38 (3): 885–912. https://doi.org/10.1111/j.1747-7379.2004.tb00223.x.

Huber, John, and Ronald Inglehart. 1995. "Expert Interpretations of Party Space and Party Locations in 42 Societies." *Party Politics* 1 (1): 73–111. https://doi.org/10.1177/1354068895001001004.

Huberman, Gur. 2001. "Familiarity Breeds Investment." *Review of Financial Studies* 14 (3): 659–80. https://doi.org/10.1093/rfs/14.3.659.

Hujo, Katja, and Nicola Piper. 2007. "South–South Migration: Challenges for Development and Social Policy." *Development* 50 (4): 19–25. https://doi.org/10.1057/palgrave.development.1100419.

Hunt, Jennifer, and Marjolaine Gauthier-Loiselle. 2010. "How Much Does Immigration Boost Innovation?" *American Economic Journal: Macroeconomics* 2 (2): 31–56. https://doi.org/10.1257/mac.2.2.31.

Ikenberry, G. John. 2001. *After Victory: Institutions, Strategic Restraint, and He Rebuilding of Order after Major Wars.* Princeton, NJ: Princeton University Press. https://press.princeton.edu/books/paperback/9780691050911/after-victory.

Imai, Katsushi S., Raghav Gaiha, Abdilahi Ali, and Nidhi Kaicker. 2014. "Remittances, Growth and Poverty: New Evidence from Asian Countries." *Journal of Policy Modeling* 36 (3): 524–38. https://doi.org/10.1016/j.jpolmod.2014.01.009.

Inglehart, Ronald, and Pippa Norris. 2017. "Trump and the Populist Authoritarian Parties: The Silent Revolution in Reverse." *Perspectives on Politics* 15 (2): 443–54. https://doi.org/10.1017/S1537592717000111.

Iosifides, Theodoros, Mari Lavrentiadou, Electra Petracou, and Antonios Kontis. 2007. "Forms of Social Capital and the Incorporation of Albanian Immigrants in Greece." *Journal of Ethnic and Migration Studies* 33 (8): 1343–61. https://doi.org/10.1080/13691830701614247.

Itzigsohn, José. 2000. "Immigration and the Boundaries of Citizenship: The Institutions of Immigrants' Political Transnationalism." *International Migration Review* 34 (4): 1126–54. https://doi.org/10.1177/019791830003400403.

Javorcik, Beata S., Çağlar Özden, Mariana Spatareanu, and Cristina Neagu. 2011. "Migrant Networks and Foreign Direct Investment." *Journal of Development Economics* 94 (2): 231–41. https://doi.org/10.1016/j.jdeveco.2010.01.012.

Jensen, J. Bradford, Dennis P. Quinn, and Stephen Weymouth. 2017. "Winners and Losers in International Trade: The Effects on US Presidential Voting." *International Organization* 71 (3): 423–57. https://doi.org/10.1017/S0020818317000194.

Jensen, Nathan M. 2003. "Democratic Governance and Multinational Corporations: Political Regimes and Inflows of Foreign Direct Investment." *International Organization* 57 (3): 587–616. https://doi.org/10.1017/S0020818303573040.

Jetten, Jolanda, Frank Mols, and Tom Postmes. 2015. "Relative Deprivation and Relative Wealth Enhances Anti-Immigrant Sentiments: The V-Curve Re-Examined." *PLoS ONE* 10 (10): e0139156. https://doi.org/10.1371/journal.pone.0139156.

Jetten, Jolanda, Frank Mols, and Niklas K. Steffens. 2021. "Prosperous but Fearful of Falling: The Wealth Paradox, Collective Angst, and Opposition to Immigration." *Personality and Social Psychology Bulletin* 47 (5): 766–80. https://doi.org/10.1177/0146167220944112.

Joly, Danièle. 1987. "Associations amongst the Pakistani Population in Britain." In *Immigrant Associations in Europe*, edited by John Rex, Danièle Joly, and Czarina Wilpert. Aldershot, UK: Gower Publishing.

Jones-Correa, Michael. 2001. "Under Two Flags: Dual Nationality in Latin America and Its Consequences for Naturalization in the United States." *International Migration Review* 35 (4): 997–1029. https://doi.org/10.1111/j.1747-7379.2001.tb00050.x.

Joppke, Christian. 1998. "Why Liberal States Accept Unwanted Immigration." *World Politics* 50 (2): 266–93. https://doi.org/10.1017/S004388710000811X.

——— 2020. "Immigration in the Populist Crucible: Comparing Brexit and Trump." *Comparative Migration Studies* 8 (1): 49. https://doi.org/10.1186/s40878-020-00208-y.

Kahanec, Martin, and Klaus F. Zimmermann. 2010. "High-Skilled Immigration Policy in Europe." Discussion paper 5399. IZA. http://ftp.iza.org/dp5399.pdf.

Kang, Jun-Koo, and Rene M. Stulz. 1997. "Is Bank-Centered Corporate Governance Worth It? A Cross-Sectional Analysis of the Performance of Japanese Firms during the Asset Price Deflation." Working paper 6238. National Bureau of Economic Research. https://www.nber.org/papers/w6238.

Kapur, Devesh. 2001. "Diasporas and Technology Transfer." *Journal of Human Development* 2 (2): 265–86. https://doi.org/10.1080/14649880120067284.

Kapur, Devesh, and John McHale. 2005. *Give Us Your Best and Brightest: The Global Hunt for Talent and Its Impact on the Developing World*. Washington, DC: Center for Global Development. https://www .cgdev.org/sites/default/files/9781933286037-Kapur-Hale-best-and-brightest .pdf.

Katz, Eliakim, and Oded Stark. 1986. "Labor Migration and Risk Aversion in Less Developed Countries." *Journal of Labor Economics* 4 (1): 134–49. https://doi.org/10.1086/298097.

Kaushal, Neeraj. 2006. "Amnesty Programs and the Labor Market Outcomes of Undocumented Workers." *Journal of Human Resources* XLI (3): 631–47. https://doi.org/10.3368/jhr.XLI.3.631.

Keck, Margaret E., and Kathryn Sikkink. 1998. *Activists beyond Borders: Advocacy Networks in International Politics*. Ithaca, New York: Cornell University Press.

Keohane, Robert O., and Joseph S. Nye. 1974. "Transgovernmental Relations and International Organizations." *World Politics* 27 (1): 39–62. https://doi .org/10.2307/2009925.

Kerr, Sari Pekkala, 2017. "Immigrant Entrepreneurship." In *Measuring Entrepreneurial Business: Current Knowledge and Challenges*, edited by John Haltiwanger, Erik Hurst, Javier Miranda, and Antoinette Schoar, 187–250. Chicago: University of Chicago Press. https://doi.org/10.7208/ 9780226454108-008.

Kerr, Sari Pekkala, and William R. Kerr. 2011. "Economic Impacts of Immigration: A Survey." Working paper 16736. National Bureau of Economic Research. https://www.nber.org/papers/w16736.

Kerr, William R. 2018. *The Gift of Global Talent: How Migration Shapes Business, Economy & Society*. Palo Alto, Californie: Stanford University Press. https://www.sup.org/books/title/?id=29770.

Keynes, John Maynard. 1919. *The Economic Consequences of the Peace*. New York: Routledge. https://doi.org/10.4324/9781351304641.

Kiewiet, D. Roderick, and Mathew D. McCubbins. 1991. *The Logic of Delegation*. Chicago: University of Chicago Press. https://press.uchicago .edu/ucp/books/book/chicago/L/bo3629025.html.

Kleinman, Ephraim. 1996. *Jewish and Palestinian Diaspora Attitudes to Philanthropy and Investment*. Tel Aviv: Hebrew University Press.

Knoll, Anna, and Andrew Sheriff. 2017. "Making Waves: Implications of the Irregular Migration and Refugee Situation on Official Development Assistance Spending and Practices in Europe." Report 2017:01. EBA. https://www.oecd.org/derec/sweden/201701-ECDPM-rapport.pdf.

Koczan, Zsoka, and Franz Loyola. 2018. "How Do Migration and Remittances Affect Inequality? A Case Study of Mexico." Working paper 18/136. Washington, D C: IMF. https://www.imf.org/en/Publications/WP/Issues/ 2018/06/14/How-Do-Migration-and-Remittances-Affect-Inequality-A-Case-Study-of-Mexico-45926.

Kogut, Bruce, and Harbir Singh. 1988. "The Effect of National Culture on the Choice of Entry Mode." *Journal of International Business Studies* 19 (3): 411–32. https://doi.org/10.1057/palgrave.jibs.8490394.

Kolenikov, Stanislav, and Gustavo Angeles. 2009. "Socioeconomic Status Measurement with Discrete Proxy Variables: Is Principal Component Analysis a Reliable Answer?" *Review of Income and Wealth* 55 (1): 128–65. https://doi.org/10.1111/j.1475-4991.2008.00309.x.

Kone, Zovanga L., and Çağlar Özden. 2017. "Brain Drain, Gain and Circulation." In *Handbook of Globalisation and Development,* edited by Kenneth A. Reinert. Cheltenham, UK: Elgar. https://doi.org/10.4337/9781783478651.00029.

Koslowski, Rey. 2003. "Challenges of International Cooperation in a World of Increasing Dual Nationality." In *Rights and Duties of Dual Nationals: Evolution and Prospects,* edited by David A. Martin and Kay Hailbronner, 157–82. The Hague, The Netherlands: Kluwer Law International.

Kossoudji, Sherrie A., and Deborah A. Cobb-Clark. 2002. "Coming out of the Shadows: Learning about Legal Status and Wages from the Legalized Population." *Journal of Labor Economics* 20 (3): 598–628. https://doi.org/10.1086/339611.

Kugler, Maurice, Oren Levintal, and Hillel Rapoport. 2018. "Migration and Cross-Border Financial Flows." *World Bank Economic Review* 32 (1): 148–62. https://doi.org/10.1093/wber/lhx007.

Kunovich, Robert M. 2004. "Social Structural Position and Prejudice: An Exploration of Cross-National Differences in Regression Slopes." *Social Science Research* 33 (1): 20–44. https://doi.org/10.1016/S0049-089X(03)00037-1.

Kustov, Alexander. 2020. "'Bloom Where You'Re Planted': Explaining Public Opposition to (E)Migration." *Journal of Ethnic and Migration Studies* Forthcoming (May): 1–20. https://doi.org/10.1080/1369183X.2020.1754770.

Kustov, Alexander, Dillon Laaker, and Cassidy Reller. 2021. "The Stability of Immigration Attitudes: Evidence and Implications." *The Journal of Politics,* (83)4: 1478–1494. https://doi.org/10.1086/715061.

Lafleur, Jean-Michel, and Leticia Calderón Chelius. 2011. "Assessing Emigrant Participation in Home Country Elections: The Case of Mexico's 2006 Presidential Election." *International Migration* 49 (3): 99–124. https://doi.org/10.1111/j.1468-2435.2010.00682.x.

Lanati, Mauro, and Rainer Thiele. 2018. "The Impact of Foreign Aid on Migration Revisited." *World Development* 111 (November): 59–74. https://doi.org/10.1016/j.worlddev.2018.06.021.

Lane, Philip R. 2006. "Global Bond Portfolios and EMU." *International Journal of Central Banking* 2 (2): 1–23.

Lane, Philip R., and Gian Maria Milesi-Ferretti. 2008. "International Investment Patterns." *Review of Economics and Statistics* 90 (3): 538–49. https://doi.org/10.1162/rest.90.3.538.

Larreguy, Horacio, and John Marshall. 2017. "The Effect of Education on Civic and Political Engagement in Nonconsolidated Democracies: Evidence from Nigeria." *Review of Economics and Statistics* 99 (3): 387–401. https://doi.org/10.1162/REST_a_00633.

Lazear, Edward P. 1995. "Culture and Language." Working paper 5249. National Bureau of Economic Research. https://www.nber.org/papers/w5249.

Leblang, David. 2010. "Familiarity Breeds Investment: Diaspora Networks and International Investment." *American Political Science Review* 104 (3): 584–600. https://doi.org/10.1017/S0003055410000201.

——— 2017. "Harnessing the Diaspora: Dual Citizenship, Migrant Return Remittances." *Comparative Political Studies* 50 (1): 75–101. https://doi.org/10.1177/0010414015606736.

Lederman, Daniel, Norman V. Loayza, and Rodrigo R. Soares. 2005. "Accountability and Corruption: Political Institutions Matter." *Economics & Politics* 17 (1): 1–35. https://doi.org/10.1111/j.1468-0343.2005.00145.x.

Lee, Melissa M., Gregor Walter-Drop, and John Wiesel. 2014. "Taking the State (Back) Out? Statehood and the Delivery of Collective Goods." *Governance* 27 (4): 635–54. https://doi.org/10.1111/gove.12069.

Leeds, Brett, Jeffrey Ritter, Sara Mitchell, and Andrew Long. 2002. "Alliance Treaty Obligations and Provisions, 1815–1944." *International Interactions* 28 (3): 237–60. https://doi.org/10.1080/03050620213653.

Legrain, Philippe. 2020. *Them and Us: How Immigrants and Locals Can Thrive Together*. London: Oneworld Publications. https://oneworld-publications.com/them-and-us.html.

Levitt, Peggy. 1998. "Social Remittances: Migration Driven Local-Level Forms of Cultural Diffusion." *International Migration Review* 32 (4): 926–48. https://doi.org/10.1177/019791839803200404.

Lewis, Karen K. 1999. "Trying to Explain Home Bias in Equities and Consumption." *Journal of Economic Literature* 37 (2): 571–608. https://doi.org/10.1257/jel.37.2.571.

Lewis, W. Arthur. 1954. "Economic Development with Unlimited Supplies of Labour." *The Manchester School* 22 (2): 139–91. https://doi.org/10.1111/j.1467-9957.1954.tb00021.x.

Light, Ivan, Richard B. Bernard, and Rebecca Kim. 1999. "Immigrant Incorporation in the Garment Industry of Los Angeles." *International Migration Review* 33 (1): 5–25. https://doi.org/10.1177/019791839903300101.

Linebarger, Christopher, and Alex Braithwaite. 2020. "Do Walls Work? The Effectiveness of Border Barriers in Containing the Cross-Border Spread of Violent Militancy." *International Studies Quarterly* 64 (3): 487–98. https://doi.org/10.1093/isq/sqaa035.

Lipset, Seymour Martin. 1959. "Some Social Requisites of Democracy: Economic Development and Political Legitimacy." *American Political Science Review* 53 (1): 69–105. https://doi.org/10.2307/1951731.

Lorenc, Theo, Stephen Clayton, David Neary, Margaret Whitehead, Mark Petticrew, Hilary Thomson, Steven Cummins, Amanda Sowden, and Adrian Renton. 2012. "Crime, Fear of Crime, Environment, and Mental Health and Wellbeing: Mapping Review of Theories and Causal Pathways." *Health & Place, Infectious Insecurities*, 18 (4): 757–65. https://doi.org/10.1016/j.healthplace.2012.04.001.

Loungani, Prakash, Ashoka Mody, and Assaf Razin. 2002. "The Global Disconnect: The Role of Transactional Distance and Scale Economies in Gravity Equations." *Scottish Journal of Political Economy* 49 (5): 526–43. https://doi.org/10.1111/1467-9485.00246.

Lucas, Robert E. 1990. "Why Doesn't Capital Flow from Rich to Poor Countries?" *American Economic Review* 80 (2): 92–96.

Lupia, Arthur, and Mathew D. Mccubbins. 2000. "Representation or Abdication? How Citizens Use Institutions to Help Delegation Succeed." *European Journal of Political Research* 37 (3): 291–307. https://doi.org/10.1023/A:1007068904236.

Makina, Daniel. 2012. "Determinants of Return Migration Intentions: Evidence from Zimbabwean Migrants Living in South Africa." *Development Southern Africa* 29 (3): 365–78. https://doi.org/10.1080/0376835X.2012.706034.

Manchin, Miriam, and Sultan Orazbayev. 2018. "Social Networks and the Intention to Migrate." *World Development* 109 (September): 360–74. https://doi.org/10.1016/j.worlddev.2018.05.011.

Marcel, Lubbers. 2000. "Expert Judgment Survey of West-European Political Parties 2000." Dataset. Nijmegen, Netherlands: NOW, Department of Sociology, University of Nijmegen.

Margalit, Yotam. 2012. "Lost in Globalization: International Economic Integration and the Sources of Popular Discontent." *International Studies Quarterly* 56 (3): 484–500. https://doi.org/10.1111/j.1468-2478.2012.00747.x.

——— 2019. "Economic Insecurity and the Causes of Populism, Reconsidered." *Journal of Economic Perspectives* 33 (4): 152–70. https://doi.org/10.1257/jep.33.4.152.

Massey, Douglas S. 1990. "Social Structure, Household Strategies, and the Cumulative Causation of Migration." *Population Index* 56 (1): 3–26. https://doi.org/10.2307/3644186.

——— 2009. "The Political Economy of Migration in an Era of Globalization." In *International Migration and Human Rights: The Global Repercussions of US Policy,* edited by Samuel Martinez. Berkeley, California: University of California Press. https://doi.org/10.1525/california/9780520258211.001.0001.

Massey, Douglas S., and Felipe García España. 1987. "The Social Process of International Migration." *Science* 237 (4816): 733–38. https://doi.org/10.1126/science.237.4816.733.

Massey, Douglas S., Joaquin Arango, Graeme Hugo, Ali Kouaouci, Adela Pellegrino, and J. Edward Taylor. 1993. "Theories of International Migration: A Review and Appraisal." *Population and Development Review* 19 (3): 431–66. https://doi.org/10.2307/2938462.

Masson-Delmotte, Valérie, Panmao Zhai, Anna Pirani, Sarah L. Connors, C. Péan, Sophie Berger, Nada Caud, et al., eds. 2021. "Intergovernmental Panel on Climate Change Report." In *Climate Change 2021: The Physical Science Basis. Contribution of Working Group I to the Sixth Assessment Report of the Intergovernmental Panel on Climate Change.* Cambridge University Press.

Mayda, Anna Maria. 2006. "Who Is Against Immigration? A Cross-Country Investigation of Individual Attitudes toward Immigrants." *Review of Economics and Statistics* 88 (3): 510–30. https://doi.org/10.1162/rest.88.3 .510.

2010. "International Migration: A Panel Data Analysis of the Determinants of Bilateral Flows." *Journal of Population Economics* 23 (4): 1249–74. https:// doi.org/10.1007/s00148–009-0251-x.

Mazzolari, Francesca. 2009. "Dual Citizenship Rights: Do They Make More and Richer Citizens?" *Demography* 46 (1): 169–91. https://doi.org/10.1353/dem .0.0038.

McAuliffe, Marie, and Binod Khadria. 2020. "*World Migration Report 2020.*" Geneva, Switzerland: International Organization for Migration. https:// publications.iom.int/books/world-migration-report-2020.

McManus, Walter, William Gould, and Finis Welch. 1983. "Earnings of Hispanic Men: The Role of English Language Proficiency." *Journal of Labor Economics* 1 (2): 101–30. https://doi.org/10.1086/298006.

Mede, Niels G., and Mike S. Schäfer. 2020. "Science-Related Populism: Conceptualizing Populist Demands toward Science." *Public Understanding of Science* 29 (5): 473–91. https://doi.org/10.1177/0963662520924259.

Mesquita, Bruce Bueno de, Alastair Smith, Randolph M. Siverson, and James D. Morrow. 2003. *The Logic of Political Survival*. Cambridge, Massachusetts: MIT Press. https://mitpress.mit.edu/books/logic-political-survival.

Messina, Anthony M. 2007. *The Logics and Politics of Post-WWII Migration to Western Europe*. Cambridge: Cambridge University Press. https://doi.org/10 .1017/CBO9781139167192.

Miller, Michael K., and Margaret E. Peters. 2020. "Restraining the Huddled Masses: Migration Policy and Autocratic Survival." *British Journal of Political Science* 50 (2): 403–33. https://doi.org/10.1017/S0007123417000680.

Mols, Frank, and Jolanda Jetten. 2016. "Explaining the Appeal of Populist Right-Wing Parties in Times of Economic Prosperity." *Political Psychology* 37 (2): 275–92. https://doi.org/10.1111/pops.12258.

Morales, Nicolas. 2021. "High-Skill Migration, Multinational Companies and the Location of Economic Activity." Working paper 19-20. Federal Reserve Bank of Richmond. https://www.richmondfed.org/publications/research/ working_papers/2019/wp_19-20.

Moriconi, Simone, Giovanni Peri, and Riccardo Turati. 2018. "Skill of the Immigrants and Vote of the Natives: Immigration and Nationalism in European Elections 2007-2016." Working paper 25077. National Bureau of Economic Research. https://www.nber.org/papers/w25077.

Mundell, Robert A. 1957. "International Trade and Factor Mobility." *American Economic Review* 47 (3): 321–35.

Nanes, Matthew, and Trevor Bachus. 2021. "Walls and Strategic Innovation in Violent Conflict." *Journal of Conflict Resolution* 65 (6): 1131–58. https://doi .org/10.1177/0022002721994667.

Neumayer, Eric. 2005. "Bogus Refugees? The Determinants of Asylum Migration to Western Europe." *International Studies Quarterly* 49 (3): 389–409. https://doi.org/10.1111/j.1468-2478.2005.00370.x.

Norris, Pippa. 2005. *Radical Right: Voters and Parties in the Electoral Market.* Cambridge: Cambridge University Press. https://doi.org/10.1017/CBO9780511615955.

Norris, Pippa, and Ronald Inglehart. 2019. *Cultural Backlash: Trump, Brexit, and Authoritarian Populism.* Cambridge: Cambridge University Press. https://doi.org/10.1017/9781108595841.

North, Douglas C. 2005. *Understanding the Process of Economic Change.* Princeton, NJ: Princeton University Press. https://press.princeton.edu/books/paperback/9780691145952/understanding-the-process-of-economic-change.

Nowrasteh, Alex, and Benjamin Powell. 2020. *Wretched Refuse? The Political Economy of Immigration and Institutions. Cambridge Studies in Economics, Choice, and Society.* Cambridge: Cambridge University Press. https://doi.org/10.1017/9781108776899.

Ocantos, Ezequiel Gonzalez, Chad Kiewiet de Jonge, and David W. Nickerson. 2014. "The Conditionality of Vote-Buying Norms: Experimental Evidence from Latin America." *American Journal of Political Science* 58 (1): 197–211. https://doi.org/10.1111/ajps.12047.

OECD. 2019. "OECD International Migration Database." 2019. https://www.oecd.org/els/mig/keystat.htm.

——— 2020. *International Migration Outlook.* Paris: OECD Publishing. https://doi.org/10.1787/ec98f531-en.

Office of Immigration Statistics. 2017. "Efforts by DHS to Estimate Southwest Border Security between Ports of Entry." Department of Homeland Security. https://www.dhs.gov/sites/default/files/publications/17_0914_estimates-of-border-security.pdf.

Oishi, Shigehiro, Ulrich Schimmack, and Ed Diener. 2012. "Progressive Taxation and the Subjective Well-Being of Nations." *Psychological Science* 23 (1): 86–92. https://doi.org/10.1177/0956797611420882.

Okawa, Yohei, and Eric van Wincoop. 2012. "Gravity in International Finance." *Journal of International Economics* 87 (2): 205–15. https://doi.org/10.1016/j.jinteco.2012.01.006.

Olivas Osuna, José Javier, and José Rama. 2021. "COVID-19: A Political Virus? VOX's Populist Discourse in Times of Crisis." *Frontiers in Political Science* 3 (June): 1–17.

Olken, Benjamin A., and Rohini Pande. 2012. "Corruption in Developing Countries." *Annual Review of Economics* 4 (1): 479–509. https://doi.org/10.1146/annurev-economics-080511-110917.

Orefice, Gianluca. 2015. "International Migration and Trade Agreements: The New Role of PTAs." *Canadian Journal of Economics* 48 (1): 310–34. https://doi.org/10.1111/caje.12122.

Orrenius, Pia M., and Madeline Zavodny. 2015. "The Impact of Temporary Protected Status on Immigrants' Labor Market Outcomes." *American Economic Review* 105 (5): 576–80. https://doi.org/10.1257/aer.p20151109.

Ortega, Francesc, and Giovanni Peri. 2009. "The Causes and Effects of International Migrations: Evidence from OECD Countries 1980–2005."

Working paper 14833. National Bureau of Economic Research. https://www
.nber.org/papers/w14833.

2013. "The Effect of Income and Immigration Policies on International
Migration." *Migration Studies* 1 (1): 47–74. https://doi.org/10.1093/migration/
mns004.

Østergaard-Nielsen, Eva. 2003. "The Politics of Migrants' Transnational Political
Practices." *International Migration Review* 37 (3): 760–86. https://doi.org/10
.1111/j.1747-7379.2003.tb00157.x.

Ottaviano, Gianmarco I. P., Giovanni Peri, and Greg C. Wright. 2018.
"Immigration, Trade and Productivity in Services: Evidence from
U.K. Firms." *Journal of International Economics* 112 (May): 88–108.
https://doi.org/10.1016/j.jinteco.2018.02.007.

Owen, Erica. 2019. "Foreign Direct Investment and Elections: The Impact of
Greenfield FDI on Incumbent Party Reelection in Brazil." *Comparative
Political Studies* 52 (4): 613–45. https://doi.org/10.1177/0010414018797936.

Özden, Çağlar, Christopher R. Parsons, Maurice Schiff, and Terrie L. Walmsley.
2011. "Where on Earth Is Everybody? The Evolution of Global Bilateral
Migration 1960–2000." *World Bank Economic Review* 25 (1): 12–56.
https://doi.org/10.1093/wber/lhr024.

Palloni, Alberto, Douglas S. Massey, Miguel Ceballos, Kristin Espinosa, and
Michael Spittel. 2001. "Social Capital and International Migration: A Test
Using Information on Family Networks." *American Journal of Sociology* 106
(5): 1262–98. https://doi.org/10.1086/320817.

Palop-García, Pau, and Luicy Pedroza. 2019. "Passed, Regulated, or Applied? The
Different Stages of Emigrant Enfranchisement in Latin America and the
Caribbean." *Democratization* 26 (3): 401–21. https://doi.org/10.1080/
13510347.2018.1534827.

Pan, Ying. 2012. "The Impact of Legal Status on Immigrants' Earnings and
Human Capital: Evidence from the IRCA 1986." *Journal of Labor
Research* 33 (2): 119–42. https://doi.org/10.1007/s12122-012-9134-0.

Pandya, Sonal. 2014. *Trading Spaces: Foreign Direct Investment Regulation,
1970–2000. Political Economy of Institutions and Decisions. Cambridge:
Cambridge University Press.* https://doi.org/10.1017/CBO9781139628884.

Pandya, Sonal, and David Leblang. 2017. "Risky Business: Institutions vs. Social
Networks in FDI." *Economics & Politics* 29 (2): 91–117. https://doi.org/10
.1111/ecpo.12088.

Papademetriou, Demetrios G, and Madeleine Sumption. 2011. "Rethinking
Points Systems and Employer-Selected Immigration." *Technical report.*
Washington, DC: Migration Policy Institute. https://www.migrationpolicy
.org/research/rethinking-points-systems-and-employer-selected-immigration.

2013. "Attracting and Selecting from the Global Talent Pool – Policy
Challenges." Report. Washington, DC: Migration Policy Institute. https://
www.migrationpolicy.org/sites/default/files/publications/GlobalTalent-
Selection.pdf.

Parker, Christopher Sebastian. 2021. "Status Threat: Moving the Right Further to
the Right?" *Daedalus* 150 (2): 56–75. https://doi.org/10.1162/daed_a_01846.

Parsons, Christopher R., and L. Alan Winters. 2014. "International Migration, Trade and Aid: A Survey." In *International Handbook on Migration and Economic Development*, edited by Robert E.B. Lucas, 65–112. Cheltenham, UK: Elgar. https://doi.org/10.4337/9781782548072.00008.

Parsons, Christopher, and Pierre-Louis Vézina. 2018. "Migrant Networks and Trade: The Vietnamese Boat People as a Natural Experiment." *The Economic Journal* 128 (612): F210–34. https://doi.org/10.1111/ecoj.12457.

Pedroza, Luicy, Pau Palop-García, and Bert Hoffmann. 2016. *Emigrant Policies in Latin America and the Caribbean*. Santiago, Chile: FLACSO.

Perea, Jose Ramon, and Matthew Stephenson. 2017. "Outward FDI from Developing Countries." In *Global Investment Competitiveness Report 2017/2018: Foreign Investor Perspectives and Policy Implications*, 101–34. Washington, DC: World Bank. https://doi.org/10.1596/978-1-4648-1175-3_ch4.

Pérez-Armendáriz, Clarisa, and Lauren Duquette-Rury. 2021. "The 3×1 Program for Migrants and Vigilante Groups in Contemporary Mexico." *Journal of Ethnic and Migration Studies* 47 (6): 1414–33. https://doi.org/10.1080/1369183X.2019.1623345.

Peri, Giovanni, and Vasil Yasenov. 2019. "The Labor Market Effects of a Refugee Wave Synthetic Control Method Meets the Mariel Boatlift." *Journal of Human Resources* 54 (2): 267–309. https://doi.org/10.3368/jhr.54.2.0217.8561R1.

Peters, Margaret E. 2015a. "Trade and Migration." *Oxford Handbook of the Political Economy of International Trade*. https://doi.org/10.1093/oxfordhb/9780199981755.013.29.

——— 2015b. "Open Trade, Closed Borders Immigration in the Era of Globalization." *World Politics* 67 (1): 114–54. https://doi.org/10.1017/S0043887114000331.

——— 2017. *Trading Barriers: Immigration and the Remaking of Globalization*. Princeton, NJ: Princeton University Press. https://press.princeton.edu/books/hardcover/9780691174471/trading-barriers.

——— 2019. "Immigration and International Law." *International Studies Quarterly* 63 (2): 281–95. https://doi.org/10.1093/isq/sqy063.

Peterson, Brenton D., Sonal S. Pandya, and David Leblang. 2014. "Doctors With Borders: Occupational Licensing as an Implicit Barrier to High Skill Migration." *Public Choice* 160 (1): 45–63. https://doi.org/10.1007/s11127-014-0152-8.

Pfutze, Tobias. 2012. "Does Migration Promote Democratization? Evidence from the Mexican Transition." *Journal of Comparative Economics* 40 (2): 159–75. https://doi.org/10.1016/j.jce.2012.01.004.

——— 2014. "Clientelism Versus Social Learning: The Electoral Effects of International Migration." *International Studies Quarterly* 58 (2): 295–307. https://doi.org/10.1111/isqu.12072.

Poirine, Bernard. 1997. "A Theory of Remittances as an Implicit Family Loan Arrangement." *World Development* 25 (4): 589–611. https://doi.org/10.1016/S0305-750X(97)00121-6.

Poprawe, Marie. 2015. "On the Relationship between Corruption and Migration: Empirical Evidence from a Gravity Model of Migration." *Public Choice* 163 (3): 337–54. https://doi.org/10.1007/s11127-015-0255-x.

Portes, Alejandro. 1995. "Economic Sociology and the Sociology of Immigration: A Conceptual Overview." In *Economic Sociology of Immigration, The: Essays on Networks, Ethnicity, and Entrepreneurship*, edited by Alejandro Portes, 1–41. New York: Russell Sage Foundation. https://www.jstor.org/stable/10.7758/9781610444521.

Portes, Alejandro, and József Böröcz. 1989. "Contemporary Immigration: Theoretical Perspectives on Its Determinants and Modes of Incorporation." *International Migration Review* 23 (3): 606–30. https://doi.org/10.1177/019791838902300311.

Portes, Richard, and Hélène Rey. 2005. "The Determinants of Cross-Border Equity Flows." *Journal of International Economics* 65 (2): 269–96. https://doi.org/10.1016/j.jinteco.2004.05.002.

Portes, Richard, Hélène Rey, and Yonghyup Oh. 2001. "Information and Capital Flows: The Determinants of Transactions in Financial Assets." *European Economic Review, 15th Annual Congress of the European Economic Association*, 45 (4): 783–96. https://doi.org/10.1016/S0014-2921(01)00138-6.

Prinz, Vanessa. 2005. ""Imagine Migration" – The Migration Process and Its Destination Europe in the Eyes of Tanzanian Students." *Wiener Zeitschrift Für Kritische Afrikastudien* 8 (5): 119–40.

Project Europe. 2010. "Project Europe 2030: Challenges and Opportunities." *A report to the European Council by the Reflection Group on the Future of the EU 2030*. LU: Publications Office. https://data.europa.eu/doi/10.2860/9573.

Qian, Nancy. 2015. "Making Progress on Foreign Aid." *Annual Review of Economics* 7 (1): 277–308. https://doi.org/10.1146/annurev-economics-080614-115553.

Rapoport, Hillel, and Frédéric Docquier. 2006. "The Economics of Migrants' Remittances." In *Handbook of the Economics of Giving, Altruism and Reciprocity*, edited by Serge-Christophe Kolm and Jean Mercier Ythier, 2:1135–98. Applications. Elsevier. https://doi.org/10.1016/S1574-0714(06)02017-3.

Ratha, Dilip, and William Shaw. 2007. "South–South Migration and Remittances." *Working paper 102*. Washington, DC: World Bank. http://hdl.handle.net/10986/6733.

Rauch, James E., and Alessandra Casella. 2003. "Overcoming Informational Barriers to International Resource Allocation: Prices and Ties." *The Economic Journal* 113 (484): 21–42. https://doi.org/10.1111/1468-0297.00090.

Rauch, James E., and Vitor Trindade. 2002. "Ethnic Chinese Networks in International Trade." *Review of Economics and Statistics* 84 (1): 116–30. https://doi.org/10.1162/003465302317331955.

Ravenstein, Ernst G. 1885. "The Laws of Migration." *Journal of the Statistical Society of London* 48 (2): 167–235. https://doi.org/10.2307/2979181.

Reher, David, and Miguel Requena. 2009. "The National Immigrant Survey of Spain: A New Data Source for Migration Studies in Europe." *Demographic Research* 20: 253–78.

Renshon, Stanley A. 2005. *The 50% American: Immigration and National Identity in an Age of Terror.* Washington, DC: Georgetown University Press. http://press.georgetown.edu/book/georgetown/50-american.

Rex, John, and Sasha Josephides. 1987. "Asian and Greek Cypriot Associations and Identity." In *Immigrant Associations in Europe*, edited by John Rex, Danièle Joly, and Czarina Wilpert. Aldershot, UK: Gower Publishing.

Rhodes-Purdy, Matthew, Rachel Navarre, and Stephen M. Utych. 2021. "Populist Psychology: Economics, Culture, and Emotions." *The Journal of Politics Forthcoming (May)*: 1–14. https://doi.org/10.1086/715168.

Riley, Dylan, and Rebecca Jean Emigh. 2002. "Post-Colonial Journeys: Historical Roots of Immigration and Integration." *Comparative Sociology* 1 (2): 169–91. https://doi.org/10.1163/156913302100418484.

Rivera-Batiz, Francisco L. 1999. "Undocumented Workers in the Labor Market: An Analysis of the Earnings of Legal and Illegal Mexican Immigrants in the United States." *Journal of Population Economics* 12 (1): 91–116. https://doi.org/10.1007/s001480050092.

Rogowski, Ronald. 1987. "Political Cleavages and Changing Exposure to Trade." *American Political Science Review* 81 (4): 1121–37. https://doi.org/10.2307/1962581.

Root, Jay. 2016. "In Texas, Lawmakers Don't Mess with Employers of Undocumented Workers." *The Texas Tribune*, December 14, 2016. https://www.texastribune.org/2016/12/14/lawmakers-go-easy-employers-undocumented-workers/.

Rose, Andrew K., and Mark M. Spiegel. 2009. "International Financial Remoteness and Macroeconomic Volatility." *Journal of Development Economics, New Approaches to Financial Globalization*, 89 (2): 250–57. https://doi.org/10.1016/j.jdeveco.2008.04.005.

Ruhs, Martin. 2013. *The Price of Rights.* Princeton, NJ: Princeton University Press. https://press.princeton.edu/books/hardcover/9780691132914/the-price-of-rights.

Salahuddin, Mohammad, and Jeff Gow. 2015. "The Relationship between Economic Growth and Remittances in the Presence of Cross-Sectional Dependence." *Journal of Developing Areas* 49 (1): 207–21.

Sangita, Seema. 2013. "The Effect of Diasporic Business Networks on International Trade Flows." *Review of International Economics* 21 (2): 266–80. https://doi.org/10.1111/roie.12035.

Santos Silva, João M. C., and Silvana Tenreyro. 2006. "The Log of Gravity." *Review of Economics and Statistics* 88 (4): 641–58. https://doi.org/10.1162/rest.88.4.641.

Sassen, Saskia. 1995. "Immigration and Local Labour Markets." In *The Economic Sociology of Immigration*, edited by Alejandro Portes. New York: Russell Sage Foundation.

———. 1996. *Losing Control? Sovereignty in the Age of Globalization.* Columbia University Press. http://cup.columbia.edu/book/losing-control/9780231106092.

Saxenian, AnnaLee. 2002. "Silicon Valley's New Immigrant High-Growth Entrepreneurs." *Economic Development Quarterly* 16 (1): 20–31. https://doi.org/10.1177/0891242402016001003.

Schewel, Kerilyn. 2015. "Understanding the Aspiration to Stay: A Case Study of Young Adults in Senegal." Working paper 107. International Migration Institute. https://ora.ox.ac.uk/objects/uuid:6b94a8a2-e80c-43f4-9338-92b641753215.

——— 2020. "Understanding Immobility: Moving Beyond the Mobility Bias in Migration Studies." *International Migration Review* 54 (2): 328–55. https://doi.org/10.1177/0197918319831952.

Schon, Justin. 2020. *Surviving the War in Syria: Survival Strategies in a Time of Conflict*. Cambridge: Cambridge University Press. https://doi.org/10.1017/9781108909716.

Schon, Justin, and David Leblang. 2021. "Why Physical Barriers Backfire: How Immigration Enforcement Deters Return and Increases Asylum Applications." *Comparative Political Studies*, June. https://doi.org/10.1177/00104140211024282.

Schulte, Bettina. 2008. "Second Generation Entrepreneurs of Turkish Origin in Germany: Diasporic Identity and Business Engagement." Working paper 56. Centre on Migration, Citizenship and Development (COMCAD) Arbeitspapiere. https://www.ssoar.info/ssoar/handle/document/35349.

Schüttler, Kirsten. 2007. *The Moroccan Diaspora in Germany: Its Contribution to Development in Morocco*. Eschborn, Germany: Federal Ministry for Economic Cooperation and Development.

Shain, Yossi. 1999a. *Marketing the American Creed Abroad: Diasporas in the U.S. and Their Homelands*. Cambridge: Cambridge University Press. http://services.cambridge.org/jp/academic/subjects/politics-international-relations/american-government-politics-and-policy/marketing-american-creed-abroad-diasporas-us-and-their-homelands?format=HB&isbn=9780521642255.

——— 1999b. "The Mexican-American Diaspora's Impact on Mexico." *Political Science Quarterly* 114 (4): 661–91. https://doi.org/10.2307/2657788.

——— 2002. "The Role of Diasporas in Conflict Perpetuation or Resolution." *SAIS Review* 22 (2): 115–44.

Shain, Yossi, and Aharon Barth. 2003. "Diasporas and International Relations Theory." *International Organization* 57 (3): 449–79. https://doi.org/10.1017/S0020818303573015.

Sharpe, Michael. 2005. "Globalization and Migration: Post-Colonial Dutch Antillean and Aruban Immigrant Political Incorporation in the Netherlands." *Dialectical Anthropology* 29 (3): 291–314. https://doi.org/10.1007/s10624-005-3477-3.

Sheffer, Gabriel. 2003. *Diaspora Politics: At Home Abroad*. Cambridge: Cambridge University Press. https://doi.org/10.1017/CBO9780511499432.

Siegel, Jordan I., Amir N. Licht, and Shalom H. Schwartz. 2011. "Egalitarianism and International Investment." *Journal of Financial Economics* 102 (3): 621–42. https://doi.org/10.1016/j.jfineco.2011.05.010.

Singer, David Andrew. 2010. "Migrant Remittances and Exchange Rate Regimes in the Developing World." *American Political Science Review* 104 (2): 307–23. https://doi.org/10.1017/S0003055410000110.

Sjaastad, Larry A. 1962. "The Costs and Returns of Human Migration." *Journal of Political Economy* 70 (5, Part 2): 80–93. https://doi.org/10.1086/258726.

Slaughter, Anne-Marie. 2004. *A New World Order*. Princeton, NJ: Princeton University Press. https://press.princeton.edu/books/paperback/9780691123974/a-new-world-order.

Smeekes, Anouk, Jolanda Jetten, Maykel Verkuyten, Michael J.A. Wohl, Inga Jasinskaja-Lahti, Amarina Ariyanto, Frédérique Autin, et al. 2018. "Regaining In-Group Continuity in Times of Anxiety About the Group's Future." *Social Psychology* 49 (6): 311–29. https://doi.org/10.1027/1864-9335/a000350.

Smith, Adam. 1776. *An Inquiry into the Nature and Causes of the Wealth of Nations. Edited by Edwin Cannan*. UK ed. edition. Chicago: University of Chicago Press.

Sobotka, Eva. 2003. "Romani Migration in the 1990s: Perspectives on Dynamic, Interpretation and Policy." *Romani Studies* 5 (13): 79–121. https://doi.org/10.3828/rs.2003.4.

Somin, Ilya. 2020. *Free to Move: Foot Voting, Migration, and Political Freedom*. Oxford: Oxford University Press. https://global.oup.com/academic/product/free-to-move-9780190054588?cc=us&lang=en&.

Spiro, Peter J. 2002. "Embracing Dual Citizenship." In *Dual Nationality, Social Rights and Federal Citizenship in the U.S. and Europe: The Reinvention of Citizenship*, edited by Randall Hansen and Patrick Weil. Oxford: Berghahn Books.

Spolaore, Enrico, and Romain Wacziarg. 2009. "The Diffusion of Development." *Quarterly Journal of Economics* 124 (2): 469–529. https://doi.org/10.1162/qjec.2009.124.2.469.

2018. "Ancestry and Development: New Evidence." *Journal of Applied Econometrics* 33 (5): 748–62. https://doi.org/10.1002/jae.2633.

Stark, Oded. 1984. "Migration Decision Making: A Review Article." *Journal of Development Economics* 14: 251–59.

1995. *Altruism and Beyond: An Economic Analysis of Transfers and Exchanges within Families and Groups. Oscar Morgenstern Memorial Lectures*. Cambridge: Cambridge University Press. https://doi.org/10.1017/CBO9780511493607.

Stark, Oded, and David Levhari. 1982. "On Migration and Risk in LDCs." *Economic Development and Cultural Change* 31 (1): 191–96. https://doi.org/10.1086/451312.

Strøm, Kaare. 2000. "Delegation and Accountability in Parliamentary Democracies." *European Journal of Political Research* 37 (3): 261–90. https://doi.org/10.1023/A:1007064803327.

Sulemana, Iddisah, Abdul Malik Iddrisu, and Jude E. Kyoore. 2017. "A Micro-Level Study of the Relationship Between Experienced Corruption and Subjective Wellbeing in Africa." *Journal of Development Studies* 53 (1): 138–55. https://doi.org/10.1080/00220388.2016.1187721.

Surak, Kristin. 2015. "Guestworker Regimes Globally: A Historical Comparison." In *Handbook of the International Political Economy of Migration*, edited by Leila Simona Talani and Simon McMahon. Cheltenham, UK: Elgar. https://doi.org/10.4337/9781782549901.00015.

Tavits, Margit. 2008. "Representation, Corruption, and Subjective Well-Being." *Comparative Political Studies* 41 (12): 1607–30. https://doi.org/10.1177/0010414007308537.

Taylor, Edward J. 1999. "The New Economics of Labour Migration and the Role of Remittances in the Migration Process." *International Migration* 37 (1): 63–88. https://doi.org/10.1111/1468-2435.00066.

Taylor, J. Edward, Jorge Mora, Richard Adams, and Alejandro López-Feldman. 2008. "Remittances, Inequality and Poverty: Evidence from Rural Mexico." In *Migration and Development Within and Across Borders: Research and Policy Perspectives on Internal and International Migration*, edited by Josh DeWind and Jennifer Holdaway. Geneva, Switzerland: International Organization for Migration.

Tesar, Linda L., and Ingrid M. Werner. 1995. "Home Bias and High Turnover." *Journal of International Money and Finance* 14 (4): 467–92. https://doi.org/10.1016/0261-5606(95)00023-8.

Tjaden, Jasper, Daniel Auer, and Frank Laczko. 2019. "Linking Migration Intentions with Flows: Evidence and Potential Use." *International Migration* 57 (1): 36–57. https://doi.org/10.1111/imig.12502.

Tobin, Jennifer L., David Leblang, and Christina Schneider. 2021. "Framing Unpopular Foreign Policies." *American Journal of Political Science* Forthcoming.

Todaro, Michael P. 1976. "Migration and Economic Development: A Review of Theory, Evidence, Methodology and Research Priorities." *Occasional paper 18*. Nairobi: Institute for Development Studies, University of Nairobi. https://opendocs.ids.ac.uk/opendocs/handle/20.500.12413/791.

Totten, Robbie J. 2017. "Statecraft and Migration: A Research Note on American Strategies to Use Immigration in Foreign Policy from the Founding Era through the Early Twenty-First Century." *Diplomacy & Statecraft* 28 (2): 344–70. https://doi.org/10.1080/09592296.2017.1309896.

United Nations. 2019a. "United Nations Population Division – International Migration Flows to and from Selected Countries." 2019. https://www.un.org/en/development/desa/population/migration/data/empirical2/migrationflows.asp.

———. 2019b. "World Population Policies." 2019. https://www.un.org/development/desa/pd/data/world-population-policies.

Uzzi, Brian. 1996. "The Sources and Consequences of Embeddedness for the Economic Performance of Organizations: The Network Effect." *American Sociological Review* 61 (4): 674–98. https://doi.org/10.2307/2096399.

Van Hear, Nicholas, Rebecca Brubaker, and Thais Bessa. 2009. "Managing Mobility for Human Development: The Growing Salience of Mixed Migration." *Human Development Research Paper* Vol. 20, No. 2009. https://mpra.ub.uni-muenchen.de/19202/.

Verba, Sidney, Kay Lehman Schlozman, and Henry E. Brady. 1995. *Voice and Equality: Civic Voluntarism in American Politics.* Cambridge, Massachusetts: Harvard University Press. https://www.hup.harvard.edu/catalog.php?isbn=9780674942936.

Vink, Maarten, Arjan H. Schakel, David Reichel, Ngo Chun Luk, and Gerard-René de Groot. 2019. "The International Diffusion of Expatriate Dual Citizenship." *Migration Studies* 7 (3): 362–83. https://doi.org/10.1093/migration/mnz011.

Vink, Maarten, Tijana Prokic-Breuer, and Jaap Dronkers. 2013. "Immigrant Naturalization in the Context of Institutional Diversity: Policy Matters, but to Whom?" *International Migration* 51 (5): 1–20. https://doi.org/10.1111/imig.12106.

Wahba, Jackline. 2014. "Return Migration and Economic Development." In *International Handbook on Migration and Economic Development,* edited by Robert E.B. Lucas, 327–49. Cheltenham, UK: Elgar. https://doi.org/10.4337/9781782548072.00016.

Wang, Hongying. 2000. "Informal Institutions and Foreign Investment in China." *Pacific Review* 13 (4): 525–56. https://doi.org/10.1080/09512740010004269.

Warren, Mark E. 2011. "Voting with Your Feet: Exit-Based Empowerment in Democratic Theory." *American Political Science Review* 105 (4): 683–701. https://doi.org/10.1017/S0003055411000323.

Weesie, Jeroen. 2000. *"Seemingly Unrelated Estimation and the Cluster-Adjusted Sandwich Estimator."* Stata Technical Bulletin. StataCorp LP. https://ideas.repec.org/a/tsj/stbull/y2000v9i52sg121.html.

Wei, Shang-Jin. 2000. "How Taxing Is Corruption on International Investors?" *Review of Economics and Statistics* 82 (1): 1–11. https://doi.org/10.1162/003465300558533.

Weidenbaum, Murray, and Samuel Hughes. 1996. *Bamboo Network: How Expatriate Chinese Entrepreneurs Are Creating a New Economic Superpower in Asia.* New York: Free Press.

Weiner, Myron, and Rainer Münz. 1997. "Migrants, Refugees and Foreign Policy: Prevention and Intervention Strategies." *Third World Quarterly* 18 (1): 25–51.

Weitz-Shapiro, Rebecca, and Matthew S. Winters. 2017. "Can Citizens Discern? Information Credibility, Political Sophistication, and the Punishment of Corruption in Brazil." *Journal of Politics* 79 (1): 60–74. https://doi.org/10.1086/687287.

Wellman, Elizabeth Iams. 2021. "Emigrant Inclusion in Home Country Elections: Theory and Evidence from Sub-Saharan Africa." *American Political Science Review* 115 (1): 82–96. https://doi.org/10.1017/S0003055420000866.

White House. 1993. "Remarks by President Clinton, President Bush, President Bush, President Carter, President Ford, and Vice President Gore in Signing of NAFTA Side Agreements." September 14, 1993. https://clintonwhitehouse6.archives.gov/1993/09/1993-09-14-remarks-by-clinton-and-former-presidents-on-nafta.html.

2021. "Executive Order on Creating a Comprehensive Regional Framework to Address the Causes of Migration, to Manage Migration Throughout North and Central America, and to Provide Safe and Orderly Processing of Asylum Seekers at the United States Border." The White House. February 2, 2021. https://www.whitehouse.gov/briefing-room/presidential-actions/2021/02/02/executive-order-creating-a-comprehensive-regional-framework-to-address-the-causes-of-migration-to-manage-migration-throughout-north-and-central-america-and-to-provide-safe-and-orderly-pro cessing/.

White, Roger, and Bedassa Tadesse. 2008. "Cultural Distance and the US Immigrant–Trade Link." *The World Economy* 31 (8): 1078–96. https://doi .org/10.1111/j.1467-9701.2008.01115.x.

Wilpert, Czarina. 1989. "Work and the Second Generation: The Descendents of Migrant Workers in the Federal Republic of Germany." In *Entering the Working World*, edited by Czarina Wilpert. Aldershot, UK: Gower Publishing.

World Bank. 2017. "Migration and Remittances Data." Text/HTML. World Bank. 2017. https://www.worldbank.org/en/topic/migrationremittancesdias poraissues/brief/migration-remittances-data.

World Bank Group. 2016. *Migration and Remittances Factbook*. 3rd ed. Washington, DC: World Bank. https://openknowledge.worldbank.org/ handle/10986/23743.

Yang, Dean. 2008. "International Migration, Remittances and Household Investment: Evidence from Philippine Migrants' Exchange Rate Shocks." *The Economic Journal* 118 (528): 591–630. https://doi.org/10.1111/j.1468-0297.2008.02134.x.

2011. "Migrant Remittances." *Journal of Economic Perspectives* 25 (3): 129–52. https://doi.org/10.1257/jep.25.3.129.

Yang, Dean, and Claudia A. Martínez. 2006. "Remittances and Poverty in Migrants' Home Areas: Evidence from the Philippines." In *International Migration, Remittances, and the Brain Drain*, edited by Maurice Schiff and Çaglar Özden. Washington, D C: World Bank and Palgrave Macmillan. http://hdl.handle.net/10986/6929.

Yang, Philip Q. 1994. "Explaining Immigrant Naturalization." *International Migration Review* 28 (3): 449–77. https://doi.org/10.1177/ 019791839402800302.

Zamora-Kapoor, Anna, and Monica Verea. 2014. "Public Attitudes toward Immigration in Turbulent Times." *Migration Studies* 2 (2): 131–34. https:// doi.org/10.1093/migration/mnu034.

Zeitz, Alexandra O., and David Leblang. 2021. "Migrants as Engines of Financial Globalization: The Case of Global Banking." *International Studies Quarterly* 65 (2): 360–74. https://doi.org/10.1093/isq/sqaa084.

Zellner, Arnold. 1962. "An Efficient Method of Estimating Seemingly Unrelated Regressions and Tests for Aggregation Bias." *Journal of the American Statistical Association* 57 (298): 348–68. https://doi.org/10.1080/01621459 .1962.10480664.

Zimmermann, Klaus F., Amelie F. Constant, and Liliya Gataullina. 2009. "Naturalization Proclivities, Ethnicity and Integration." Edited by Amelie F. Constant, Martin Kahanec, and Klaus F. Zimmermann. *International Journal of Manpower* 30 (1/2): 70–82. https://doi.org/10.1108/01437720910948401.

Zipf, George Kingsley. 1946. "The P1 P2/D Hypothesis: On the Intercity Movement of Persons." *American Sociological Review* 11 (6): 677–86. https://doi.org/10.2307/2087063.

Zolberg, Aristide R. 2000. "The Dawn of Cosmopolitan Denizenship." *Indiana Journal of Global Legal Studies* 7 (2): 511–18.

Index

Index

CPSIA information can be obtained
at www.ICGtesting.com
Printed in the USA
BVHW051944310123
657545BV00009B/130